Developments in Object Relations

Developments in Object Relations provides a highly accessible account of how British Object Relations developed in the second half of the twentieth century, focusing on the generation who took up where Klein and Winnicott left off. Complementing and building on its predecessor, *An Introduction to Object Relations*, it gives an overview of the development of Object Relations with special reference to the Independent and Kleinian traditions.

An introductory chapter defines the key features of Object Relations. The emergence of Object Relations is then described as emerging theoretically from some of Freud's papers and clinically from the controversial work of Sandor Ferenczi. Gomez brings clarity to a complex field, discussing what is powerful and problematic about the two main strands in British psychoanalysis. Kleinian and Independent approaches are consistently compared and contrasted, so that readers can develop a clear idea of each. Rather than preferring one to the other, they are presented as different approaches to what is fundamental in psychoanalysis. Chapters on Bion and Masud Khan bring the work of each tradition to life in a fascinating and informative way. Gomez concludes by summarising the claim of psychoanalysis to offer a new way of understanding human reality, particularly useful for readers interested in her second book, *The Freud Wars*.

Developments in Object Relations will be of great help to psychoanalysts and psychotherapists who work psychoanalytically, particularly those in the process of training, those who have recently qualified and those who are rethinking their position on the different, strongly held views they encounter. This book is particularly timely when psychoanalytic approaches are under attack from treatments claiming to offer quicker and easier solutions.

Lavinia Gomez worked for thirty years as a psychotherapist and supervisor and as a trainer at a number of psychotherapy training organisations. She is the author of *An Introduction to Object Relations* (1997) and the Routledge title *The Freud Wars* (2005). These reflect her interests in Object Relations and in philosophy, especially the philosophy of psychoanalysis and the legitimacy of psychoanalysis as a subject.

Developments in Object Relations

Controversies, Conflicts and Common Ground

Lavinia Gomez

Routledge
Taylor & Francis Group
LONDON AND NEW YORK

First published 2017
by Routledge
2 Park Square, Milton Park, Abingdon, Oxon OX14 4RN

and by Routledge
605 Third Avenue, New York, NY 10017

Routledge is an imprint of the Taylor & Francis Group, an informa business

British Library Cataloguing-in-Publication Data
A catalogue record for this book is available from the British Library

Library of Congress Cataloging-in-Publication Data
A catalogue record for this title has been requested

ISBN: 978-0-415-62917-1 (hbk)
ISBN: 978-0-415-62918-8 (pbk)
ISBN: 978-1-315-31664-2 (ebk)

Typeset in Times New Roman
by codeMantra

In memory of our granddaughter,
Rumer Louise Gomez, 2015–2016

Contents

Preface

My first book, *An Introduction to Object Relations* (1997), was written many years ago. I had always intended to write a follow-up volume but much has happened, personally and professionally, to get in the way. There were a number of philosophical questions left hanging at the end of the *Introduction*: what is the basic human unit – the individual, the mother–infant duo or the group? What is the basis of Object Relations thinking and beyond that, of psychoanalysis itself? My second book, *The Freud Wars* (2005), turned aside from Object Relations to explore these issues.

This book returns to the subject matter of the *Introduction* to explore the work of the generation of psychoanalysts who came after the Object Relations pioneers. The 'Controversial Discussions' of 1941–1945 proved a watershed in psychoanalytic theory, practice and organisation in the British Psychoanalytical Society. The present book considers the Kleinians and the Independents, two of the three groupings which emerged as a result of these often fractious discussions. The conflicts and differences that developed between these two approaches in the second half of the twentieth century remain live issues to this day.

My intention is the same as in my previous writings – to explore complex ideas in a way that renders them accessible without misleading simplification. To get the most out of this book, readers need to be familiar with basic Object Relations terms and theories: it would be useful to have read the *Introduction* or an equivalent work. To retain a proper focus it has been necessary to select what could not be left out rather than include everything I might have wished to, and this inevitably differs from what others might have chosen. The theorists whose work is discussed seem to me to offer an interesting range of thought in the area with which I am concerned; psychotherapy with children or with groups is largely omitted.

An Introduction to Object Relations is addressed to counsellors and psychotherapists of all orientations who draw on Object Relations in their work. This book, however, deals with Object Relations in terms of the psychoanalytic tradition within which it developed. Accordingly, I refer to 'patients' rather than 'clients' throughout, and sometimes use the term 'psychotherapist' or 'therapist' as more inclusive alternatives to 'analyst'. As to the thorny issue of 'he' and 'she', I generally use 'he' when referring to patients and infants, and 'she' for parents and therapists.

While my views have changed and developed since my first book was published, I still believe that a short initial biography helps to contextualise theories. Since, however, some of the theorists I write about in this book are still living or have died only recently, it would not always be appropriate to include the same amount of biographical detail as in the *Introduction*. My hope is that this book will help to develop knowledge and interest in Object Relations, as well as psychoanalysis more generally, and encourage readers to explore the original texts of these important practitioners for themselves.

References

Gomez, L. (1997) *An Introduction to Object Relations*, London: Free Association Books and New York: New York University Press.

——— (2005) *The Freud Wars: An Introduction to the Philosophy of Psychoanalysis*, London and New York: Routledge.

King, P. and Steiner, R. (1991) *The Freud-Klein Controversies 1941–45*, London and New York: Routledge/Tavistock.

Acknowledgements

First of all, thanks to the Routledge staff – they have been helpful, flexible and easy to communicate with throughout the writing of this book. Thanks also to Penguin Books for permission to use part of Winnicott's poem in Chapter 7. Every effort has been made to contact the other copyright holder. Routledge would be grateful to hear from any copyright holder who is not here acknowledged and will undertake to rectify any errors or omissions in future editions of this book.

I began this book in the throes of convalescence from surgery, presuming that writing it would take about the same length of time as my other books. As time went by, however, it became clear that recovery was not going to come quickly; and finally, recuperation turned into permanent retirement from clinical work and teaching. Writing thus took on a new importance that was both exciting and imprisoning – it was my exclusive activity when my energy was at its best.

This book therefore took a lot more time and effort than I had expected. Several people helped and encouraged me, and amongst these I particularly want to thank David Dyke and David Smart. They joined me in regular (and very enjoyable) sessions of reading, rewording, discussing and suggesting improvements of all kinds. Their input has made the book far better than it otherwise would have been, and I am extremely grateful to them.

Thanks also to my larger family, who have been particularly important during the writing of this book.

Chapter 1

Introduction

The emergence of Object Relations

Psychoanalysis became established in Britain early in the twentieth century. Ernest Jones worked with the British Medical Association to facilitate its recognition as a valid medical treatment and set up the London Psycho-Analytical Society in 1913. This was composed largely of non-practising members of the public with an interest in the field. The British Psychoanalytical Society arose out of this in 1919, welcoming men and women members from medical and non-medical backgrounds but with stricter conditions of membership than its parent body. Shortly after, Jones established the Institute of Psychoanalysis as an administrative and training body, together with a clinic offering subsidised psychoanalytic treatment. *The International Journal of Psychoanalysis* was published from 1920, and *The International Library of Psychoanalysis* in 1921. By the early 1920s there was thus a solid platform from which the Society's work could be developed.

In the decade preceding the Second World War, however, a crisis was building up. Following Nazi attempts to extinguish psychoanalysis as a 'Jewish science', a number of Central European analysts emigrated to America and the UK. Several came to London, including Melanie Klein in 1926 and Sigmund Freud and his family in 1938. With the outbreak of war in 1939 and the death of Freud a mere three weeks later, a period of open conflict in the British Psychoanalytical Society erupted. Controversy centred on the impact of the new Kleinian thinking on the established Freudian group. While some of the Society's members were excited by Klein's radical new ideas, others denounced them as a gross and misguided departure from Freudian orthodoxy. The presence of Anna Freud, newly bereaved and with her own very different approach to psychoanalysis with both children and adults, made for discussions which were personally as well as theoretically charged. Melitta Schmideberg, Klein's daughter, became involved in the controversies when she arrived in London in 1933. Her views, and especially those of her analyst, Edward Glover, diverged increasingly from her mother's. Schmideberg and Glover were not inclined to mince their words and became Klein's most outspoken critics.

It was as though the external conflict was being mirrored in the London psychoanalytic world, its members agonising over whether psychoanalysis would even survive the war. London was traumatised by the blitz, there was a scarcity of patients, and those analysts who remained in London and kept the Society going resented colleagues leaving for safer parts. In an attempt to address the divisions a series of 'Controversial Discussions' was initiated in London during the 1940s (see King and Steiner 1991). The British School of Object Relations emerged from these.

The points of dispute focused on the disparities between Kleinian and Freudian thinking. These held implications for the official stance of the British Psychoanalytical Society with regard to theoretical outlook, clinical practice and the teaching of trainees, and for who held power in the organisation. Their differences mainly involved their respective views of child development and destructiveness. The Freudians saw Eros and the Death Drive as psychobiological urges impelling psychical life, directed towards increasing integration on the one hand and progressive dissolution on the other. Klein reconceptualised the drives in terms of human relations, as love and hate, leading the Freudians to accuse her of confusing descriptive with conceptual terms. They also disagreed with the centrality of phantasy in the Kleinian framework and with her concept of innate internal figures. Her descriptions of imagined violent attacks on the internal mother disturbed them, and they doubted whether very young infants had the mental capacity for such sophisticated emotions as envy, as Klein maintained. Communication was hampered by key terms carrying different shades of meaning to the different parties, adding to the already toxic mix of professional and personal dynamics.

Clinically, Klein homed in on the patient's most pressing anxieties, expressed through unconscious phantasy, while her Freudian colleagues aimed to foster positive relations before venturing into more difficult territory; and unlike the Freudians, Klein sought to interpret all clinical material in terms of the transference relationship. With so much disagreement about Klein's most important concepts and techniques, there was particular objection to children being exposed to such a controversial approach. Klein had developed her play technique as a direct parallel to adult free association, enabling her to use the same principles in the analysis of children as with adults. Her rigorous here-and-now transference interpretations centred on the aggressive or sexual impulses causing the most immediate anxiety. Anna Freud, on the other hand, worked with children through a modified approach based on kindly guidance and explanation. She thought the child's real dependence on his parents prevented the development of transference.

The society did its best to contain the conflicts without the organisation disintegrating. The outcome was the formation of separate groupings in the Society. There were the Freudian[1] or Viennese group, with Anna Freud as its main proponent, and the 'Kleinists', or Kleinians, with Klein as their leader. The Kleinian group originally included Winnicott, Heimann and Bowlby, but only for a short time; they were unable to accept some of its core ideas. They joined the largest group, composed of analysts who did not wish to belong to either faction, known as the 'Middle Group'. This mainly comprised the mostly British analysts who had belonged to the Society before the discussions took place, retaining the typically Anglo-Saxon attitudes of pragmatism and flexibility. They had already contributed work on infant psychology and development, which stood as a background to the work of both Freud and Klein (e.g. Middlemore 1941; and see King and Steiner 1941: 240, 262 fn. 15). The Middle Group hoped to mediate between the other two sections to keep communication open and reach some compromise. This proved unworkable, and as the group became more organised it was renamed the 'Independents'. Its members sought to have neither an internal hierarchy nor a set theoretical position, remaining open to thinking from different sources. They took a more 'independent' attitude towards defined texts and tenets than members of the other two groups. As Winnicott gained increasing influence he became the *de facto* leader of the Independent school.

Like many of the Freudians, the Independents abhorred the idea of primary destructiveness and envy. They also envisaged ego/object structures developing through responsive care from a state of primary narcissism. If, as Winnicott reminds us, an infant cannot exist without such care, can we identify an infant psyche distinct from the quality of care in the early weeks? It is this which shapes the individual subject that the infant becomes; the 'good-enough' mother enables him to develop in a healthy way.

This arrangement of three distinct groupings enabled the society to remain as a single organisation, and the formal 'Gentleman's Agreement'[2] on which it was based was only abandoned comparatively recently. The Independents continue to take up concepts from other approaches as they see fit but eschew any idea of an innate destructive drive. By contrast, it is less common for Kleinians to make use of non-Kleinian concepts. The Contemporary Freudians, meanwhile, take material from the other two approaches into their own mode of work, based on the ego as a system rather than on object relations. This means that they do not belong in a book focusing on the British School of Object Relations. The same applies to other psychoanalytic approaches, such as Attachment Theory, Ego Psychology, Existential Psychoanalysis and Self Psychology. Although a number of these include aspects of Object Relations in their overall approach, internal and external subject-object relations are not central to their conception of the psyche, and they do not belong to either the Kleinians or the Independents.

What is Object Relations?

Object Relations embraces a spectrum of thinking and practice, from the Kleinian to the Independent, and is defined differently by different people. My own working definition remains broadly the same as it was in the *Introduction*:

- The psychological person, or personal sphere, is made up of relationships and evolves within a matrix of relationship. A person deprived of this could not realise the potential for relationship: even if they survived physically they would not have the capacity to lead a fully human life.

- The need for relationship is primary: nothing else can replace it. René Spitz (1945) coined the term 'hospitalism' for the mental and physical 'failure to thrive' seen in infants confined to impersonal institutions, or given insufficient emotional care. This occurred in the Romanian orphanages of the Ceaucescu era, for example.
- Finally, Object Relations thinking is not the same as interpersonal thinking: unconscious processes are fundamental. Object Relations speaks of projection, repression, phantasy, splitting – all essentially unconscious mental concepts. Unconscious material appears in dreams, slips of the tongue, free association and so on. When what was previously unconscious emerges into consciousness, different modes and rules apply.

In summary, then: an Object Relations approach is a British psychoanalytic development in which unconscious relationship is fundamental. As experiencing and social beings we develop in a matrix of relationship; the person is first and foremost a seeker not of pleasure but of relationship. Material needs must be satisfied for our physical survival, but how we relate to ourselves and others is at the core of what makes each of us a human individual.

Preview

The first main chapter of this book, 'Beginnings', starts by looking at the developments in psychoanalysis which led to the emergence of Object Relations. In theoretical terms, Object Relations emerged through a range of key papers by Freud and clinically, through the practice of Freud's younger colleague, Ferenczi. In the following chapter, 'The Kleinian and Independent Frameworks', the two schools of British Object Relations, are introduced. Their overall frameworks, similarities and differences are clarified, providing a platform from which readers can engage effectively with the work of the practitioners considered.

There is then a complete chapter on Bion, probably the most influential psychoanalyst apart from Freud and Klein. The subsequent chapter focuses on 'Further Kleinian Developments', and we then proceed to the Independent school. As with Bion, a whole chapter is given over to Masud Khan, a fascinating and innovative figure and perhaps the best-known analyst of his day, but shunned in later years because of his flagrant malpractice. Following this, the work of two other important Independent practitioners is discussed.

The book ends with a chapter on 'Approaches to Practice', leaving the reader with a vivid sense of each modality. Leading Kleinian and Independent analysts give an explication of their own approach, together with how each viewed the other. Papers by Bion and Khan bring their respective clinical styles to life, illustrating issues raised in the first part of the chapter and in the book as a whole. A general discussion sums up the Kleinian and Independent approaches overall.

Finally, an Appendix is included which sketches out the main arguments of *The Freud Wars*, mentioned several times in this book, for interested readers. The appendix explores the ground of psychoanalysis, at the same time introducing a philosophical evaluation. Taking the controversies in the *New York Review of Books* during the 1990s as a starting point, *The Freud Wars* examines how psychoanalysis and its central concept, the unconscious, can be accounted for: it becomes clear why there is no common agreement as to whether it is a scientific or a humanities subject. By investigating Freud's writings to unearth his philosophical commitments, implicit foundations can be found and constructed which show that psychoanalysis can be seen as a valid area of study which is neither a science nor a humanities subject: it arises from a conceptual point before the mind/body, hermeneutic/scientific distinction is located in Western thought.

Notes

1 The Freudian group later became the 'Contemporary Freudians'.
2 In fact, the 'Gentleman's Agreement' was made between Anna Freud, Melanie Klein and Sylvia Payne, as leading representatives of the three groups.

References

King, P. and Steiner, R., eds (1991) *The Freud-Klein Controversies 1941–45*, London and New York: Tavistock/Routledge.

Middlemore, M. (1941) *The Nursing Couple*, London: Hamish Hamilton Medical Books.

Spitz, R. (1945) 'Hospitalism – An Inquiry into the Genesis of Psychiatric Conditions of Early Childhood', *Psychoanalytic Study of the Child* 1: 53–74.

Chapter 2

Beginnings

Theoretical beginnings: Freud (1856–1939)

The enormously wide-ranging and innovative work of Freud means that there is scarcely a serious review of therapeutic thinking that does not have to start with his writing. His thinking can be complex and his writing dense, and because several papers are outlined, this chapter makes more demands on the reader than those that come later; nevertheless, it lays essential ground for the change in Freud's thinking that led into Object Relations.

Object Relations as a field is widely understood to have commenced with his ground-breaking papers 'On Narcissism' (1914, S.E.14) and 'Mourning and Melancholia' (1915, S.E.14). These are the papers in which he first conceives the psyche (misleadingly translated as 'mind') as a group of personal elements relating to each other. At the centre is the ego or 'I', an organised dynamic structure made up of a number of interconnecting subjective figures or significant figures. As early as 1914, Object Relations began to take shape as a new conceptualisation of the human psyche based on conscious and unconscious connections within and between people.

Freud's first attempted theory of the psyche was as close as he could get to an entirely physical account. In his *Project for a Scientific Psychology* (1950/1895, S.E.1) the psyche is imagined as a quasi-physical apparatus regulating itself through an unknown form of energy. Freud never managed to finish this and appears to have tried to suppress it. However, many of its patterns reappeared in a theoretical work which he began immediately afterwards, *The Interpretation of Dreams* (1901, S.E.4–5). The centrepiece of this work is chapter 7, 'The Psychology of the Dream-Processes', particularly section B (S.E.5: 533–549). It is here that he shifts the physicalistic concepts of the *Project* to the psychical level. He uses the same sequence of steps as in the *Project* to map out how the stimuli impacting on the sense-organs move from the mental level of perception to straightforwardly physical motor activity – from perception to thought to action. In the metapsychological portions (the bedrock theoretical level) of this long work he likens the psyche to a 'compound microscope or a photographic apparatus' (S.E.5: 536) which gives us pictures which are not physically real, but which can be treated as representing something material. He begins to clarify his conception of the psychical zone as the unconscious yet somatic region between the physical and the conscious. He describes psychical processes as unitary, but with mental and physical aspects (1940a, S.E.23).

Freud envisages two forms of energy or drives (mistranslated as 'instincts'): the self-preservative drives, such as hunger and aggression, and the sexual drives, which include all forms of social and personal attachment and have the preservation of the species as their aim (S.E.14: 78). Freud divides psychical processes into conscious, pre-conscious and unconscious systems. The unconscious levels of mind have their own laws and ways of acting: in the regions of the dream and the neurotic symptom there is no negation, no contradiction, no differentiation between thought and reality. One layer of unconsciousness consists of that which was once conscious and may become so again – the repressed unconscious. The other is the unconscious 'proper', 'primal phantasies' which have never and will never become conscious, but which shape and colour the upper layers of awareness. Primal phantasies are inherited collective myths in the form of rudimentary portrayals of notions such as the mother's body (internal and external), parental intercourse and castration (ibid. 269). It is these that promote the psychic organisation that is typical of human beings, regardless of experience.

This theoretical framework, known as 'Libido Theory', acts as the backdrop for his later version of the Life and Death drives (*Beyond the Pleasure Principle*, 1920, S.E.18) and the development of his tripartite structure of the psyche (*The Ego and the Id*, 1923, S.E.19). As noted above, a framework for an Object Relations approach begins to appear from 1914, within a libido theory context, in 'On Narcissism' and 'Mourning and Melancholia'. It is consolidated in the late 'Splitting of the Ego in the Process of Defence' (1940b, S.E.23).

We shall now take a brief look at these papers to see how this view of the psyche developed.

'On Narcissism: An Introduction' (1914, S.E.14)

In Freud's earlier theoretical framework, narcissism encompasses both 'primary' and 'secondary' narcissism, before and after the infant perceives himself as separated out from the rest of reality. In primary narcissism, other people are included as the objects of the sexual drives (love and attachment), and as parts of the self from which they are not yet viewed as separate. Freud generally sees this as the most primitive form of psychic organisation. Once external objects become distinct from the self, 'object libido' may be redirected towards these separate objects or else returned back to the self or ego, now distinct from these objects; this happens when external attachments become too disappointing or too difficult to be borne. This development is what is normally spoken of as 'narcissism', noticeable because of its inappropriateness. Where we might expect someone to feel naturally for other people, the narcissistic person seems to feel mainly or only for himself. In Freud's terms this is 'secondary narcissism', a developmental process that defends against external relations, which are experienced as untenable. 'On Narcissism' thus develops a more complex view of the individual as the ego and his objects: instead of simply internal and external objects, self and other, there are different components of each to which the ego can relate, together with a particularly tricky kind of psychic organisation which Freud calls 'auto-erotism' (1905, S.E.7: 181–183).

Freud saw infantile sexuality as different from adult or genital sexuality, with 'erotic' meaning the form of sensuality which develops later into adult sexuality. He describes 'auto-erotism' as an alternative perspective on primary narcissism, with energy derived from the auto-erotic drives or instincts, which are there 'from the very first' (S.E.14: 77). Initially this energy, libido, is sent out from the ego to the 'erotogenic zones', or centres of erotism, which are also felt to be aspects of the ego itself (ibid. 84). There is the mouth in the oral stage, the anus in the anal stage and the penis in the phallic stage, as well as the whole body in the 'polymorphously perverse' stage of development where the whole body is the locus of proto-erotic sensuality. Thus we can see auto-erotism as primary narcissism from the point of view of the energy which is sent out, the libido. The alternative is to see it from the point of view of the ego, as the structure from which the libido is sent out, in which it is stored and which paradoxically also receives it back again.

This looks at first like another kind of narcissism; but in auto-erotism the libido is thought of as cathected or sent out to the body parts which are seen as part of the ego, whereas in primary narcissism it is stored up in the ego or ego-id as a whole. In auto-erotism, therefore, the ego begins to look like an object which one can have a particular view of, or relation to, from the vantage point of the libido, the energy contents of the ego. The drives take what looks like an object as their target, but this is a very different kind of target from an external object: 'its ideal prototype is that of the lips kissing themselves' (S.E.7: 182).

Thus Freud sees psychic development as starting with primary narcissism, where all libido is stored up in the original ego-id. But from another point of view, the libido is cathected or attached to the ego, which is now seen as a structure; this makes a little more sense of Freud's oscillation between treating the beginning of psychic structure sometimes as the ego and sometimes as the ego-id. Auto-erotism is 'self-love', or love of the ego or self which, bearing in mind that the ego is 'first and foremost a body-ego', makes the idea of the 'lips kissing themselves' more understandable. Eventually object libido develops, where the libido is cathected to objects clearly recognised as separate – resulting in object-love, or love of an object (usually a person). It is this form of libido, finally, which is sent back to the ego as secondary narcissism (S.E.14: 77). So primary narcissism is the natural beginning of object relating, whereas secondary narcissism, or narcissism as it is often referred to today, is a pathological structure, a defence against healthy object-relating. It is in this paper that Freud begins to develop the idea of the ego as a complex structure with changing roles; he describes it as the original object of its own attachment.

'Mourning and Melancholia' (1915, S.E.14)

This paper is often seen as the real beginning of Object Relations. Here, Freud presents the psyche not as a system for regulating the strength of desires or 'excitations' but as a system of attachments or cathexes of various parts of the psyche to each other. These internal objects are external figures that have been internalised or taken into the ego to exist there in representational form, with each internal object being a split-off part of the ego. It is in this paper that the super-ego is also hinted at as 'conscience', a semi-autonomous voice in the ego derived from the internalised father. Its counterpart is the adored and admired 'ego ideal', from the internal mother, an imaginary inspiring figure which we try, but inevitably fail, to live up to.

The essence of this paper is that mourning can help us understand neurotic symptoms, just as dreams can: the structure of mourning reflects that of the symptoms of melancholia (now termed depression) in the same way that the structure of dreams mirrors that of hysterical symptoms. In Freud's theory, dreams have overt and covert meanings, with hidden 'laws' applicable only to the unconscious; so too does melancholia or depression. He describes melancholia as the turning-in on the ego of the grief and anger that was triggered originally by loss – of a person, of a hoped-for good marriage which turns out badly, or an important possession like a job. Taking the simple example of ordinary bereavement, Freud describes the typical symptoms of mourning as non-pathological. We would not even think of treating them, he says, because 'it never occurs to us to regard it as a pathological condition ... We rely on its being overcome after a certain lapse of time, and we look upon any interference with it as useless or even harmful' (S.E.14: 243–244).

In the normal state of grief and mourning, melancholia or depression is not involved. In time, the reality of the loss comes to be accepted and the mourner moves through mourning. While not forgetting the loss, its memory does not induce the acute pain, disorientation and anger that it did in the early days; real rather than idealised memories predominate, and the individual has become free to make new attachments. This happens because the mourner is able to separate himself psychologically from the loved object. At first the mourner may carry the assumption that the object is alive – even consciously, as in séances, for example – or that the mourner himself is dead – usually unconsciously, with a sense of deadened flatness coming from an inner representation of the lost object (see Ogden 2002). The work of mourning enables the individual to convince himself finally that he is alive and the loved person dead, and to come to terms with these facts. No-one, however, completely fulfils the task of mourning. There will always be an undercurrent of loss remaining, unconsciously if not consciously.

While Freud and his readers took this attitude for granted, it is of course very different today. Even slightly prolonged grief is often seen pathologically as depression and treated before a natural recovery is possible. The bereaved may be routinely offered anti-depressants, with the apparent aim of getting 'back to normal' as soon as possible and minimising the effects of the loss, rather than allowing for the process of mourning to run its course with personal rather than chemical support. Although this may be an advance in some situations, the readiness with which it is resorted to is likely to result in less resilient and nuanced personalities.

As a variant of the mourning process, Freud describes the situation where the loss is not straightforward; the bereaved person may have only 'lost' the partner in the abstract, in the sense of losing his attention and so feeling rejected and abandoned. In this case, it is not so easy to understand and accept what feels like a loss, but does not look like one from the outside. Both mourner and lost object are alive but set on different courses; the mourner is predominantly furious with the abandoning object of love, so is left embroiled in feelings of rage, loss and abandonment.

In melancholia or depression, whether arising from the death of a loved person, their involvement in other activities or the loss of a crucial factor in the individual's identity, the emotions are the same as in normal mourning, but reversed. Instead of being directed healthily towards their instigator they are turned inwards onto their possessor, for fear that even more may be lost if these feelings are openly acknowledged. In this case it is more likely that the melancholic or depressed person 'may [know] *whom* he has lost, but not *what* he has lost in him' (S.E.14: 245) – what function the now absent person played for the one feeling abandoned. The 'bereaved' person may become highly self-critical, complaining or implying that he is a worthless and despicable person whom anyone would reject if they could. He may not be able to live normally, make new attachments, or even to eat or sleep well. 'In mourning it is the world that is poor and empty; in melancholia, it is the ego itself' (ibid. 246). This, at any rate, is how it feels to the depressed person, and it is this that makes it a pathological reaction. Thus psychic health depends not on being 'happy' but on being able and willing to accept reality. In depression, the view of 'reality' itself is manipulated in order to try to make life more bearable for the quasi-bereaved person, left feeling defeated.[1]

Freud depicts depression as a blind alley from which the sufferer can only emerge once its tangles are unravelled and the emotions understood, redirected and worked through. If the original situation involves two people, both may suffer unnecessarily – one from depression, the other from outbursts or undercurrents of anger and blame. In this further step, Freud describes how the depressed person takes into himself the attributes he sees in the lost person, believing himself to possess them, generally at an unconscious level: 'we perceive that the self-reproaches are reproaches against a loved object which have been shifted away from it on to the patient's own ego' (ibid. 248). No wonder life is difficult for both the patient and the 'loved object'.

The true state of affairs is revealed by the fact that, apart from the depressed individual, the person most likely to suffer from this state is the inattentive partner. He[2] is the target of hidden but effective revenge, often unacknowledged or even unconscious, because otherwise the depressed individual would appear powerful and independent rather than a blameless victim of neglect. In a form of regression, an ordinary object cathexis has reverted to a simple identification, where the ego makes itself one with the abandoned object. Both are dead, or deadened, rather than the survivor being alive and the other person lost, or dead (see Ogden 2002). 'The shadow of the object fell upon the ego' (S.E.14: 249) is Freud's striking metaphor. Instead of the mourner gradually accepting that the object has gone, its shadow is taken in and retained indefinitely. As long as this continues, mourning cannot be completed.

There is now quite a complex 'psychic apparatus': the beginnings of a subdivided 'I', with both an example to aspire to – the ego ideal – and the ever-present voice of criticism – the conscience – both of which arise from identification with, or taking in of, the parents, and beyond them, society itself. Thus in normal development the 'shadow' of the parents and society falls upon the ego, just as it does pathologically in melancholia or depression.

From the study of 'melancholia', therefore, Freud has taken some aspects of the processes of narcissistic object-choice to set out the final picture of mourning gone wrong. Yet interestingly Freud also suggests that if it is not too severe it may pass without treatment: 'The fact that it [melancholia] passes off after a certain time has elapsed without leaving traces of any gross changes is a feature it shares with mourning' (ibid. 252). For both, 'time is needed for the command of reality-testing to be carried out in detail' (ibid.) before it can be truly accepted that the loss is something that the individual can come to terms with. As hysteria did with dreams, Freud's study of melancholia illuminates processes similar to mourning in normal life.

'Splitting of the Ego in the Process of Defence' (1940b, S.E.23)

In this fragment of a paper, one of the last of Freud's writings, the emphasis shifts away entirely from the id and its drives, to the ego and its 'behaviour' – predominantly, its ways of relating: this is what makes it embryonically object-relational. Although Freud did not get further than the beginning of this paper, he describes the splitting of the ego exceptionally clearly, depicting it as an alternative defence to repression. Freud sets out the example of a boy first seeing a girl's genitals, with no penis, and at around the same time being threatened with castration (by the father, as Freud declares is usually the case) if he continues masturbating. The boy takes from these two events that the father's threat is all too real: here is a castrated being! There are two apparent choices – he must either be ready to lose his penis through literal castration if he goes on masturbating, or give up the gratification he derives from masturbating in order to keep his penis. Neither appears possible; and the route the boy takes is to do both at once, which is also, as Freud says, to do neither. In one part of the ego he recognises what he takes to be reality and the prohibitions that go with it – in this case, the terrible imagined punishment for masturbation, which makes him do his best to stop;

in another part of his ego he denies his knowledge that some people have no penis and continues masturbating. He cannot both masturbate and not masturbate at the same time, so he solves his problem by various forms of displacement.

Freud gives an intriguing example of this kind of solution. A boy became terrified of punishment by his father, which he envisaged as being *eaten* by him. Freud notes a Greek myth in which this is represented. 'Kronos, the old Father God, swallowed his children and sought to swallow Zeus like the rest, [but Zeus] was saved by the craft of his mother and later on castrated his father' (S.E.23: 278). Eventually, he went on to become an adult with a morbid fear of his little toes being touched 'as though, in all the to and fro between disavowal and acknowledgement, it was nevertheless castration that found the clearer expression …' (ibid.).

In Freud's example castration is first portrayed as being swallowed – an example of regression to the earlier oral stage, with the penis being represented by the whole body. Then, in the settled adult neurotic state, the little toes stand in for the complete body, and beyond that, the penis, while their being touched represents the penis being cut off. Freud implies here that the fear of castration is an ancient and powerful dread, appearing at every stage of history and probably in every part of humanity. The girl, too, he suggests, sees herself as a mutilated and damaged object, because she also must have been castrated – by the mother, he says, so that she usually remains free to become erotically attached to the father and thereafter to other men.

In this day and age, not everyone agrees with this; many, but not all, think that Freud was looking at women through the lens of cultural patriarchy rather than that of physical difference. Nevertheless, we see that Freud's theoretical development of the psyche has gone through various stages. At first, there is a comparatively simple psychic apparatus which has at least two parts, ego and id, which may perhaps start out as one. A mysterious energy is experienced as desire if it falls between two points. When excitation is either too high or too low, the individual feels the urge to regulate it and keep it at its comfortable middle point: it is this that Freud sees as the impulse to act to fulfil a desire. The focus is on the instincts or drives, and whether and how they fall into the self-preservative or sexual/libidinal categories. We have to remember that when Freud mentions 'libido' he is referring to all the attachment drives.

Freud seeks to divide the drives into two groups: libido theory encompasses the self-preservative (hunger and aggression) and the erotic drives. Later (1920, S.E.18: 44), he develops the concepts of Eros, the 'life' drive, which seeks for union on an ever greater scale, and Thanatos, the 'death' or destructive drive, in which destruction is sought by the method of dismemberment towards an ever simpler state, ending with inanimacy. Thus Freud came to see putting together and taking apart as the active principles of all psychic life.

Regarding the psychic apparatus, Freud becomes increasingly engrossed in his idea of the ego rather emphasising the id as the locus of the drives. At first, we must remember, the ego is simply the 'I', the organised element of the psyche that experiences life from its own point of view, consciously and unconsciously. From being devoted, constitutionally, to the protection of itself as a psychic organisation, as an individual organism and as the means of promoting the continuation of the species, the ego comes to direct its drives towards different kinds of objects. These include not just the external satisfiers of needs and desires, but also oneself, as one is, was or would like to be – as we also see in the melancholic reaction to loss ('the shadow of the object …').

Freud then subdivides the psyche into id and ego, and then also super-ego and ego ideal, the representatives of the critical and admirable qualities of the parents and through them, society; even now we can see that depression may take the form of a savage super-ego attacking the ego, with all the oedipal aggression the child feels towards his parents redirected towards himself. And finally, as the id drops out of the immediate picture, the ego itself is seen as setting up internal splits: not only do we internalise objects, such as the super-ego and its corollaries, but the ego or experiencer is itself divided, so that more than one psychic reality or point of view can exist in the same personal reality. The example which Freud gives in 'The Splitting of the Ego' is one of fetishism, where an object which the individual identifies with – often a possession or non-sexual body-part of a sexual partner – takes on libidinal charge: the penis is kept safe from castration, psychically speaking, because its significance has been displaced elsewhere, while the separateness of the external object is maintained.

In these few papers, Freud moves from the libido theory, where the psyche is driven by a few simple forces, to an emphasis on subjectivity and the ego, with all its subdivisions and developments. This is no easy transition, and the following summary may make the whole a little easier to grasp. It is nevertheless worth reading these three original papers to experience the development of Freud's thinking. Ogden (2002) may also be helpful in this.

Summary

Freud's partial move from 'instinct theory' or libido theory to an ego-based psychology proceeds in widely spaced steps, of which these papers offer a sample:

- In his *Project for a Scientific Psychology* (1895), Freud seeks to explain the psychological world in entirely physical terms. Not surprisingly, this does not succeed: psychology cannot be reduced to the material, except in broad, group-based areas. Social sciences can, for example, treats its data in the same way as the ordinary physical sciences, with probability taking the place of absolute causality. Individual psychology, however, cannot be treated satisfactorily as a science. *The Freud Wars* (2005) deals with this.
- In *An Interpretation of Dreams* (1901), Freud shifts his view of how perception leads to reasoned action from material to virtual terms, using the images seen in an apparatus such as a telescope as an analogy. From this point on, there is no thought of reducing the psychological to the physical.

- In 'On Narcissism' (1914), Freud begins to focus on the ego's cathexes (attachments). He sets out the stages as (i) primary narcissism, in which the whole of the libido is stored up in the ego/id; (ii) auto-erotism, in which the ego sends cathexes out to parts of the body known as the erotogenic zones; since these are still felt to be part of the ego or subjective individual, this is compatible with primary narcissism. The earliest organisation is the oral, in which the infant is subject to urges to suck or bite, or metaphorically to incorporate or reject; (iii) object relating proper, where the target of the drives is a separate person, or part of a person; (iv) secondary narcissism, in which the attachment to an object is drawn back into the ego and refocused on itself. Examples in (iii) and (iv) take up the oral, anal and phallic stages, preceding the Oedipus Complex and oedipal stage.
- In 'Mourning and Melancholia' (1915), Freud articulates and clarifies the idea of the internal object suggested in the Narcissism paper: the 'shadow of the object falls upon the ego', or at least on part of it. This shadow may be the conscience, later termed the super-ego, the ego-ideal, its idealised counterpart, or a significant external object which has been either physically or emotionally unavailable. In each case, the ego treats this lost object as though it were a part of the ego itself – the critical or wonderful object of its attachment with which it identifies.
- In 'Splitting of the Ego in the Process of Defence' (1940b), Freud describes the splitting of the ego itself into parallel strands, each with its own object relations. Because the unconscious does not recognise logic or negation, these strands neither contradict nor cancel each other out, however logically incompatible they may be. This is a way of avoiding the Scylla of castration anxiety (which eventually wins out metaphorically) and the Charybdis of rejecting reality as perceived by the ego, which would entail the real dangers and the terrors of psychosis. In this part of a paper, the focus is entirely on the ego; the id and its instincts are taken for granted as a theoretical background.

In a Freudian approach, the relational template is authoritative father (analyst) and passionate child (patient). Under Object Relations, this gradually changes into a relational template of our earliest connections – mother and infant, in all their varying emotional ramifications. Where Freud finds the child within the adult, focusing on the classical Oedipus Complex, Object Relations theorists see the infant in the child. The different ways in which Klein and Winnicott do this initiate the Kleinian and Independent strands of Object Relations.

Clinical beginnings: Sandor Ferenczi (1873–1933)

Ferenczi was the eighth of twelve children born to parents who moved from Poland to Hungary to escape the increasing anti-Semitism in their homeland. They changed their name from 'Fränkel' to the Hungarian 'Ferenczi', in tune with the nationalist trend of the day; Hungarian had only recently replaced German as the official language of their new country. Bernath, Ferenczi's father, threw himself into the political milieu with enthusiasm, managing a bookshop which sold radical political literature and inviting prominent Hungarian figures to speak locally. He died when Ferenczi was fifteen, four years after the death of a younger sister, so Ferenczi suffered the loss of close family members at an early age. As one of the middle children in a large family, he must have experienced a complex network of relational dynamics, but probably not much maternal intimacy. His background may throw some light on his enduring emphasis on relationship over theory in psychoanalysis, in contrast to Freud, who as consistently championed theory as the bedrock of practice. Freud was the eldest son in a smaller, more spaced family, and he experienced different pressures: much was expected from him academically, for example. While he took the view that developments in psychoanalytic theory would lead to advances in technique, Ferenczi proclaimed that new theory would emerge out of changes in practice. Disagreement gradually soured what had been one of the closest of Freud's collegial relationships: he used to allude to Ferenczi as his 'favourite son', wishing that he might marry into his family. Both probably felt abandoned and let down by the other.

The falling-out with Ferenczi was one of a succession of schisms between Freud and erstwhile favoured colleagues. Ferenczi made a sustained effort to reorient the style, focus and accessibility of psychoanalysis (Haynal 1988). He complained that psychoanalytic therapy was becoming an 'educative' rather than a therapeutic procedure. It is not difficult to see how this could have happened. As the only form of psychoanalytic training in the early twentieth century, analysts routinely incorporated teaching and supervision into the analyses of trainees, and were concerned to make their work with students as rigorous as possible. Ferenczi declared that this had produced a generation of analysts who duplicated their own experience by prioritising intellectual understanding over emotional experience, insisting on long and 'deep' treatments regardless of expense or need, and misusing their power by imposing punitively rigid boundaries and withholding responses under the aegis of therapeutic neutrality. His mission became to extend psychoanalysis to those who were more disturbed than the usual psychoanalytic patients, and to make it more effective at less cost in money, time and suffering.

Ferenczi's practical innovations developed from his conviction that the outer causes of neurosis were more rather than less important than the inner causes, and therefore that the vehicle of therapeutic change must be at least as much external as internal. In an early example of Object Relations thinking, he argued that neurosis was the consequence of a lack of love in early life, and that the imbalance of the drives that Freud held ultimately responsible was negligible by comparison. Accordingly, he set out to make good this deficiency, on the basis that the deprived patient can only gain sufficient therapeutic benefit by real new experiences: simply gaining insight through analytic interpretation could not be enough: 'Psychoanalytic cure is in direct proportion to the cherishing love given by the psychoanalyst to the patient' (Ferenczi and Rank, 1925), he wrote, introducing the technique of gratifying the patient's wishes on occasion rather than routinely frustrating them. Freud, characteristically, advocated the latter in his theoretical writing, but was less thorough-going in practice.

The term 'psychotherapist' is perhaps more appropriate for Ferenczi than 'psychoanalyst', reflecting as it does his emphasis on helping the patient live with himself, as against the Freudian focus on gaining self-knowledge. Nevertheless, the two aims are not as distinct as is sometimes portrayed. Ferenczi frequently stressed the need for the beginning analyst to gain the foundational experience of holding out against the pressure of the patient's pleas before experimenting with less conventional modes of working. Freud, meanwhile, is known to have lent his patients money, given them food and joined with them in social events. Vienna was a far smaller social milieu than London between the wars, so it was much more likely that Freud would come across his patients outside of sessions. Thus Freud and Ferenczi had nearly as many points of agreement as disagreement, although their disputes were painful, acrimonious and damaging to the psychoanalytic movement as a whole.

Ferenczi's 'active interventions' led him to the highly unusual step, for that time, of offering very flexible forms of relating. These included affectionate embraces, physical relaxation, 'forced' or guided fantasy, even 'mutual analysis', such was the urgency he saw for analysts not to misuse their power over patients. He experimented with extending and increasing the frequency of sessions for patients who found separation difficult, and setting tasks and time limits for those whose resistances led them to 'misuse' free association – deliberately remaining at a superficial level, for example, or circling around a single topic or semi-compulsive action. His aim seems to have been to try to circumvent his patients' efforts to avoid a true emotional meeting with the analyst and with his or her own unconscious processes, as far as this was possible by practical means. For years he saw patients on weekends, in the night and even on holiday. His exhausted state is clear from a card he wrote in 1930 to the maverick psychiatrist Groddeck, whose ideas Freud also made use of: 'I dedicate four and sometimes five hours to my main patient "The Queen"... Psychoanalysis, as I'm now practising it, takes much more out of one than previously has been assumed' (Fortune 2002); and in the following year, 'For the first time for years, I am on holiday without my patients' (ibid.). Two years later he died of pernicious anaemia, aged 60.

There is no doubting Ferenczi's courage, commitment and imagination. But perhaps we can also understand the horror with which Freud foresaw the collapse of his newly respectable profession, with its very survival hanging in the balance as a so-called 'Jewish science' under increasingly anti-Semitic regimes. The Freud-Ferenczi dispute is now taken as having been almost inevitable, given their equal commitment to opposing, if complementary, trends within psychoanalysis. Nevertheless, the whole messy affair disturbed the psychoanalytic establishment greatly, and a general retrenchment followed Ferenczi's death. His name was largely edited out of psychoanalytic history, rumours were circulated that he had gone mad and any mention of touch, active techniques or over-experimental attitudes became taboo. Nevertheless, similar concerns were to resurface in the work of Balint and Winnicott, in the anti-psychiatry movements of Thomas Szasz in America and R.D. Laing in the UK, and in the rise of the 'growth movement' and humanistic psychology which spread from America to Europe in the 1950s and 1960s. All these tendencies were explicitly or implicitly proposed as an antidote to psychoanalysis as it was often seen at this time: paternalistic, ineffective and frankly boring. But it is also thanks to Ferenczi that supervision has become accepted as an ordinary professional requirement rather than a mark of failure, and that addressing the therapist's 'counter-transference' is now seen to be just as important for successful therapy as working with the patient's transference.

Freud was not unaware of the effect of the analyst's behaviour on the therapeutic outcome, but his main focus was always on interpretation. He tended to rely on the analyst's 'tact' to provide what Ferenczi spells out as 'empathy', and this is what seems to have caused him to vary considerably in his approach. He alternated between being dogmatic and open-minded, appearing almost overconfident in his own views and abilities at one moment, only to announce at the next moment (or the next page) that he expected psychoanalysis to look vastly different after it had had time to develop further.

Throughout his working life, Ferenczi's approach was to build, rebuild and take forward the therapeutic relationship with his patients at both the conscious and unconscious levels, coming to theoretical questions from a clinical standpoint. He saw the practice of psychoanalysis as centred on relationship, developed through the elaboration and intensification of the transference relationship and resolved through its careful dissolution, leaving the patient free to seek genuine satisfaction outside the world of analysis. Ferenczi gave credence to the 'real' relationship which develops alongside the transference relationship, and in this he was closer to Freudian than Kleinian thinking. He thought it was possible for people to see others as they were in the present, as well as through the lens of past relationships, and that this was not entirely a matter of superficiality and depth. He thus allotted comparable if not equal weight to the conscious and unconscious strands of the therapeutic relationship (see Ferenczi 1980, 1994, 2014).

Ferenczi's work was taken on by a far larger number of analysts than is often realised. A few stayed behind with him in the increasingly dangerous Hungary – Ferenczi did so at the behest of Freud, who feared that psychoanalysis would die out completely without someone as committed as Ferenczi on the ground. A sizeable group of independent-minded European analysts emigrated to America, including Margaret Mahler, who specialised in a detailed programme of early development from her closely observed work with infants, and Clara Thompson, who with Karen Horney, Erich Fromm and Harry Stack Sullivan developed an interpersonal ego psychological strand to American psychoanalysis.

Melanie Klein was analysed by Ferenczi for fourteen months; his warm and empathic nature seems to have helped her find the confidence to become a leading psychoanalyst rather than remain a depressed single parent with a possessive and dogmatic mother. Following the disintegration of her disastrous marriage

Klein resettled in Berlin, continuing analysis with the steady and reliable Karl Abraham, who sadly died not long afterwards. Ernest Jones, the leading British psychoanalyst, invited her to London in 1926, a time when Berlin in turn had become a centre of the anti-Semitism from which she and others had escaped from Hungary. He also assisted Ferenczi's faithful admirers Michael and Alice Balint to emigrate, but to avoid overt clashes between them and those most loyal to Freudian methods, encouraged them to settle in Manchester rather than London. Taking the Freudian side in the dispute, Jones played a leading role in denigrating Ferenczi's reputation.

Less directly but no less definitely, Ferenczi's work influenced Winnicott, who paid him the unusual compliment of refusing outright to read his work for fear that it might say just what he himself was planning to write. Ferenczi also influenced Ronald Fairbairn, the first psychotherapist to work out a complete new model for an Object Relations psychoanalysis (see Fairbairn 1952; Gomez 1997). Ferenczi ultimately fell from the heights of his position as Freud's 'favoured son' to the depths of one whose name became synonymous with either betrayal or madness. Nevertheless, his works give a fascinating insight to the mind of an innovative if eccentric theorist, as well as the clinical initiator of Object Relations.

Conclusion

Freud never abandoned his libido theory but added to it by developing the concept of the ego, rebalancing his focus from the id and its drives to the ego and its object relations (see Balint 1986: 35–39). Although Klein and Winnicott take at least aspects of drive theory as given, one consequence of the development of Object Relations was for the bodily aspect of psychical processes to be pushed to the background as further complexities were discovered in the psychological realm. Freud defines psychical reality as holding both biological and psychological aspects, so to disregard its physical side would be as significant a loss as to omit its subjective side – as Freud attempted to in his original *Project for a Scientific Psychology*. This seems to have happened to some extent, although both Klein and Winnicott attempted to retain the bodily aspect of psychoanalysis in different ways.

With Freud's theoretical innovations and Ferenczi's practical insights, the stage is set for the emergence of Object Relations.

Notes

1 See Ogden 2002: 779, on the alteration of 'loss' to 'abandonment' in melancholia, together with the sense of lifelessness and other differences found in examples of melancholia as opposed to mourning.

2 Although in this book in general 'he' represents the patient or infant and 'she' the therapist or mother, at this point these terms are reversed, since we are discussing Freud's example of a depressed wife and inattentive husband.

References

Freud's papers are all taken from the *Standard Edition of the Complete Psychological Works of Sigmund Freud*, 24 volumes, London: Hogarth, abbreviated as S.E. (Volume).

Balint, M. (1986/68) *The Basic Fault: Therapeutic Aspects of Regression*, London: Tavistock.

Fairbairn, R. (1952) *Psycho-Analytic Studies of the Personality*, London: Routledge and Kegan Paul.

Ferenczi, S. (1980) *First Contributions to Psycho-Analysis*, London: Karnac.

——— (1994) *Final Contributions to the Problems and Methods of Psycho-Analysis*, London: Karnac.

——— (2014) *Further Contributions to the Theory and Technique of Psychoanalysis*, London: Karnac.

Ferenczi, S. and Rank, O. (2006) *The Development of Psycho-Analysis*, USA: Kessinger Publishing. First published (1925) by The Nervous and Mental Disease Publishing Company, Washington, USA.

Fortune, C., Ed. (2002), Ferenczi, S. and Groddeck, G., *The Ferenczi-Groddeck Correspondence 1921–1933*, London: Open Gate Press.

Freud, S. (1950/1895) *Project for a Scientific Psychology*, S.E.1: 281–397.

——— (1901) *The Interpretation of Dreams*, S.E.4–5.

——— (1905) *Three Essays on the Theory of Sexuality*, S.E.7: 123–245.

——— (1914) *On Narcissism: An Introduction*, S.E.14: 73–102.

——— (1917/1915) *Mourning and Melancholia*, S.E.14: 237–258.

——— (1920) *Beyond the Pleasure Principle*, S.E.18: 1–65.

——— (1923) *The Ego and the Id*, S.E.19: 19–47.

——— (1940a) *An Outline of Psycho-Analysis*, S.E.23: 144–207.

——— (1940b) *Splitting of the Ego in the Process of Defence*, S.E.23: 271–278.

Haynal, A. (1988) *The Technique at Issue: Controversies in Psychoanalysis from Freud and Ferenczi to Michael Balint*, London: Karnac.

Ogden, T. (2002) 'A New Reading of the Origins of Object-Relations Theory', *International Journal of Psycho-Analysis* 83: 767–782.

Chapter 3

The Kleinian and Independent frameworks

This chapter gives a brief overview of the Kleinian and Independent approaches, as shown in the work of their originators, Klein (1882–1960) and Winnicott (1896–1971). It is not a comprehensive introduction and readers are assumed to have a basic knowledge of their theory and practice (see Gomez 1997); the aim is rather to outline each approach so that readers can engage more fully with the subsequent material.

Object Relations arose from Freud's earlier work, but differs from it in its vocabulary and assumptions, its contents and attitudes. Freud expresses his early theoretical framework, his libido theory, physicalistically,[1] while his clinical concepts are expressed in mentalistic terms; these are more concrete than the terminology of Object Relations, however, which is consistently experiential. Object Relations extends Freud's later refocusing on the ego rather than the id and on relational structures and processes rather than on drives. The clinical template reflects the containing mother–child relationship rather than Freud's more patriarchal father–child model.

Klein and Winnicott came from very different backgrounds; it is easy to contrast Klein's childhood and family life as unhappy and Winnicott's as happy, but this is not entirely accurate. Certainly, Klein faced repeated losses in her life, from the deaths of a sister and a brother in early life to a disastrous marriage followed by an unsuccessful love affair. She also lost two of her three children – her son Hans in a climbing accident and her daughter Melitta, also a psychoanalyst, through estrangement. Having migrated from Vienna to Berlin and thence to London, Klein encountered fierce opposition when she first introduced her ideas to the British psychoanalytic world (King and Steiner 1991; Grosskurth 1986). She quickly gathered a group around her, however, and became one of the leading members of the BPAS. With only two short periods of personal psychoanalysis, she transformed herself from a depressed single mother dominated by her own mother to a leading figure in psychoanalysis. Her developmental scheme is original, coherent and detailed. It is also rather grim: to progress from a 'paranoid-schizoid' to a 'depressive' position does not suggest an optimistic view of life. Nevertheless, despite the considerable difficulties she faced, both personally and professionally, she did not revert to the depression of her early adult years, remaining productive until the end of her life. Concepts such as 'projective identification' and the 'paranoid-schizoid' and 'depressive positions' sparked the imagination of many of her colleagues, and have been taken up throughout the psychoanalytic world.

Winnicott, by contrast, came from a middle-class background in Plymouth. As the only boy, he was expected to take over from his father in the family business. But he was determined to study medicine, disliking the thought of lifelong dependence on doctors after breaking his collar-bone as a child. This alone throws doubt on his supposedly idyllic childhood, as does his trepidation at telling his father of his career intentions. Winnicott came to psychoanalysis through paediatrics, 'with a knack for getting mothers to tell me about their children and about the early history of their children's disorders' (1962 in 1982: 172). As a paediatrician, he saw many thousands of babies with their mothers over his years in London hospitals. He married twice and had no children; his protégé, Masud Khan, suggested he was impotent (Cooper 1993: 35). It is said that he was too anxious to tell his father about his separation from Alice Winnicott, his first wife, staying with her until his father's death. His second marriage, however, was stable and happy, with Clare Winnicott becoming a major exponent of his work and protector of his reputation.

Winnicott was analysed first by the Freudian James Strachey and later by the Kleinian Joan Rivière. Especially at the beginning of his psychoanalytic career, he greatly admired Klein's theories. They offered an example of what he was sure was needed in psychoanalysis – a theoretical framework providing a convincing account of emotional disturbance going back to infancy. Klein herself supervised his work with children before she eventually excluded him from the Kleinian group of the BPAS, since he did not accept some of her central concepts, such as innate destructiveness and envy, or see the paranoid-schizoid position as a normal phase of infancy. Winnicott became the leading figure in the Middle or Independent group and introduced a developmental scheme of his own, less comprehensive than Klein's and based on hers to a considerable extent. He includes eloquent accounts of a variety of early experiences and psychic states, with enigmatic phrases such as 'potential space', 'subjective object' and 'transitional phenomena' pervading his work.

Winnicott came to find Klein difficult as a person but he always retained a deep respect for Klein's work; she, however, barely mentions his.

The Kleinian view of the psyche

Klein sees the ego, or self, as existing from birth, taking a variety of subject–object forms and constantly influenced by the life and death instincts. Apart from external objects (significant others), she also describes internal objects, both whole objects and part objects, good and bad, deriving not only from the infant's rudimentary sense of the mother but also from a primitive awareness of the major body parts and functions.

The 'paranoid-schizoid' and 'depressive' positions are the main features of the Kleinian framework (Klein 1952). Klein's concept of 'position' refers to a particular psychic constellation that the individual moves into and out of, in contrast to Freud's stages of sexual development which the infant grows into and through. 'Paranoid' designates the projection of badness – one's own hatefulness – into external figures, and 'schizoid',[2] the defence of splitting. The characteristic features of this position are therefore an overriding fear of persecution by the oppressive and terrifying bad object and perfect, all-encompassing bliss.

The 'depressive' position, which had always been a minor part of the infant's ways of experiencing, begins to predominate over the paranoid-schizoid position at about three months of age. This brings a move from part-object to whole-object perception, and the new possibility of ambivalence. Badness is mitigated by goodness, but goodness is also offset by badness. The dominant anxiety is now that one's aggression may damage those discovered to be 'good' as well as 'bad' – loved as well as hated – the nucleus of depression. Emotional life becomes less extreme and the new awareness that others have feelings too makes possible mixed feelings and more mature emotional states: bearable disappointment, emotional integrity and ethical responsibility.

At the same time, the infant's complex internal objects come into focus, influenced by experience from the external world. Rather than the primitive two-person mode relationship of the paranoid-schizoid position, the three-person relationship of the depressive position allows the possibilities of envisaging relationships from which the infant himself is excluded. Oedipal dynamics and the development of the superego are thus taken back from early childhood to infancy. As part of this, the mother and her 'insides' make up the infant's most important object: the infant becomes fiercely curious about what the mother's body may contain – the father's penis and unborn children, for example. This leads Klein to take up Freud's 'Wissentrieb' – the 'knowledge' drive – renaming it the 'epistemological instinct'. Whereas Freud saw it as a part of Eros, Klein sees the urge to know (first and foremost what is in the mother's body) as an intense oral- and anal-sadistic drive: the infant has an urge to rip apart the womb to find and destroy his rivals. Bion develops this idea further as 'K' (see Chapter 4).

We never grow out of these positions but our personality does, of course, develop. The Kleinian Ronald Britton analyses how our changing states of mind build increasing maturity (1998). Paranoid-schizoid and depressive positions alternate, with increasing elaboration and sophistication at each step. The former breaks up what could become rigid, and the latter brings new coherence to what would otherwise be chaotic. Splitting, we should note, is not always bad: 'functional' splitting enables the infant to begin to make sense of his world – himself included – by dividing it into 'good' and 'bad'. Its function is to bring order to chaos, to protect 'good' objects from 'bad', and at an extreme, to break up the most frightening emotions into smaller segments. But when emotions that could be lived with are split off, it becomes defensive, impoverishing the ego while adding to the sense of hostility coming from the outside world.

Envy, finally, is a particularly problematic emotion, deriving from the death instinct. Klein believes that every infant feels envious of the bountiful, beautiful breast which seems to contain all that he could ever possibly need or wish for, but which is not subject to his control. Envy makes a good experience bad and interferes with the early splitting which every baby needs.[3] The title of Klein's seminal paper 'Envy and Gratitude' (1957) expresses the contrast between envy, which leads us to wish harm to those who could help us, and gratitude, where love engenders further love. Gratitude arises from the realisation that other people are also individuals with their own hopes, fears and needs, rather than either rivals to or servers of the self, with no legitimate needs of their own.

Winnicott's framework

Winnicott gives an entirely different sense of the earliest weeks and months – he sees Klein's paranoid-schizoid position as a picture of a baby in distress. The basic psychological unit is not the infant alone, but mother and infant together: 'For me, there is no description of an infant that leaves out the behaviour of the person caring for the infant; or in an object-relationship, the behaviour of the object' (Winnicott 1959: 445). For the most part, Winnicott presumes, the 'good enough' mother gives her baby sufficiently responsive and loving care for him to develop in a healthy way. Winnicott's benign perspective is in sharp distinction to the Kleinian focus on anxiety and how it is experienced.

For Winnicott, the quality of care is always more important for psychical development than constitutional factors, but he does not ignore what is inborn: 'It can be assumed that inheritance is of utmost importance, but the psychologist cannot lean on the inheritance factor until everything that is possible has been done in terms of psychology' (1989: 457). This 'inheritance factor' includes genetic predispositions and vulnerabilities, but also Eros, the life drive, to which he affords both erotic and aggressive roots, while the death or destructive drive is jettisoned entirely. Where aggression becomes destructive, he sees it as a pathological distortion of normal, life-affirming aggression, the outcome of care that is lacking or distorted.

When things go well, the 'good enough' mother's 'maternal preoccupation', lasting from the last weeks of pregnancy through the first few weeks of birth, enables her to intuit the child's needs and desires with unusual accuracy, so that he is afforded a 'brief experience of omnipotence', where it seems to him that his own desires bring about their satisfaction. Winnicott sees the infant as relating first to the 'environmental mother' and later also to the 'object mother'. The environmental mother is a 'subjective object', a sense rather than a figure, barely distinguishable from the infant's own experiential world in the early weeks after birth. She manages the infant's experience, ensuring that he is not overwhelmed by inner factors such as hunger or fear, or by external factors such as constant disturbance. The main task of the environmental mother is 'holding', screening what reaches the child so that he can relax into a state which Winnicott describes not as *dis*integrated but as *un*integrated, with the protection necessary varying with each mother–child relationship.

The object mother, by contrast, is the mother that the child meets with the excitement of his needs, at the same time making sense of them: the feeding mother, for example, who recognises and satisfies his hunger – or fails to do so. Her task is predominantly to bring the world to the child, at first in close attunement to his needs. After 'holding' and 'object-presenting', the remaining maternal function is 'handling'. What is crucial here is the sensitivity with which the mother deals with the child's physicality, so that he develops a firm sense of 'indwelling' in the body, the opposite of depersonalisation. Gradually, if the care the child receives is sufficient in these three respects, the child moves smoothly from the 'absolute dependence' of the earliest period to 'relative dependence', when he can hold the mother in mind for long enough not to fall into despair at her temporary absences.

Psychosis, the most severe pathology of the self, is described by Winnicott as an 'environmental deficiency disease' (1949, in 1992: 246) rather than a genetic roll of the dice. When the very young infant's needs are not adequately met, the sense of 'wrongness' runs throughout his unified experiential world: inner and outer reality have not yet separated out. It is only at a later stage that he is capable of feeling that it is his mother, or he, that is wrong or inadequate. Like all states of mind, psychosis is not usually total; there may be 'mad' points or areas in the personality, which Winnicott saw as deeply connected with the environment as originally perceived by the infant. Above or around these points, however, healthier growth can take place. Psychotic symptoms tend to break out first in adolescence or early adulthood, when the psyche has to manage the impact of hormonal turmoil as well as new expectations of separation and independence.

If all goes sufficiently well, the infant lays down a sense of continuity and reality throughout the early period; it is this simple sense of aliveness that Winnicott defines (1960) as the 'True Self'. When he begins to express himself deliberately – calling or crying for company, food or help, for example – he does so naturally from this sense of himself. When his care is erratic, or worse (again, what this means will vary with each mother–infant pair), the sense of omnipotence he has taken for granted is periodically interrupted, forcing the infant to focus prematurely on his mother's state: only if she is 'all right' will he be able to risk relaxing into himself. After a critical point, the mother's mood routinely becomes the basis of his actions and reactions, and in order to get his own needs met he has to do all he can to meet hers first. A compliant 'False Self' develops in the place of, or alongside, the 'True Self'. Individuals affected in this way feel fake, unreal or fraudulent as human beings; since their pathology began so early, it can also be entrenched. It is terrifying for them to risk letting go, even if they have some awareness of the existence and function of their 'False Self'. There is not a clear point when 'true' becomes 'false'; the quality of selfhood lies along a continuum (1982: 142–143). At the 'true' or healthy end, there may be only a slight 'falseness' to the self which is little different from ordinary politeness. Its self-explanatory nature makes the false self one of Winnicott's most influential concepts.

As the self is crystallising out, many children select an external object which they use as an emblem of the inner good mother, to support them in her absence or at times of anxiety. This may be a soft toy or blanket, the pattern on the curtain or the sound of a musical box – anything which clearly has a reality of its own rather than being solely imaginary. This is particularly widespread in the Western world, where babies are expected to manage without their parents for far longer periods of time, and more often, than in other societies. The baby may be anywhere from 'four-to-six-to-eight-to-twelve-months', says Winnicott, stressing individual variation. He terms whatever the child uses for support a 'transitional object' (1971), referring to its location in the intermediate zone where inner and outer reality overlap and material objects are accorded a special subjectivity. This is carried over into childhood as play, and into adulthood in areas such as culture, religion or even a favourite mug. Psychotherapy, too, is seen at its best at 'play', in the sense that the patient works to resolve his early conflicts in the transference as the child might in an imaginative game. In these areas, we are not expected to account fully for our emotions or our preferences; they represent the bond felt with our earliest carer.

At the start of the period of 'relative dependence' – a phase which never completely ends – the mother's identification with her baby is naturally waning. She realises, rightly, that he does not need her as urgently or as constantly as he once did, and the child gains confidence as his own resources prove increasingly adequate. His former illusion of omnipotence gives way to 'disillusionment', and so long as his frustration is not too severe he gains strength from this. As his confidence in his abilities grows, he comes to achieve what Winnicott calls 'unit status': he perceives himself, like others, as a 'whole object' with changing combinations of qualities. This awareness of the 'other' heralds in 'the stage of concern', the equivalent of the phase when Klein's depressive position comes to predominate. As in Klein's account, painful feelings of loss and guilt accompany concern for others, although it is this more positive aspect that Winnicott emphasises. The child's main anxiety comes to rest on the destructive effects of his anger on those he now realises he also loves; the same applies to the psychoanalytic patient revisiting early stages of development. The urge for reparation comes to the rescue: if hate can damage, love can restore. Babies at the weaning stage often try to feed their mother, and this progresses into childhood efforts to prepare food for parents. Love is expressed by doing for others what one enjoys being done for oneself: food is one of the most basic symbols of love and care.

Similarities and differences

For both Klein and Winnicott, the key event of the first year of life is the move to whole-object relating: from absolute to relative dependence, or from the dominance of the paranoid-schizoid to the depressive position. The changes affect the defences used against the anxiety that threatens the infant's wellbeing. During the initial period, his main recourse is to split off the menacing impulses and qualities and project them into others, so convincingly that the 'other' may even take them up. This powerful and primitive process is known as 'projective identification', and is explored in detail in the chapter on Bion. In the second phase, however, the infant is more able to acknowledge that these impulses belong to himself alone. Recognising that the targets of his aggression are also people that he loves, repression begins to take the place of splitting and denial. Instead of manipulating his view of the external world, he takes the need for change into himself, pushing the threatening emotion down to unconscious levels. This represents a new attempt to uphold external reality and take responsibility for his own feelings.

Both Klein and Winnicott, too, place physical experience at the heart of their developmental frameworks, expanded to include a sense of self and other. Klein attributes a rudimentary sense of self and other to the infant from birth, Winnicott after initial non-differentiation followed by a period of 'omnipotence'. This comparatively minor difference largely underpins what is often described as Klein's prioritising of the infant's constitution in psychic development, and Winnicott's prioritising of the environment. Neither does so explicitly, and both state the importance of both factors, so it is worth going into a little more detail.

Klein states that the ego is called into being by the traumatic effects of birth; it is described as the 'organized part of the self, constantly influenced by instinctual influences but keeping them under control … [It] directs all activities and establishes and maintains the relation to the external world' (Klein 1959: 249). Once created, the ego's first task is to project outwards the destructive drive, or death instinct, in aggressive phantasies,[4] in order to protect both the ego and the infant from destruction from within (1958). The ego's next action is to take in the breast, token of the nurturing mother, as an inner centre and safeguard, though the breast, too, is quickly divided into 'good' and 'bad' breasts; thus, she explains, object relations begin at birth. The infant's initial need to expel destructiveness explains why the Kleinian infant can seem to have a surplus of hate over love; for Winnicott, it is the other way around, since he did not believe that birth is normally traumatic, and he maintained that the human race would not have survived without 'good-enough' mothering being the norm.

Klein's focus is always on the infant as an individual. Since a subject cannot exist without an object, she includes internal objects as parts of the self in relation to the ego, together with an expectation of an external object after birth. Her speculations on psychic processes in the newborn child suggest that she assumes external conditions at birth have a fundamental influence on the infant's basic tendencies, apart from the constitutional balance and strength of the drives (1957: 178–180). Thus Klein sees the ego or self developing as subject–object structures or relationships from 'what is given' at the outset (that is, birth), internally and externally; from then on, perceptions are coloured by projection and introjection. Her work can, however, be read as though she is speaking of the infant in distinction to either the mother or the environment. The Kleinian focus on primitive infantile 'mechanisms' means there is little sense of the environment as part of the individual, although the ego or self does, for Klein, imply maternal and paternal inner objects or expectations, and even those of unborn siblings, too.

In Winnicott's work, by contrast, there is minimal sense of the very young infant as an individual apart from his environment. 'There is no such thing as a baby …' (1992: 99), he declares in one of his best-known phrases. Throughout his work, there is far more sense of continuity and flow between external and internal, mother and child, therapist and patient. Winnicott believes Klein to be seeing only part of the infant when she blocks out the '*dependence of the infant on the mother*' in favour of '*primitive mechanisms that are personal to the infant*' (1959: 448). The upshot of this, he says, is that in 'choosing the latter course Klein involved herself in an implicit denial of the environmental factor, and consequently she disqualified herself from describing infancy itself, which is a time of dependence' (ibid.). He is saying that through confining herself to the infant as a discrete individual, Klein is looking at only part of the infant. The matter is partially resolved when we consider that Klein sees the ego/self as including the earliest environment. Winnicott believes the same, but sees the ego as emerging at a later stage out of the dual unity of mother and child as an undifferentiated whole. These views, which theoretically only differ to a minor degree, mean that the Kleinian emphasis is on the ego or subject, and how he treats the object, while the Winnicottian approach has a greater emphasis on how the world, or object, has treated the subject.

Clinical approaches

These developmental schemata have distinctive implications for clinical practice. Since the Kleinian view is that what originates in the infant himself has the greatest influence on his development, the same applies in psychotherapeutic treatment. A great deal of care is taken to distinguish what belongs to the patient and what to the therapist: therapeutic change must come from the patient accepting, understanding and taking responsibility for himself. A Kleinian therapeutic session will tend to focus on the 'here-and-now' transference communications, so that the patient's relational structures can be recognised in the interaction between therapist and patient. Accurate and empathic interpretations offer the patient the opportunity to acknowledge and understand an increasingly wide range of split-off and repressed impulses, feelings and thoughts, to accept disowned as well as cherished aspects of himself and to take responsibility for his own responses and also those he elicits in others. The counter-transference is the therapist's primary resource but can never be fully relied on: she must also listen for confirmations of her hypothesis in the patient's material.

In Winnicott's clinical approach, the most important factor is the impact of the therapeutic setting, just as for him, the quality of care has the major influence on the infant's psychical development. This differs from the Kleinian reliance on the consistency of the session and the presence of the psychotherapist as agents of containment: for Winnicott, the therapeutic setting is centred on the therapeutic relationship but goes beyond it. The quality of the 'holding environment' constitutes the main vehicle of therapy, and may even involve a setting which does not allow for the regular sessions with the therapist that Kleinian work is built on. Independent therapists are more improvisatory in their approach than their Kleinian colleagues, both in drawing theoretical conclusions from therapeutic interactions and in making practical arrangements. Especially with patients whom they consider to need something different from the orthodox setting, they may modify the circumstances in which sessions are held – their length, for example – and beyond that, if necessary, the patient's pattern of everyday life. This is particularly likely to be needed with patients suffering from psychotic or False Self disturbances, who may go through a period of 'extreme dependence' (Winnicott 1982: 151–152) while they are relinquishing the False Self and beginning to live from a weak and undeveloped True Self. Counter-transference, while important, is used as much to facilitate empathy on the part of the psychotherapist as to reach a detailed understanding of the patient's inner world.

The ultimate aim for the Independent psychotherapist is for the patient to become authentically himself; in Kleinian work, it is for him to increase his insight and capacity to be in touch with his internal and external world. For both groups, however, what most assist him in reaching these ends are first, his own commitment to his psychological development, and second, the depth and sensitivity of the psychotherapist's understanding and acceptance of the patient and how effectively she conveys this to him, implicitly and explicitly, consciously and unconsciously.

Summary

The approaches of Klein and Winnicott are thus relational in subtly different ways. Klein sees the original ego as including internal objects and with a special need to eject hate and incorporate love – though this will also engender the need to project love, to make the external world less hateful and introject hate, to keep it separate from the external world. Where Klein sees love and hate as primary urges, Winnicott describes healthy aggression as life-affirming, and destructive only when distorted by bad experiences. These differences reflect, in part, where each learned the most about infantile processes. For Klein, it was through the analysis of children as young as two and a half, in which she treated free play with small toys and play materials as the equivalent of the adult's free association. These children may well have been the offspring of parents who were psychoanalytically-informed, well-educated and able to access costly treatment for their disturbed children; Klein treated children without their parents being present, so she could see regression in the child alone. Winnicott, meanwhile, must have been strongly influenced by the streams of mothers who brought their babies and young children to be treated in hospitals in deprived areas of London where he worked as a paediatrician. It is likely that these were the sources of the ideas most closely associated with Winnicott – the 'good-enough mother' and the 'transitional object' (1971). Since mother and child would always be seen together, he would notice the constant communication between the two, and it would seem natural to consider mother and infant as a dual unit. Yet he too treated children as well as adults psychoanalytically, or psychotherapeutically, apart from their parents; he also noted that it was easier to see primitive infantile processes in adults in regression rather than in babies themselves.

In the Kleinian approach, finally, the therapeutic setting is strictly maintained, since it is this which provides the stable container for the living out of the transference/counter-transference process, supplying the material which both therapist and patient are trying to understand. In Winnicott's approach, it is the nature of the therapeutic setting which provides what the patient needs to take the next maturational step. This reflects the need for change in the mother's mode of care, the only possible aspect of the mother–infant dyad which could be influenced or worked with. For more personal reasons, perhaps, the key concept of the Kleinian approach is anxiety; for Winnicott's, it could be creativity, or 'transitional' or 'potential space'.

These frameworks have remained separate approaches in psychoanalytic psychotherapy. Both have been influenced by the other approach and both have led to further developments, but in the time we are concerned with, the second half of the twentieth century, Kleinian practitioners tended to stay more within their own parameters while Independents were more open to different theoretical approaches. Independent theorists such as Green and Ogden, whose work will be described later, built their new concepts from a starting point which includes Kleinian as well as Independent ideas. Distinctive examples of Kleinian and Independent therapeutic work are discussed in Chapter 8.

Notes

1 Strictly speaking, in this context 'physicalistic' does not mean in physical terms, but in terms of the kind of science of which physics is the prime example.
2 Klein described the initial position as the 'paranoid' position before she added the term 'schizoid', taken from Fairbairn's work (Fairbairn 1952).
3 Chaucer, Milton and Blake all deemed envy the worst of all the sins.
4 At this stage, phantasy is experienced as if it had been acted upon.

References

Britton, R. (1998) 'Before and after the depressive position; Ps(n)→D(n)→Ps(n+1)', in *Belief and Imagination: Explorations in Psychoanalysis*, London, New York and Canada: Routledge.

Cooper, J. (1993) *Speak of Me As I Am: The Life and Work of Masud Khan*, London: Karnac.

Fairbairn, R. (1952) *Psychoanalytic Studies of the Personality*, London: Routledge and Kegan Paul.

Gomez, L. (1997) *An Introduction to Object Relations*, London: Free Association Books and New York: New York University Press.

Grosskurth, P. (1986) *Melanie Klein: Her World and Her Work*, London: Hodder and Stoughton; Cambridge, MA: Harvard University Press.

King, P. and Steiner, R., eds. (1991) *The Freud-Klein Controversies 1941–45*, London and New York: Tavistock/Routledge.

Klein, M. (1952) 'Some Theoretical Conclusions Regarding the Emotional Life of the Infant, in 1988: 61–93.

——— (1957) 'Envy and Gratitude', in Klein, 1988: 176–235.

——— (1958) 'On the Development of Mental Functioning', in Klein, 1988: 236–246.

——— (1959) 'Our Adult World and Its Roots in Infancy', in Klein, 1988: 247–263.

——— (1988) *Envy and Gratitude and Other Works*, London: Virago.

Winnicott, D. (1949) 'Mind and Its Relation to the Psyche-Soma', in 1992: 243–254.

——— (1959) 'Melanie Klein: On Her Concept of Envy', in 1989: 443–464.

——— (1960) 'Ego Distortion in Terms of True and False Self', in 1982: 140–152.

——— (1962) 'A Personal View of the Kleinian Contribution', in 1982: 171–178.

——— (1971) 'Transitional Objects and Transitional Phenomena', in *Playing and Reality*, London: Tavistock.

——— (1982) *The Maturational Processes and the Facilitating Environment*, London: Hogarth and the Institute of Psychoanalysis.

——— (1989) *Psycho-Analytic Explorations*, London: Karnac.

——— (1992) *Through Paediatrics to Psychoanalysis*, London: Karnac. First published (1958) by Tavistock Publications Ltd. (London).

Chapter 4

Wilfred Bion and his development of psychoanalysis

The originality and influence of Bion's work merits a complete chapter, and this also allows a more rounded picture of a specific Kleinian approach. We begin with an account of Bion's life as a context for his work. His main concepts are then examined and his most significant contributions to psychoanalysis evaluated. Much of his writing is dense and obscure but highly original, and includes rethinking the development of the psyche. Bion's huge output includes fiction and poetry which, unfortunately, lie outside the parameters of this book.

While Klein brings Freud's focus on the child and the Oedipus complex back to infantile anxieties, Bion takes Klein's work back to explore the very beginnings of psychical processes. He centres his concept of the psychical on the making and breaking of links, both within the psyche itself and between the psyche and its objects – people and part-people, thoughts and emotions, both normal and pathological. Linking is driven by his version of Klein's epistemological instinct, which he terms 'K'. He gives the drive for knowledge a new importance, placing it on a level with the drives for love and hate. The Kleinian concepts of containment, counter-transference and projective identification are also redefined and elaborated; he explores all these ideas through his counter-transference with his patients, particularly the more disturbed amongst them, and also by continuing self-scrutiny, thought and reflection.

Bion's earliest work focuses on new ways of working with groups, after which he turns to individual psychoanalysis, psychosis and a new model of the psyche. His thinking in this area takes up Freud's original idea of the psychical as the zone between the mental and the physical. He sees the most primitive states as pre-differentiated 'proto-mental' states (1961: 101–104), and their corresponding 'proto-physical' counterparts. Like the majority of his concepts defining his model of the psyche, he is referring not so much to actual processes but to tools which assist thinking in this complex area. Bion is the only Object Relations practitioner to explore how psychical processes develop and to find his own way of expressing this.

Life

Bion was born Wilfred Ruprecht Bion in India in 1897. His autobiographical writings (1991a/1982, 1991b/1985) offer a detailed picture of his life. His father Frederick was a successful civil engineer and, apart from his mother Rhoda, an

Indian ayah (nurse) also looked after him and his sister in their earliest years. Bion was close to his ayah and absorbed much of the atmosphere of Indian mythology from her.

His parents appear in his autobiographical writings as conventional Edwardians, impervious to the intelligence and sensitivity of their son. Bion's father comes over as particularly unimaginative, but Bion experienced his mother differently:

> My mother's attitude … was not an 'attitude' at all; his was. She loved us; he loved his image of us. She knew she had two nasty brats and could tolerate that fact; my father bitterly resented the menace of any reality which imperilled his fiction.
>
> (1991a: 28)

Bion views himself harshly, even as a child, recalling his childhood sadism in his relationship presumably to his younger sister Edna, under the eyes of their parents: 'After much painful experience I learned how to curl myself into a tight ball of snowy innocence and launch myself, with a small sharp piece of ice in the middle, at my foe' (ibid.).

This vivid description does not suggest a happy home life, nor did things improve in later years. After starting at a rather soulless-sounding boarding school[1] in England at the age of eight, Bion never returned to India. However, he always maintained a special feeling for the extremes of heat and cold, sun and dark, and the stories his ayah had told him.

Once started at school Bion saw his family only occasionally, as was then normal for children whose parents lived abroad. School life comes over as a continuation of the confusing unhappiness of family life, but without the love of his mother. In particular, he seems to have been prey to tormenting guilt from a muddle between sexuality, death and religion, and the lack of an understanding adult to talk to. There was the occasional weekend visit by his mother, whom he failed to recognise on her first visit, after three years apart. He writes about his sometimes dangerous pranks with the schoolboy chums he stayed with in the holidays, punctuated occasionally by deep yearnings for his mother and sister as he saw the affection within his friends' families. Bion's female relatives seem idealised in these memories, while his father does not get a mention.

Bion's writing brings to life with precision and clarity the experiences and ways of thinking of a child, a teenager and later a young adult in the ghastly surroundings of the First World War. Although constantly worried that he was a mere 'cringing rat' he acted with sufficient bravery to be recommended for a Victoria Cross, the highest award in the UK honours system. This alarmed him: many VC recipients met their deaths soon after in efforts to be worthy of the decoration, and to his relief the award recommended was downgraded to a Distinguished Service Order. Bion felt some concern about his indifference as to whether he lived or died, and was also aware of his tendency to cut off emotionally, to become depersonalised, to take refuge in dark humour at the worst times. Yet he always reclaims his sensitivity, as in a poignant description of his mother's death, years later in 1939. They had become distant during Bion's school years and found it hard to talk to each other thereafter. But a connection of sorts seems to have been re-established at the end: '... her eyes rested on a vase of spring flowers ... "The heads of the flowers are drooping. I can hold them up no longer. Will you hold them up for me?" She lost consciousness and died soon after' (ibid. 266).

Bion's sense of inferiority continued at The Queen's College, Oxford, where he started immediately after he was demobilised in 1919. Surely, he thought, the other students were better equipped by school and family tradition to make use of this wonderful place: 'Oxford was kind and tolerant ... Oxford was marvellous' (in Bléandonu 1994: 35), a view he kept throughout his life. But he suffered from flashbacks – vivid nightmares which would today be put down to post-traumatic stress – and he feared he was losing his mental grip. He graduated in Modern History in 1921 with an ordinary rather than an honours degree. This mediocre result is not surprising, given that his military involvement meant that he started the course later than most students and with the burden of war trauma – but he was pleased to be able to put 'BA' after his name.

After Oxford, Bion returned to his old school for a short stint of teaching. It is not surprising that a troubled young man, stranded at the beginning of adult life, should return to the place where he had spent most of his childhood. But his post ended shockingly with an accusation that he made 'sexual approaches' to one of the students there (Bion 1991b: 16–17). Although it sounds improbable, the allegation may have had its roots in sexual confusion, especially in relation to a boy for whom Bion had a special feeling. It awakened all the old sexual guilt that had been covered over by the war, and he left teaching with the aim of training in medicine in order to become a psychoanalyst – an ambition fostered unusually early, at school.

Despite his disappointing degree, University College London (UCL) accepted Bion readily in 1924, given his war experience and sporting excellence – perhaps they saw more in Bion than he did himself. He graduated from UCL in 1930.

Once embarked on his medical training, life improved for a period. Bion started achieving more in line with his abilities – he was awarded a gold medal for surgery, for example. He admired the university intellectual circle, working with Wilfred Trotter, brother-in-law to the leading British psychoanalyst, Ernest Jones, and was also impressed by Captain (Dr) J.A. Hadfield, a founder member of the Tavistock Clinic, recently formed as an innovative psychological clinic in London. But Bion still judged himself as harshly as ever, and it must have been a wonderful surprise when he was sent flowers by the sister of an old friend who had offered him hospitality after his school debacle. He took this as an unambiguous declaration of love, and indeed the two young people did become engaged in the late 1920s. He describes her repeatedly as his 'beautiful' fiancée but accords her no other attributes whatsoever. Disastrously for Bion, she broke off their relationship in a way which he found unbelievably humiliating: he heard that she was already in love with someone else even as she accepted his proposal.

Bion met the couple by chance some time later. After an awkward encounter he fantasised: 'If I had had my service revolver on me I would have shot him' – despatching the new partner efficiently and finally but without continuing torture; then with excruciating detail he mentally transferred to her a wound that could never be healed: 'I would have shot her through the knee in such a way that the joint could not be repaired and she would have had a permanently rigid leg to explain to her future lovers' (Bion 1991b: 29–30).

It was not the shock of this failed relationship that first sent him to seek psychological help, but apparently his worry about what he saw as his academic and sporting failures. He says little about his psychotherapy and even less about his 'psychoanalyst', whom he merely dubs 'Mr. Feel-it-in-the-past'. Despite the derogatory nickname he was apparently 'far from unknown or unimportant' (Bléandonu 1994: 42): one wonders who it could have been. Although they began with twelve sessions or so in mind, the treatment continued for seven or eight years (ibid. 41) – the length of time he had lived with his parents – despite Bion's acute financial difficulties. For whatever reason, he did not ask for help from his parents, although they would probably have been in a position to give it.

Apart from any other gains, this therapist helped him get started with building a private practice: this was before the days of organised and lengthy therapeutic training, so personal analysis was central to preparation for work as a psychoanalyst. But in an echo of his schoolteaching days, the work finished with an unpleasant ethical disagreement about the common habit of paying for referrals, a practice Bion saw as unequivocally unethical. He removed himself to another of the university élite, Dr Hadfield, the only staff member with an active interest in psychodynamic work, even if it does seem to have been more from an academic than a clinical angle. Hadfield must also, of course, have been a military man, which would have counted quite a lot for Bion, traumatised as he was by his war experiences. And most importantly, he was a founder member of the Tavistock Clinic, set up to provide psychological help for the general population of London in 1920.

Bion joined the Tavistock Clinic in the early 1930s, as a junior 'assistant doctor'. One of his later referrals, intriguingly, was Samuel Beckett; his therapy with the inexperienced trainee was not a great success, and both remained discreetly quiet about their mutual involvement (ibid. 45–46). The Tavistock post did not pay enough to live on, so Bion added medical work to make ends meet until 1935, when he took up work with delinquency. This was at the new Portman Clinic which specialised in forensic psychology and was (and remains) closely connected to the Tavistock. He worked there until 1940, when he was again called up for the Second World War, this time as an army psychiatrist.

In 1937 he began to pursue his psychoanalytic training with more earnestness, first meeting the eminent John Rickman and soon beginning work with him. Bion appreciated Rickman's experience, his straightforward manner and their shared army past. However, in 1939 Rickman ended the work: he thought they had gone as far as they could, given their common background (Bion 1991b: 66), and the onset of war also complicated matters as Rickman and Bion became colleagues in the area of military psychiatry. Rickman was at that time working with Melanie Klein, in whose work Bion was also becoming increasingly involved.

Bion was then without an analyst for several years. He closed down his practice and took up the role of military psychiatrist in a small team, developing an early model of 'milieu therapy' as a pragmatic way of treating the streams of traumatised soldiers. This is written up as the 'Northfield Experiment' in *Experiences in Groups* (1961) – the easiest to read of all his psychotherapy books. Despite its apparent success, this first attempt at Bion's own form of 'group therapy' was stopped abruptly after no more than six weeks; Bion felt bitterly unrecognised and unappreciated by his army superiors. Even worse, he was the only military psychiatrist to leave the army without having been promoted. It must have been particularly galling that, apart from his former analyst Rickman, colleagues such as Siegfried Foulkes and Patrick de Mare took up and developed this work from 1944, after Bion had left the scene; this speaks for its fundamental promise. Perhaps Bion's brusque manner, his problems with guilt and aggression, his opposition to what he saw as misused authority might have provoked those to whom he was accountable; or maybe his gifts simply did not emerge sufficiently clearly until he had found his true metier, individual psychoanalysis.

One thing did go right for him, if not for long. In the late 1930s, after the earlier disaster with his 'beautiful' fiancée, he met a leading actress, Betty Jardine (Elizabeth Kittrick Jardine), and they married in 1940. Tragically, she died of a pulmonary embolism a few days after the birth of their daughter near the end of the war, while Bion was working in Normandy. He was horrified when several people, including Betty's parents and, he asserts, his own,[2] suggested that the child might be adopted or otherwise brought up away from him (Bléandonu 1994: 65; Bion 1991b: 61).

Having vowed to himself, even more than to Betty's memory, that he would take responsibility for his daughter, he could think of nothing to say to these tactless suggestions but a peremptory 'No'. He spent all their savings (£8,000) on a cottage in Iver Heath, just outside London. Bion lived there with Parthenope, the name Betty and he had chosen for their baby if she was a girl. Rather eerily this means 'the lost siren', a name Bion had found in Virgil's writings, of which he was particularly fond. Although Betty had clearly agreed with him, this demonstrates that he was not a partner to stand back: Betty's suggestions are not mentioned. He asked the kindly woman who had looked after Betty during her pregnancy to care for their daughter, and she stayed on as a general housekeeper well after she would have been needed as a childminder.

Her family came to live at the cottage as well (1991b: 63), so Bion had to work hard to support them all while in analysis himself. He rented rooms in Harley

Street for the sake of the prestige and the money that the address would eventually bring in, but for some time it meant that he had to work very long hours; his only free times were Saturday and Sunday afternoons. He saw as much of Parthenope as he could, and at first they seem to have become very close:

> I became aware of a sense of gratification when the bus stopped beneath a magnificent beech tree and I got off to be met by a small figure, now a toddler, doing her best to run to meet me. Her eyes were almost closed in the throes of concentration required for mobility and the equal necessity for concentration on where she was going. At last the perilous ten yards would be achieved and tiny arms strove to meet round my neck. A rapid change into week-end clothes, and then the cycle ride.
>
> (Ibid. 66)

Bion had bought a bicycle and fixed a child seat on it with the express purpose of riding with Parthenope into the nearby village for tea on Saturdays. He greatly enjoyed these expeditions, though he must have longed for Betty's presence with them. Yet while he is joyfully aware both of his own gratification and his daughter's joy at being with him, he shows little sign of sensing what it might be like for her growing up without a mother and barely seeing her father, however good her everyday carer might be.

At times, however, Bion shows a painful awareness of the extremes of love and cruelty within him. In contrast to the happy meetings at the bus-stop, he writes of a disturbing episode that must have happened only a few months earlier.

> That something was wrong … was brought home to me one week-end when I was sitting on the lawn near the house and the baby was crawling … on the opposite side of the lawn. She began to call out to me; she wanted me to come to her.
>
> I remained sitting. She now made to crawl towards me. But she called to me as if expecting me to come to fetch her.
>
> I remained sitting.
>
> She continued to crawl and now her calls became distressful.
>
> I remained sitting.
>
> I watched her continue on the painful journey across the vast expanse, as it must have appeared to her, that separated her from her Daddy.
>
> I remained sitting but felt bitter, angry, resentful. Why did she do this to me? Not quite audible was the question, 'Why do you do this to her?'
>
> The nurse could not stand it and got up to fetch her. 'No,' I said, 'let her crawl. It won't do her any harm.' We watched the child crawl painfully. She was weeping bitterly now but sticking stoutly to her attempt to cover the distance.
>
> I felt as if I were gripped in a vice. No. I would *not* go. At last the nurse, having glanced at me with astonishment, got up ignoring my prohibition,

> and fetched her. The spell snapped. I was released. The baby had stopped weeping and was being comforted by maternal arms. But I, I had lost my child.
>
> ... It was a shock, a searing shock, to find such depth of cruelty in myself.
>
> (Ibid. 70)

In this brutal confrontation of himself he discounts the implied infrequency of such behaviour. His daughter was showing that he was already a key person in her life, and this must have been borne out of consistently loving behaviour from him. The 'nurse' was astonished at his response to his daughter, and had no qualms about disobeying her employer. Although she must have been aware that he needed her as much as or more than she needed him, her astonishment shows that his harshness was unusual. We can understand Bion's reaction as a repetition of the abandonment and isolation he had suffered as a child; but he was still in the business of judging himself negatively, and of course he does not consider that harsh feelings enter into all parent–child relationships even in the easiest of circumstances. Perhaps he thought that, as the exceptional man he was, he should never have failed in this respect.

Bion's self-criticisms continued, eventually becoming slightly mitigated. In later life he concluded that

> To this day I retain a certain confidence that no matter how dangerous or how unpleasant my contemporaries may be, I myself am even nastier. I cannot feel confident that I am more *dangerous* because my malice is tempered by cowardice. The resultant cunning is not without its value; I probably owe more to this quality than I have ever admitted.
>
> (Bion 1991a: 28)

It is evidently rather humiliating to be glad that he was 'less dangerous'. This is one of the only times he accords himself any useful quality whatsoever, even though he describes it as morally ambiguous. He has become prone to admitting and retracting a self-description in the same sentence, in this case the last one in the quotation, and in the previous one the question to himself that was 'not quite audible'. This is another example of opposites coming together, and personality deficits paradoxically turning out to provide opportunities.

When the war had ended Bion began analysis with Melanie Klein. His only female analyst, she was to become the foremost theoretical influence in his psychoanalytic life. He was not an easy patient: 'When I was given an interpretation I used very occasionally to feel it was correct; more usually I thought it was nonsense', though such interpretations 'later seemed to have been correct' (Bion 1991b: 68). Despite her value to him as an analyst – and a female one – who could stand up to him, he found her a tiresome colleague after his analysis. A letter to his wife from a Congress in Geneva observes: 'I must find a way of explaining to M.K. that I need sleep and then use it for writing!' (ibid. 114). 'Melanie is extremely demanding. I suppose it is because she has had so many attacks and so little genuine happiness in her life, but I always feel sucked dry' (ibid. 116).

As his practice gradually developed, Bion worked hard to develop his new group dynamic methods at the Tavistock Clinic (Bion 1961) as well as undergoing training at the Institute of Psychoanalysis. But even while he was at home he seems to have been largely absorbed in his work, to the detriment of his family life. He gives a vivid description of his small daughter's intense effort to remain completely quiet, the condition on which she was allowed to stay with him and paint while he was writing. He describes the outward signs of her effort with sharp clarity but gives no thought to what it might mean to a small child to be allowed such strictly provisional time with her only parent, who was so often out or 'busy'. He seems to have grown increasingly distant from her – not that this was an unusual state of affairs for the fathers of small children at that period.

Bion seems to have fallen head over heels in love with a childless young widow whom he met at the Tavistock in 1951, when Parthenope was about six. He and Francesca married very quickly, and Francesca seems a most kind and affectionate person. It is touching to learn that she made the kind of bond with Parthenope that led Bion to thank her for having 'given Parthenope back to me and made me feel what it is like to have a child' (Bléandonu 1994: 103) – a sense he had evidently all but lost.

After their marriage the new family moved to Redcourt, a larger house near West Croydon on the other side of London. They were apparently not in a position to have a honeymoon for about seven years, when they finally took a week abroad together. It is touching to learn that instead Francesca took Parthenope for a seaside holiday after their wedding, leaving Bion alone to work. In 1952 they had a son, Julian, and in 1955 a daughter, Nicola. Not much is said about these children, but like Parthenope they appear to have gone to boarding school, probably at the same age as Bion had done.

His relationship with his children, however, was far closer and more loving than his parents' could have been with him. Bion wrote imaginative and sympathetic letters to his own children when they were away from each other, including about the agonies of home-sickness, which he remembered as 'the most ghastly feeling I ever knew – a sort of horrible sense of impending disaster without any idea what it was or even any words in which to express it …' (1991b: 173). Nevertheless, he also saw it as character-building: '… I believe it is from one's ability to stand having such feelings and ideas that mental growth eventually comes' (ibid.)

Of course, it would not be fair to judge him by the conventions of today: he was merely doing what all parents do, trying to give his children the best possible start in life. However critical we might feel of Bion, his relationship with his family was complex; and but for boarding schools, housekeepers and helpful wives, we would miss out on the flair, originality and richness that we enjoy thanks to Bion's thinking and writing.

In 1968, when the children were in their teens, Bion accepted various working trips to South and North America, settling with Francesca in Los Angeles shortly afterwards. Although there were 'good' reasons for this (it gave Bion more peace to work and write), it repeated his own experience of his family being spread across two continents. Francesca tells us that the wide spaces and hot climate of California resonated with his early memories of India (Bion 1991a: 7). He received glowing invitations and acclamations from Brazil, where he lectured from time to time, until he and Francesca returned to Oxford, his *alma mater*, in 1970.

Not surprisingly, Parthenope seems to have had a difficult relationship with her father as an adolescent, to the extent of becoming estranged from him for a period when she went to study philosophy in Italy. However, she eventually trained as a psychoanalyst, perhaps in identification with the father she seems never to have had enough of. She and her younger daughter died in a traffic accident in 1998; her memorial photograph shows a generous, kind, intelligent face very like her father's. More conventionally, Julian studied medicine and Nicola worked in publishing.

By the time Bion and his wife returned to Britain, Bion was over seventy, though barely slowing down. In 1979 he died of leukaemia, a mere week after being diagnosed. This was shortly before various planned trips, some for work and one, poignantly, to India for the first time since the age of eight; perhaps he had had some idea that there was not much time left to fit this in. Francesca continued her unstinting support by organising and editing his autobiographical writing. Hopefully she found some happiness with work and family, after the sudden loss of her husband and two decades later, of Parthenope and her daughter.

Bion's contributions to psychoanalysis

Bion defines the space in which psychoanalytic concepts reside as 'O', the unknowable, the ineffable, an ultimate form of truth: it is to this that 'K' is directed. He suggests that through 'K' we have both an unquenchable thirst to know reality ('truth') and through 'minus K' or 'anti-K' (-K)[3] an unending urge to avoid the pain it brings us. He draws from Kant's opposition of 'phenomena', or appearances, and 'noumena', the original forms that phenomena are appearances of, asserting that we do not have access to a truly objective reality: we only know reality through our sense organs and our psyche and through the reflection that takes observation further towards knowledge. Conversely, his 'Notes on Memory and Desire' (1967, in Bott Spillius 1994: 17–21) gives a concise and pragmatic guide for therapists to develop their therapeutic presence, untrammelled by any deliberate considerations which disturb simply being a responsive presence. His thinking is philosophical and meticulously exact: practical, and yet at times close to mystical. It is not surprising that he has had such wide-ranging influence, yet without generating a specific band of followers.

Bion's groupwork

The Northfields Experiment

Bion's first professional psychoanalytic work was in the sphere of groups, and it was in his groupwork that he began to form and apply his innovative psychoanalytic thinking. Groupwork was a natural sequel to a childhood spent largely in school groups followed by service in the army. As an officer he was given responsibility for subordinates from the start. It was not surprising, then, that after his medical and initial psychoanalytic training he took a particular interest in soldiers rendered unable to function through trauma and in the kind of help they needed to return to normal life: this can be seen as an extension of the responsibility he felt for 'his' men when they were getting into difficulties. Accordingly, he did not seek psychological depth for its own sake, but more pragmatically focused on 'ego-building', helping the demoralised men to leave behind their psychological collapse and regain the capacity for useful work with an adequate degree of confidence.

Bion spent a scant six weeks putting his thoughts into practice in the 'Northfields Experiment', as it was known, before it was closed down – apparently without explanation (Bion 1961: 11–26; Bléandonu 1994: 61). In later years, Bion believed it was because of the release of strong and disturbing feelings and attitudes which spread like a chain reaction through to his superiors. But the Northfields Experiment was only the first of several such schemes developed around the same time, as a result of the proliferation of 'war neuroses' or 'shell shock' as it was termed, in both the first and second world wars. These experiments formed the groundwork for milieu therapy and therapeutic communities as well as more normal therapy groups, staff support groups and other ways in which groups came to be used as the therapeutic agent.

Bion ran and wrote up the experiment with John Rickman, his previous analyst. The group comprised around a hundred soldiers in need of psychological rehabilitation. There was a contradiction internal to the task from the start, which made intense negative transference all but inevitable. None of the patient–soldiers would have wanted simply to maintain their disabling neurotic symptoms, nor would any type of 'cure' be attractive, since it would lead to the soldier having to return to the dangers and trauma of the battlefield. The psychiatrists-in-charge could readily be seen as useless, sadistic or dangerous.

This was an issue which Bion also grappled with, as of course he did not wish to make the men he was working with fit again simply so that they could be injured or killed. He resolved it for himself, at any rate partially, by redefining his task as 'to produce self-respecting men socially adjusted to the community and therefore willing to accept its responsibilities whether in peace or in war' (Bion 1961: 13). This problem, together with the very short time the experiment was in practice, makes it surprising that Bion was able to draw any conclusions at all from it; that it was possible to do so appears to be due in large part to the close adaptation of the running of the group to the specific needs of the participants.

The group was set up as a continuation of the men's previous army experience, complete with a leader who could be trusted and respected. As a first step, it was known as the 'training wing' of the Northfields Military Hospital, differentiating it from wards for patients being treated for physical injuries or infections. The idea was that the vehicle of therapy should be the way in which the participants' days were organised, encouraging a more functional organisation of the personality and discouraging neurotic forms of behaviour and thinking. It was also important that Bion set up a formal mechanism whereby the group could become a self-critical community, through a midday 'parade' at which relevant information was given out and where any of the men could comment on any aspect of the 'experiment'. For the rest of the day, the men were expected to attend and join in at least one of a number of activity groups which they had chosen themselves, with more being set up by demand. There were the inevitable attempts at sabotage: one group asked for a 'dancing' group, obviously meaning it as a joke, but one which backfired when it was taken as seriously as any other activity asked for. Gradually it became a perfectly functional relaxation group where ballroom dancing could be practised at the end of the day. As Bion says, the mere fact that this was what they asked for revealed their low morale and how 'unmanly' they felt to be unable to face the terrors and hardships of fighting.

The men also had to do an hour's physical training each day: they were expected to exert themselves physically and could only avoid this through production of a medical certificate. There was a 'rest-room' overseen by a nursing orderly, where any of the men who felt unable to attend their normal groups could pursue quiet activities such as reading or letter-writing, or play games such as draughts. The only rule was that they should not talk loudly or act in a way that disturbed the other users of the room – some of whom might genuinely be feeling ill, traumatised or severely depressed. Bion himself chose a couple of men each day, no doubt very carefully, to accompany him on a general look around the community 'just to see how the rest of the world lives' (ibid. 17). This indicates how the 'training wing' was a world in itself, reflecting aspects of the outside world, so that all participants could learn not just about their wing but about the world at large. Records were kept of the whole community by the men themselves, in the form of little flags representing what each individual was doing and when. 'By a happy thought a supply of flags bearing the skull and crossbones was prepared, ready for the use of such gentlemen as felt compelled to be absent without leave' (ibid.), while those who spent excessive time in the rest-room were quickly discovered since the orderly in charge automatically took down their names.

In this way a simple structure, together with informal self-critiques, enabled badly damaged individuals to come to feel a part of something, recover some self-respect and regain the ability to live normally. Inevitably, there was some testing out at first; but by refusing to take responsibility for what happened on himself beyond the few basic ground rules and turning the running of the wing over to the group at large, Bion established a setting in which changes happened speedily. From being a desultory psychiatric ward where few participants discharged their official responsibilities, it became a coveted place to belong to, active and purposeful: 'The atmosphere was not unlike that of a unit of an army under the command of a general in whom they have confidence, even though they cannot know his plans' (ibid. 21).

For this to happen in a mere six weeks, and despite the inevitable transference problems, was truly remarkable. Bion made imaginative modifications of psychoanalytic ideas to suit the needs and circumstances. Whatever the reasons it seems a great waste that the Northfields Experiment was discontinued so quickly, although at least the work was developed further by others.

The Tavistock Groups

After this disappointment, Bion continued his work on groups at the Tavistock Clinic, where in 1948 he was asked to set up a variety of therapeutic and staff groups. The aim of these groups was clearly to be therapeutic in the longer term, rather than the psychological 'first aid' of the Northfields Experiment. Instead of working to increase participants' confidence and self-respect, Bion used these groups to explore and understand the primitive dynamics that arose in the course of therapy. His vignettes of 'groups of which I am a member' are sharp and witty, and each point is made with acute clarity. It sounds as though he had a very clear idea indeed of what he was doing, but without setting up his own agenda.

Bion's premise was that the therapeutic value of any group depended on the insight of its members, particularly the analyst: 'in group treatment many interpretations, and amongst them the most important, have to be made on the strength of the analyst's own emotional reactions' (ibid. 149). The analyst functions, in effect, as the recipient of projective identifications (see Bléandonu 1994: 87). This is what Bion means by 'counter-transference', which, together with projective identification, transference and containment, he treats as the cornerstones of successful therapeutic work. The more insight the analyst can gain into the primitive processes of the group life, the more scope there is for change.

Bion suggests that the character of each group – the essence of what is there for the analyst to perceive in the counter-transference – resides at the 'proto-mental' level. This term, and its counterpart 'proto-physical', indicate a point before the mental and physical systems are clearly differentiated: they do not refer to the mental and the physical as such, but 'that which will become mental' and 'that which will become physical'.

Bion explores these new ideas further: 'Starting, then, at the level of proto-mental events we may say that the group develops until its emotions become expressible in psychological terms …' He is saying that 'proto-mental' processes include an emotional perspective, and may evolve further until they reach the level of the mental: only then can they be expressed. Furthermore, 'It is at this point that I say the group behaves "as if" it were acting on a basic assumption' (1961: 101). Bion uses the 'basic assumption' to indicate the most fundamental level of behaviour that makes psychological sense. He is speaking of the level of phantasy, the location of the psychotic or very primitive anxieties of infantile life, before fact and fiction, reality and hallucinated wish have grown apart. These fears, hopes and wishes are not articulated, but can be deduced from the group acting 'as if' its members held the relevant belief in common. This means that being part of a group can be both confusing and frightening, with chaotic and undefined anxieties pressuring members to act 'as a group' in ways which may be uncharacteristic of them as individuals.

Bion conceives the basic assumption to be unconscious, just as phantasy is, and presumably situated near the junction of the psychological and the physical. It must be the proximity of these two barely differentiated modes of being which enable unconscious emotional anxieties to be expressed physically as 'conversion symptoms'. Accordingly, Bion believes that some 'basic assumptions' can be linked with particular illnesses or physical states as well as types of neuroses or mental states. Some endorsement of his views has been developed in relation to diabetes and heart disease – the typical 'broken heart' of the new widower, for example (Murray Parkes et al. 1969); Bion suggests a similar basis for developing tuberculosis (1961: 108). Epidemiological studies on a sufficiently large scale might identify more of these kinds of links.

At the Tavistock, Bion took the aim of the group to be solely and absolutely the study of group tensions. Prospective participants were told this, of course, but inevitably they did not expect him to keep to this task with such alarming thoroughness. For example, at the start of a group Bion did not make any remarks or interventions whatsoever, until he felt sufficiently sure of what was happening beneath the surface of the group; he would then be in a position to make a coherent suggestion, or interpretation. Most of his groups thus began with a bewildered silence, broken only by a few brave individuals trying to make sense of what was going on: Bion might simply observe that the group seemed to expect him to take responsibility. As group members floundered about in confusion and frustration, the underlying anxieties emerged ever more clearly until they could be interpreted.

Participating in these groups was thus a powerful experience, affecting people both physically and psychologically: 'two members developed duodenal ulcer symptoms before the group finished, and three decided to have personal analyses subsequently' (Pines [ed.] 1985: 82 in Bléandonu 1994: 67). Although Bion did not claim that his method of conducting groups was curative, it certainly enabled participants to gain a marked increase in self-knowledge through highly disturbing feelings and urges being uncovered. These reactions must have been incidents of the 'proto-mental/proto-physical' states in which disturbed reactions are initiated. Their latent physical and psychological natures would spread through the group by a subtle process of communication that might involve projective identification and body language.

Bion divides groups into two types: the rational and functional 'work group' and the three types of 'basic assumption group'. The work group represents the functioning of the group at the level of the ego: members recognise that learning, understanding and thus progress comes through experience, and that language is needed as a means of rational communication. This is the aspect of the group that functions adequately and is committed to its given task, whether that be psychotherapy or a practical task of some kind. In the basic assumption groups, by contrast, uncomfortable aspects of reality are to be avoided at all costs; the events which they are built on play out the phantasy to which human beings are uniquely liable, at the level of Klein's infantile phantasies involving part-objects and psychotic anxieties. At this primitive level, it is assumed that learning and progress will happen by magic rather than through experience, and language is used as a form of action rather than as communication. Instead of facing up to unwelcome realities and acting rationally, the neurotic individual does all he can to change his personal experience, using denial, projection and especially projective identification in his attempts to move the goalposts.

The first of the basic assumption groups is the 'dependency' group. Here, members behave as though one member of the group is a godlike figure who could give the rest of the group the change they seek without any effort on their part. In Bion's Tavistock groups, every attempt would be made to get him to take up the role of the all-knowing 'doctor' with avidly receptive 'patients'. But as he consistently proved disappointing in playing this part, other participants were sometimes 'groomed' for the job. This tendency, commonly seen in groups, reflects a general regression to the oral stage and the utter dependency of the infant on the parent. Bion gives the example of the church as a group with a 'valency' for dependency alongside more grounded features. Just as no child can do without an adult, no church can do without a deity – a point not lost on Freud, either.

Next comes the 'pairing' group, where factions, subgroups, and especially quasi-couples tend to form, apparently communicating with each other in some private language. Bion suggests that the root of the pairing is unconsciously assumed to be sexual in nature. Those excluded from the special pair may hope to be chosen as the one to be attached to the powerful leader or charismatic leader-participant, with the idealisation and hidden sexual gratification that is part of this. Negative feelings can run particularly high as participants not 'chosen' in this way are prey to the assaults of envy, humiliation and rage as others get the 'goods' they were hoping for.

In another form there is the hope that the chosen 'pair' will bring forth a saviour or 'messiah'; this may be a person or an idea which the group participants hope will save them all, again without their having to do anything towards this. Language, again, is used to create notions of the subgroup or the messiah rather than to further the task in hand. Bion's example of a social group with the 'messiah' valency is the aristocracy or a related institution, such as the House of Lords. These may be tolerated or even encouraged because of the widespread hopes for rescue by the 'highest' person, the one who is closest to royalty (or God), or the individual with the 'best' idea. Although the group 'messiah' may be something or someone not yet in existence, it is always the product of an individual (or oedipal pair) of particular excellence.

Groups need a minimum of three members, Bion states, or the dynamics are solely those of the pairing couple. This means that there are likely to be oedipal dynamics in most groups.

The final example is the 'fight-flight' group, where the only forms of interaction appear to be aggressive or fearful. Again, we can see that this is a familiar form of human response, created by splitting and projecting unwanted characteristics into the excluded group: human beings seem unable to live without a 'them' and 'us'. It is not difficult to see why Bion chooses the army as the everyday example of a work group with a particular leaning towards this kind of distortion of reality: the leader may seem impossibly wonderful, the enemy unrealistically evil.

These concepts relate most clearly to the work of Freud and Klein, both central figures in Bion's thinking. The work group mirrors the proper functioning of the ego, while the basic assumption groups reflect the atmosphere and processes of the early paranoid-schizoid position, characterised by splitting, projection and paranoia. If the task of the group is to discover and reflect on the basic assumption elements hidden within it, a great increase in self-knowledge, humility and self-understanding can be achieved – one can encompass and take responsibility for the regressive, neurotic aspects of oneself from a more mature point of view.

Individual psychology

Projective identification, container–contained and reverie

Bion considers these three fundamental concepts in some detail. Together, they make up the key to the way he approaches child development as well as clinical work. The latter two formulations are essentially his own, and he extends the original Kleinian view of projective identification while offering a new perspective on it. He divides this operation into normal and excessive forms: here, we shall look at the normal version, and at the excessive form in the section on psychopathology.

Bion expresses the operation of projective identification by the dual symbol ♀♂: the female or Venus sign followed by the male or Mars sign. This does not denote gender but merely that the container is prior to the projector, and that the container is penetrated by a projected communication, whether or not words are exchanged. Projective identification is the means by which 'container–contained', actually functions, as psychic growth in action. Emotional growth begins with the assumption that the infant has only one, unconscious, resort in the face of unbearable, chaotic experiences – to attempt to relocate them in the adult who is at hand. No good will come of this unless the adult, with the more mature and resilient psyche, can take in the full horror of the infant's feelings, reflect upon them without feeling overwhelmed or panicked and return them to the child in a detoxified, safer form. If successful, the infant is then able to take in a more mature sense of hunger, or cold, or fear, together with a sense that this experience can be managed – to take in that bit of the adult mind, which he can then go on to digest and make his own.

Bion's term 'reverie' is the counterpart of this: it refers to the accommodating state of mind in which the containing mother or therapist can make sense of her infant's or patient's most difficult feelings. By eschewing frantic anxiety or automatic action, the containing adult is able to see what is troubling the infant for what it is, rather than as something actually life-threatening, and engage with it appropriately. The same process takes place in the therapeutic setting, and it is with reference to this that Bion suggests the therapist rid herself of 'memory and desire'. Bion's aim is for the therapist to reach a kind of meditative state, the 'evenly suspended attention' that Freud writes of, in which the relevant aspects of the unconscious material of the patient can register. He calls this state 'faith' (F): 'By rendering oneself "artificially blind" through the exclusion of memory and desire, one achieves F; the piercing shaft of darkness can be directed on the dark features of the analytic situation' (Bion 1970: 57). The aim is to bring to bear not an increase but a 'diminution of the "light" – a penetrating of darkness; a reciprocal of the searchlight … So that, if any object existed, however faint, it would show up very clearly' (Bion 1974: 37).

Bion is remembered as advocating a state 'without memory or desire' in which the psychotherapist is most receptive to what may arise within himself from the effects of the patient's words and way of being. Sometimes it can be thought that he is recommending that therapists block out what they know about the patient, or work against their desire that he should get better. But 'without memory' is not the same as forgetting: it is rather, for example, not deliberately reminding oneself of what the last session was about. Listening for something in particular blocks openness to the present, so if the therapist can refrain from this, she has a better chance of encountering the patient as he is today, rather than as he was a week ago or a day ago. Similarly, being without desire includes such simple and concrete examples as not waiting for an opportunity to voice an insight you have thought of, or clock-watching through sessions, waiting for the end to come. It is almost always counter-productive if therapists try too hard to 'help' their patients. Much of the most useful work emerges out of beam states of confusion, inadequacy, or overtly negative transference. Eschewing memory and desire is the counterpart for the therapist of free association for the patient. All too often we meet with a resistance in ourselves, an impulsion to say something, which might be an avoidance of uncomfortable or painful emotion. Following Bion's recommendation allows anxiety, anger and doubt to come to the fore although, as Bion warns us, it is anything but easy (1967, in Bott Spillius 1994).

It may be noticed that Bion's outlook is very similar to Winnicott's, both in atmosphere and conceptually. Both write poetically – Winnicott almost always, and Bion at times – with the meaning of what they are communicating being expressed by the rhythm and association in the words rather than through logic alone. Conceptually, both are concerned with the close attunement between mother and baby, or therapist and patient, as the basis for mental growth. Bion's containing mother and Winnicott's 'ordinary devoted mother', Winnicott's 'primary maternal preoccupation' and Bion's reverie, Winnicott's 'there is no such thing as a baby' and Bion's basic capacity for linking, are all reminiscent of each other. Although both were deeply influenced by Klein, Winnicott moves on to emphasise the aspects that she focuses on less: environment rather than individual responsibility, concern and creativity rather than destructiveness, play rather than mental conflict. Although Bion remains firmly in the Kleinian tradition, his work and thinking demonstrate not only the minutely detailed analysis typical of it, but also, at times, the inspirational and poetic qualities more commonly associated with the Independent approach. Thus Winnicott typically conveys an atmosphere, while Bion also dissects and analyses what goes to make up the atmosphere.

It is of course Klein whom Bion acknowledges as the major influence on his work: 'Even when I do not make specific acknowledgement of the fact, Melanie Klein's work occupies a central position in my view of the psychoanalytic theory of schizophrenia' [his usual term for psychosis] (Bion 1953 in 1984: 23). As Klein took Freud's theoretical work backwards into infancy and its pathological development, psychosis, so Bion's work on psychosis delves into what makes up the rudiments of psychic activity as well as introducing new ideas from clinical work with psychotic patients.

Linking and the 'K' connection

Bion places great emphasis on the linking process, both in the mental and the psychotherapeutic settings: without the ability to form connections there could be no relationship, thought or emotion. He is one of the first to rearticulate that links (or attacks on them) are made to functions rather than to objects – to feeding, rather than the breast, for example. He includes the capacity to make conceptual links as a vital capacity that human beings are born with.

The process of linking starts with curiosity – with the baby's innate interest in the world and his experiences. Bion draws this concept from Klein's 'epistemological instinct'. She understands this drive as connected with sadism, the turning outwards of the Death Drive, rather than an aspect of Eros, as Freud does. Bion terms it 'K' or 'Knowledge', the urge to know subjective and objective reality, and ultimately 'O', the unreachable truth behind appearances. Essentially, it can be seen as curiosity which, for Bion, is as basic as love and hate – thus he uses the initials 'LHK' in his analysis of psychological processes. These appear in both positive and negative modes. Bion believes there are positive versions of hate, and negative versions of love but doesn't say a great deal about these, but describes K frequently in both its forms. In the positive mode of K, the emphasis mirrors Freud's description of Eros as bringing disparate elements together in ever-increasing unities. In the negative mode, it reflects the destruction or avoidance of linking of Freud's Death Drive and its perpetual regression to ever simpler states, ultimately inanimacy.

The basic psychical terms in which Bion thinks are, as we have seen, the operations of projective identification, container–contained and reverie, and the drives LHK. These are not so much observable events as concepts which Bion thinks are necessary if we are to find a way of characterising what is happening at the unconscious level of the psyche. All are based on the urge for or against linking, or connecting, in order to make contact with another element or object, and this is therefore the most fundamental element. Similarly, the three operations, L, H and K, are all implied in each other, with reverie being the active aspect of containment, and projective identification the mechanism by which 'container–contained' enables communication of both emotion and meaning. Emotion and meaning are the constituents of psychical development, and therefore apply both to the formation of the infant as subject and to what may happen in the therapeutic situation.

Pathological processes

The destruction of 'reality' in psychotic states

The major part of Bion's work life was spent deciphering the pathological versions of normal processes. With linking as the basic process, and K as the fundamental element, psychic pathology is based on attacks on linking (1959) and on K in the negative mode, or -K. Characteristically, Bion took this task to its extreme, analysing not just neurotic but frankly psychotic processes.

The first psychotherapeutic work with overtly psychotic people was carried out in the 1950s by the American Harry Stack Sullivan, but it was a form of treatment which developed away from British Object Relations. Klein, by contrast, takes the opportunity to 'stand on Freud's shoulders' to explore the subtler signs of more pathological transference, setting the scene for developing unmodified psychoanalytic work with this most disturbed group of patients through her own work with very young children. Bion was one of the first psychoanalysts to carry out psychoanalytic work with psychotic patients, joining other eminent Kleinians such as Hanna Segal and Herbert Rosenfeld. Amongst the Independents, Winnicott, Marion Milner and André Green did so too, though in a different way.

Bion examines in detail the pathological versions of the basic psychical processes. With the container–contained interaction being the vehicle for developing psychological health, failures of containment engender psychological fragility and a disturbed relation to reality. Instead of linking, the fundamental psychic process is compulsive splitting. Aspects of experience, from both the internal and external worlds, tend to fall apart or be driven apart into ever smaller fragments in an attempt to render them manageable. Attacks on linking take the place of continual impulses to create links with K, or curiosity, becoming anti-K or minus K (-K): reality itself becomes the enemy.

Bion refers to the early defence of splitting as an attack on linking. In healthy linking, the divisions tend to fall along the object's natural lines of demarcation, making it easier to reconnect them when the subject is ready to do so. This kind of thinking, even if concrete, allows for some symbolisation to endure, and the level of destructiveness is not enough to prevent the container–contained interaction from promoting relationship and self-acceptance.

In the psychotic mode, however, splitting is insistent and random, and projective identification is at its most virulent. Container–contained interaction, or the seeking of love and understanding, feels too dangerous to risk. Instead of the psyche continuing to develop, it starts to atrophy and take on abnormal forms. Imprisoned within a hatred of reality, the psychotic person lives in a world of 'bizarre objects', tiny capsules of meaningless terror, split until they can be split no more. Their meaninglessness is implied by their 'bizarreness', the fallout of failed containment. The subject is left in a state of 'nameless dread' – a kind of terror that cannot be controlled or contained even by descriptive words such as anxiety or fear, confusion or loss. The links with thought and language have been destroyed, leaving only 'nameless' and 'dread' to describe it.

Bion describes its development in clear, third-person terms:

> Normal development follows if the relationship between infant and breast [i.e. the feeding relationship] permits the infant to project a feeling, say, that it is dying into the mother and to reintroject it after its sojourn in the breast has made it tolerable to the infant psyche. If the projection is not accepted by the mother the infant feels that its feeling that it is dying is stripped of such meaning as it has. It therefore reintrojects, not a fear of dying made tolerable, but a nameless dread.
>
> (1984/1962: 116)

This is obviously not a state in which relationship and development can take place, but rather one in which reality, internal and external, cognitive and emotional, has to be avoided. The infant may come to use words, since there will be some healthy development entwined with the pathological, but may expect them to behave as though they were things and be bewildered when they do not. Because reality is avoided, learning from experience cannot take place: to the extent that the pathological dominates normal development '-K' has won out over 'K'.

While 'bizarre object' seems to be Bion's original expression, the evocative 'nameless dread' was first used by the psychoanalyst Karin Stephen, sister-in-law of the writer Virginia Woolf. Bion describes the experience in an eerily precise and clarifying way, another example of his acute attunement to his patients and his belief that bringing the most primitive and the most sophisticated parts of the mind together facilitates psychological growth. He writes of 'bizarre objects' as fragments of the already broken-up capacity for perception, expelled by projective identification:

> Each particle is felt to consist of a real external object which is incapsulated [*sic*] in a piece of personality that has engulfed it … The object, angered at being engulfed, swells up, so to speak and suffuses and engulfs it: to that extent the object is felt to have become a thing … This suffusion of the piece of personality by the contained but controlling object leads the patient to feel that words are the actual things they name.
>
> (1984/1956: 39–40)

Here, Bion shows acute sensitivity to the nature of the disturbed patient's presence and the atmosphere of their relationship. He listens for the music of their conversation, or the images behind the scenes being alluded to. Making himself receptive to his patient, he enters into his own reverie, however briefly, and then responds to the patient's strange form of object relating.

Bion maintains that pathological projective identification differs both in extent and type from the normal kind, and we can see this in the example above. Essentially, while normal projective identification has communication as its aim, the pathological kind aims primarily to avoid emotional pain by controlling others. The psychologically frail individual may be especially prone to attempt to solve his problems by the outward movement of projective identification (exporting parts of himself into the surrounding world and significant adults) but at the same time less able to be helped by projective identification in the reverse direction. Anything outside his own control becomes ever more persecuting as his pathological development proceeds. Thus, in Bion's view, the 'schizophrenic', or psychotic patient, makes use of a form of projective identification which is abnormal both in type and degree. His previous difficulties with reality make it difficult for both patient and therapist to distinguish between each other's reality. A similar problem arises for the patient with the discrimination of objects in the external and the internal worlds: feelings, thoughts, sensations and emotions might be treated as the same as each other, or in the same concrete way as external objects, while all experiences are seen as frightening or hateful – alive, in some way.

Such states should be treated like any other, in Bion's view. If a psychotherapist is able to take in the difficult communications received and reflect upon them (enter into reverie), she may become sufficiently attuned to the damaged individual to start to return his utter dread to him in a less frightening and more defined form. In return, the patient's fragmented objects may begin to join together to form a more realistic picture of himself and his world. With enough experiences of this kind, the differences between external and internal, mine and yours, animate and inanimate, become clearer as the baby or patient increasingly takes in parts of the more mature psyche, with their greater emotional capacities and ordered and balanced contents. Fear and distress, anger and envy, can be accepted and learned from, albeit reluctantly, rather than avoided at all costs.

Bion is not so naïve as to believe in outright 'cure', that psychotic symptomology can disappear without leaving a trace, yet he retains a reasonable optimism regarding work on the cutting edge of psychoanalysis:

> I am not yet prepared to offer any opinion about the prospects of treatment [of psychotics] except to say that two of the three schizophrenics of whom I am speaking are now earning their living. I believe that if the course I have indicated above is followed, there is reason to anticipate that the schizophrenic may achieve his own form of adjustment to reality, which may be no less worthy of the title of 'cure' because it is not of the same kind as that which is achieved by less disordered patients.
>
> (1984/1967: 34)

Another apt example is given in a section of a session 'The imaginary twin' (ibid. 4–5), in which he describes working with a patient who was highly narcissistic. The work gradually develops from apparently mundane and predictable oedipal material to the kind of description that only Bion can compose. Although this analysand was not psychotic, this illustrates how Bion worked with all his patients.

> There was still the dreary monotone of associations but there was now a quality which derived from what I can best describe as the rhythm of his associations. It was as if two quite separate co-existent scansions of his material were possible. One imparted an overpowering sense of boredom and depression; the other, dependent on the fact that he introduced regularly spaced pauses in the stream of his associations, an almost jocular effect as if he were saying 'Go on; it's your turn'.
>
> (1950 in 1984: 5)

This illustration also shows us what Bion means by recommending psychotherapists to be in the state of 'Faith', 'without memory or desire' (1967, in Bott Spillius 1994: 17–21). The therapist's 'free-floating' attention and relaxed reverie makes it possible to tune into the different strands and themes of the patient's material, even those that seem to oppose each other. We can see how the playfulness in Bion's reflection might return his insight to the patient in the same vein, so that he too could see the dual messages he is giving and build on the playful aspect.

Bion presumes that we all have something like a psychotic aspect that may develop to a greater or lesser extent, depending on our constitution and our childhood circumstances, particularly the extent to which the container–contained relationship was able to evolve in our early years.

Bion's psychical concepts

In this section we shall examine the kind of mental apparatus Bion constructs to account for how human beings develop psychically. Like Freud's metapsychology and Klein's internal objects, these concepts are inferred from reflections on clinical observations, and cannot be observed directly.

In this part of the chapter we shall be exploring what Bion terms alpha and beta elements and functions and the preconceptions, conceptions and concepts that follow on from them, and return briefly to the proto-mental/proto-physical states.[4] We have already touched on this level of Bion's thinking in the section on groups. The basic assumptions, the unspoken but shared basis for the group's actions and communications, are said to be 'proto-mental' – that is, a 'system … in which physical and psychological or mental are undifferentiated' (1961: 102). There would thus seem to be no difference between the 'proto-mental' and the 'proto-physical' systems, except that one will go on to become mental, and the other physical. Both belong to the unitary concept of the 'person', where mind and body co-exist prior to their differentiation.

The proto-mental and proto-physical stages are also terms that Bion uses specifically with reference to the group, especially the 'basic assumption' aspect of the group. This suggests that he sees the group as prior to the individual: there is no possibility of a human individual emerging from anywhere but a pre-existing human matrix. It is another way of saying, like Winnicott, that 'there is no such thing as a baby'. The concept of the 'proto-physical' is also particularly useful when thinking about psychosomatic symptoms, where emotional conflicts become 'converted' into physical states (1961: 106–108).

The 'alpha' and 'beta' elements are the next stages in what will become emotional rather than physical states. Bion names the stimulus, which as yet has no meaning, the beta element; on its own, it does not lead to thinking or learning – it needs the input of a containing mind to enable this to develop. Beta elements are raw sensory or affective impressions, odd and unrelated bits of experience which do not as yet fit together. They are the stuff of bizarre objects and so cannot be described any further – they are not linked with any function, element or way of being. Therefore, Bion sees them not as observable phenomena but as 'things in themselves', a term that Kant also uses when he contrasts the world of 'phenomena', or appearances, with 'noumena', for what they are appearances of – something that no human being can get a full grasp of, since any view is by necessity partial (Gardner 1999; Honderich 1995: 657–658).

If human beings were only capable of generating beta elements, or bizarre objects, there would be no psychology, no dreaming, no thinking and no possibility of learning by experience. It is the power of the container–contained interaction which enables all these things to arise through the contribution of the containing mind of the mother, or therapist. For example, instead of the indescribable sense impression of pain, the reverie of the more sophisticated and mature containing mind affords the pain some kind of meaning: it may be hunger, or the need for contact or it may be actual physical pain. The mother empathises with the baby's sense of wrongness which, as Bion says, can be as acute as a feeling of impending annihilation, and she is able to recognise it for what it is. She can then return this 'sense of wrongness' back to the baby, not as disconnected beta elements but as more connected alpha elements. No longer bombarded by beta elements, the baby in turn begins to make sense of the world, including his own experience. Alpha elements, in their new and integrated form, become primitive alpha functioning which, with repetition, becomes smoother and less deliberate.

It is through the conglomeration of alpha elements into an organised form of functioning that Bion sees thoughts arising. It is not that the child becomes capable of thought, but that the alpha elements-made-function makes thoughts a necessity. The mind cannot hold the experience returned in this more mature arrangement except in the new form of thought: '"[T]hinking" … developed in response to the challenge presented by the existence of "thoughts"' (Bion 1977: 84). Thoughts bring thinking into being, rather than the other way around, with the inevitability of all other kinds of human functioning, given a normal brain and an adequately containing adult.

Beta elements cannot be thought and cannot be remembered: they can only be the material for projective identification, on its outward movement; and there can be no such thing as beta functioning, as the elements remain disparate and unconnected. It is only when they are returned to their owner modified into alpha elements or integrated into primitive alpha functioning that they can be thought about, dreamt about, remembered. One can imagine Bion's small daughter dreaming about going to meet her father at the bus stop, probably with each element remaining largely undisguised at this early stage (see children's dreams, Gomez 1997: 20–21, and 2005: 91). Alpha elements (the components of alpha functioning) do not have to be expelled through projective identification because they have been made tolerable and usable: if Bion's daughter were in a state of longing for her then-absent father, she would have the capacity to conjure up a sense of him, consciously or unconsciously, and thus gain comfort. His absence would no longer be experienced as a snowstorm of bizarre objects but would be transformed into organised material for dreaming and phantasy, emotion and memory, unconscious and conscious thinking. Alpha functioning is what lifts the mere bombardment of stimuli into a human experience.

Bion also extends his schema with 'preconception', 'conception' and 'concepts'. These form the spectrum of the most primitive to the most sophisticated thinking, with each leading on to the next. The preconception is 'hard-wired' into the brain, and thus psyche: the infant does not have to learn certain ways of behaving (e.g. sucking and clinging) or the accompanying expectations of an external object. This hypothesis reflects Bion's and Klein's view that the depressive position and its recognition of a separate reality always accompany the paranoid-schizoid depression to at least a minimal degree. Bion would define the expectation of satisfaction derived from sucking as a preconception, together with the breast which goes with it.

However, once the infant experiences his first feed, the situation changes. He finds an object in reality – breast or bottle – and this changes forever the in-built preconception which existed before this event had taken place. Bion terms the object that sufficiently matches the infant's preconception a 'realisation' – the counterpart in reality of something that was previously purely imaginary, or abstract. But, while the positive realisation brings security and satisfaction, the child's capacities develop more from the anticipated object which is *not* there than from the one that is, in ordinary circumstances: it is the negative realisation which is the more formative, provided it is not overwhelmingly frequent or intense. The experience of frustration forces into existence some image or sense of what it is that is missing, and the breast or bottle now bears a status in the child's psyche which it could not have had before. The baby may soon go about the business of using his own resources to provide a temporary positive realisation – the thumb for example. The breast or bottle which does arrive is a positive realisation; the one that does not is just as real, but a negative realisation.

Thus, when the preconception meets a negative realisation the result is a thought, which sets thinking going. The thought is of the bad object, with 'object' standing for the whole experience rather than simply the objective means of satisfaction (absent in this case). The bad object is a candidate for expulsion through projective identification, and this only changes when the child learns that it is the experience that is bad rather than the object itself. This can only come about if there is an adult sensitive enough to help the child to bear negative experiences such as loss and frustration. Otherwise, Bion explains, 'The failure to bring about this conjunction of sense data, and thus a common-sense view, induces a mental state of debility in the patient as if starvation of truth was somehow analogous to alimentary starvation' (Bion 1962: 119). He is saying that the deprivation of experienced reality is as detrimental to the child's psychological development as the deprivation of food is to his or her physical development. The infant is left 'starving' for reality.

Conclusion

Bion was an original, independent-minded thinker who was eminent in many areas of life: in medicine, in classical studies, philosophy, literature and the arts, as well as in the deeper levels of mathematical and scientific thinking. But psychoanalysis was his primary commitment.

Although his autobiographical writings appear highly self-revealing there are strange gaps and obfuscations. Members of his family are rarely mentioned: we do not know whether he ever saw his sister Edna after starting at boarding school. There are also odd factual discrepancies in relation to his parents. According to the official records, Bion's mother died in 1939 and his father in 1944, while Parthenope was not born until 1945; however, he maintains that both parents suggested Parthenope should be adopted (1991b: 61), and claims to have supported his father in the Iver Heath after the war (ibid. 61). His parents appear to have been comfortably off financially, but Bion seems to have struggled, at least until his practice was established: he barely had time to see Parthenope, for example.

This accentuates the impression of an intensely private man for whom it was important to be self-sufficient, as do his early loneliness and his devotion to psychoanalysis. Yet it is a mistake to divide the brilliant and innovative intellectual from the somewhat neglectful family man: those who contribute the most to their main field of work have another part of their life which, by definition, suffers. We cannot criticise the familial choices he made without acknowledging that different choices would have been to the detriment of all those he taught and worked with, and to psychoanalysis as a whole.

Regarding his psychoanalytic contributions, one must marvel at the breadth and depth of his thinking. His clinical work is remarkable, from his early work on groups and their 'basic assumptions' to the introduction of K as a basic urge on a par with love and hate. A major feature in his approach is the questioning, and then resolving, of how the categories of human experience emerge from a prior unity. He describes all pathological conditions as founded in the perversion or subversion of K into -K, bringing the roots of cognition and emotion together; his concepts of the proto-mental and proto-physical track these modes of experience back to a stage before they became differentiated. He explores his subject by going back to the very beginning and rethinking it from there – for example, that psychical processes depend on linking. All these points involve new thinking about the basic nature of the psychical and how it could develop, with concepts as original as Freud's metapsychological theories and models.

As he moved between psychoanalytic and philosophical thinking, Bion was not content merely to clarify existing concepts but was driven to reformulate them or develop them anew. His theory of thinking as arising from thoughts, rather than the other way around, reflects both Freud's and Kant's assertions that what we call 'reality' arises from the nature of the human psyche before it is 'conditioned' by experience. This endows psychic growth with a circular structure, the psyche itself only emerging from a group of other psyches, thus emphasising the social nature of human beings.

Although Bion is following Freud in this, he always remains his own person. The open and unbounded quality of the knowledge or 'truth' that we search for psychoanalytically, the indescribable, ineffable, 'O', appears to conflict with his insistence that mathematics is at the root of all thinking and all thought. It would have been interesting to see whether he might have reconciled these claims, given more time, or whether he would have left them as an unanswerable paradox. Like Freud, he seems to have been more interested in developing his own thoughts than in ensuring their consistency at all costs.

It would also have been fascinating to learn more about his views on pathological processes other than the psychotic, such as perversion, as well as on the work of contemporaries other than Freud, Klein and a few of his Kleinian colleagues. The eccentrically original nature of his thinking means he did not attract followers. There is no 'Bionic' school of psychotherapy, but he has surely taken Object Relations thinking, and even psychoanalysis itself, further forward than any other individual after Freud and Klein.

Notes

1 While having 'no intention of sparing [the school] from criticism', Bion also describes it as 'extremely enlightened' (1991a: 85).
2 This must have been a mistake on his part; we know that his mother had died in 1939 and his father lived only until 1944 (Bion family tree, http://www.sumgenius.com.au/robinson_family_tree.htm). Perhaps Betty's parents stood in for his own 'mother and father', or perhaps a bitter aftertaste towards his parents escaped in this slip.
3 Fisher (2006) makes a convincing case for '-K' to be termed 'anti-K' rather than the more usual 'minus K', since it acts against the perception of reality rather than signifying a lack of reality. This is not the main point of his paper, but an interesting aspect.
4 In his 'grid' (1977), Bion depicts in tabular form how thinking develops from sense impressions, to isolated thought components, to connected phantasies and dreams, and thence to the sophistications of scientific and finally mathematical thinking, and orders the level of psychological work from simple naming to identifying the defensive purpose and the language in which they might be expressed (see Bléandonu 1994: 165–172). It has not been taken up in the practical way Bion intended, and he came not to think highly of it himself (*Journal of Melanie Klein*, Spring 1999).

References

Bion family tree, http://www.sumgenius.com.au/robinson_family_tree.htm.
Bion, W. (1950) 'The Imaginary Twin', reprinted in *Second Thoughts* (1984).
——— (1953) 'Notes on the Theory of Schizophrenia', reprinted in *Second Thoughts.*
——— (1956) 'Development of Schizophrenic Thought', reprinted in *Second Thoughts.*
——— (1959) 'Attacks on Linking', reprinted in *Second Thoughts.*
——— (1961) *Experiences in Groups and Other Papers*, London: Tavistock.
——— (1962) 'A Theory of Thinking', reprinted in *Second Thoughts.*
——— (1967) 'Notes on Memory and Desire', in E. Bott Spillius (ed.), 1994, *Melanie Klein Today: Volume 2: Mainly Practice*, London and New York: Routledge.
——— (1970) *Attention and Interpretation*, London: Tavistock.
——— (1974) *Brazilian Lectures 1*, Rio de Janeiro: Imago Editora, reprinted (1990) London: Karnac.
——— (1977) *Seven Servants: Four Works by Wilfred Bion*, New York: Jason Aronson.
——— (1984) *Second Thoughts*, London, Karnac. First published (1967), London: William Heinemann Medical Books.
Bion, W. ed. F. Bion (1991a), *The Long Weekend, 1897–1919: Part of a Life*, London and New York: Karnac. First published in 1982, Abingdon: Fleetwood Press.
——— (1991b) *All My Sins Remembered* and *The Other Side of Genius: Another Part of a Life*, London and New York: Karnac. First published (1985) Abingdon: Fleetwood Press.
Bléandonu, G., trans. C. Pajaczkowska (1994) *Wilfred Bion: His Life and Works, 1897–1979*, London: Free Association Books, New York: Guilford Press. First published (1990) as *Wilfred R. Bion: La vie et l'oeuvre. 1897–1979*, Paris: Editions Bordas.

Bott Spillius, E. (ed.) (1994) *Melanie Klein Today: Volume 2: Mainly Practice*, London and New York: Routledge.

Fisher, J. (2006) 'The Emotional Experience of K', in Mawson, C. (ed.), *Bion Today*, 2011: 43–63.

Gardner, S. (1999) *Routledge Philosophy GuideBook to Kant and the Critique of Pure Reason*, London, Canada and USA: Routledge.

Gomez, L. (1997) *An Introduction to Object Relations*, London: Free Association Books and New York: New York University Press.

——— (2005) *The Freud Wars: An Introduction to the Philosophy of Psychoanalysis*, London and New York: Routledge.

Honderich, T. (ed.) (1995) *The Oxford Companion to Philosophy*, Oxford and New York: Oxford University Press.

Murray Parkes, C., Benjamin, B. and Fitzgerald, R.G. (1969) 'Broken Heart: A Statistical Study of Increased Mortality Among Widowers', *British Medical Journal* March 22, 1, no. 5646: 740–743.

Pines, M. (ed.) (1985) *Bion and Group Psychotherapy*, London: Routledge and Kegan Paul.

Chapter 5

Further Kleinian developments

Since the Controversial Discussions of the 1940s, Kleinians have produced an impressive body of creative and innovative work. Its members follow Klein in aiming to use the same principles for working with children and with psychotic, borderline and narcissistic patients as with neurotic adults. This entails sessions with a bounded and consistent time and space in which there is an emphasis on understanding and interpreting the patient's inner world. Kleinian practitioners usually focus on 'here-and-now' transference interpretations: the psychotherapist or analyst makes use of clues taken from her own emotional shifts in the session, as well as conscious communications to and from the patient, to reach an understanding of how the patient is unconsciously inviting her into a specific form of relationship derived from his past. Once the dynamics have become sufficiently clear, she may then interpret his actions or impulses, trying to express them in a way he can accept.

Kleinians were the first to bring infant and child observation into psychotherapeutic training (see Bick 1964). This gave prospective Kleinian psychotherapists and psychoanalysts a firm grounding in how ordinary babies and children develop, as well as substantial training in linking theory and clinical work. Infant and child observation involves regular practice in simply watching and listening without interfering – a difficult but essential requirement for any psychotherapist. It also assists in developing sensitivity to the countertransference, a primary resource for all practitioners, but especially Kleinian.

Work with children and with more disturbed adults has spread from the Kleinian group through psychoanalysis as a whole. The two kinds of work are closely related theoretically and practically. They draw on the understanding of the primitive psyche, where symbolic functions may be limited or distorted, so that the therapist has to pay acute attention to what exactly the patient might be communicating, verbally and non-verbally. It may be in a very different 'idiom' from that of ordinary speech. Both children and psychotic patients, for example, may move around the room, hide under a table, use objects to communicate or interact in other non-verbal ways. There is the risk that interpretations may be understood concretely: an observation along the lines of 'you feel I'm intruding into your space' may be experienced as an actual bodily violation. With these groups of patients there may be the need to liaise with parents, carers or other professionals. Klein began the custom of avoiding more than essential guidance, believing that even young children and psychotic patients are well able to appreciate the different 'rules' that apply to the psychoanalytic setting and to ordinary life.

Working with these patients is complex and demanding, and Kleinian work is often intensive – with three or more sessions a week. Although this kind of work is very different from that offered by counsellors and psychotherapists who see people once or twice a week, it is nevertheless useful for all practitioners to have some knowledge of the complexity and depth of work at this level. It assists in the understanding of less disturbed patients and, just as all psychotic people have non-psychotic aspects to their personality, so 'ordinary' people have pockets of narcissism and other deep disturbance in theirs.

Freud considered that patients with narcissistic or psychotic pathology lay beyond the scope of psychoanalytic treatment because of their difficulties in making relationships, including transference relationships. Kleinians disagree, holding that while narcissistic and psychotic transferences are obscure and complex, they certainly exist. Kleinians began to work with these patients, seeking to understand the often bizarre unconscious phantasies underlying their communications. The psychotherapist has to be acutely aware of her own as well as the patient's changing and often disturbing reactions in sessions, remaining ready to link current material with past events. The way the patient treats the therapist or analyst will reflect his early experiences of containment, or more often the lack of it. Whatever kind of patient she may be working with, the Kleinian therapist will focus on what the greatest anxiety seems to be and interpret how that is lived out between patient and therapist.

Special attention is given to what the patient does or says immediately following an intervention: the Kleinian practitioner requires evidence to back up her sense of the patient's dynamics. If her intervention generates more material, this is usually treated as a confirmation of the observation or interpretation; if the patient becomes blocked, it may suggest the contrary. If he reacts negatively, however, the therapist needs to consider whether she is misunderstanding the patient, whether she is overwhelmed and so unable to work at her best, or whether the patient is resisting confrontation with a painful but significant truth.

Kleinian therapy can be denigrated as rigid and persecutory. The pragmatic Michael Balint, an early Independent, went so far as to assert that the Kleinian approach, with its continual, authoritative 'here-and-now' interpretations given in 'mad' sounding language, tends to confirm its own theory. It is the centrality of the transference, he said, rather than the state of the patient, which leads to so many interpretations involving envy and hate on the one hand and idealisation on the other (Balint 1968: 104–107). In fact, of course, more depends on the individual therapist or analyst than on any other factor. John Hill, a Kleinian analyst, describes the contrasting styles of a number of different Kleinian therapists and supervisors he has known in his paper 'Am I a Kleinian? Is anyone?' (Hill 1993). He is critical of the tendency to idealise Klein and overuse well-known lines of interpretation, such as envy. Although firmly committed to the Kleinian approach, he advocates that practitioners make use of Kleinian thinking rather than follow any set way of working; he clarifies and differentiates better Kleinian therapy from worse.

This chapter discusses the work of Rosenfeld and then that of Heimann and Joseph together, all younger colleagues of Klein. Herbert Rosenfeld analyses the finer points of projective identification and distinguishes between destructive and libidinal narcissism, thick-skinned and thin-skinned variants. Paula Heimann's ground-breaking paper on counter-transference leads into Betty Joseph's paper on 'Transference: The Total Situation', laying the ground for the characteristic Kleinian 'here-and-now' transference interpretation. In the interests of privacy I shall only give biographical material that is widely available.

Herbert Rosenfeld (1910–1986)

Herbert Alexander Rosenfeld was born into a middle-class Jewish family in Nuremberg, Germany, in 1910. He studied medicine at various German universities, graduating with a medical diploma in psychiatry at the University of Munich in 1934. It was here that his interest in psychology began, but he was unable to follow it up since Nazi racial laws prevented Jewish doctors from having personal contact with their patients. The proliferation of these laws led him to move to the UK in 1935 – one of the earlier Jewish refugees to take note of the warning signs – and he had to retake his medical exams, which he did in Glasgow in 1936. He returned to London to train with the Tavistock Clinic, which enabled him to remain in the UK as a psychological specialist. This meant he entered the field of psychotherapy rather earlier than he had expected.

In the months before starting his Tavistock training, Rosenfeld took up short-term locum posts at the Warneford, a small hospital in Oxfordshire, and at the Maudsley Hospital in London. In each he was allowed to treat psychotic patients with basic psychotherapy, although at neither hospital was this expected to be a productive way forward. Rosenfeld's facility for creating a constructive and friendly rapport with patients seen as more-or-less untreatable came to the fore, and in each place the work was successful, in that some of the patients' most overt symptoms retreated or diminished. However, he was only able to treat one patient at the Warneford, whereas at the Maudsley several came his way. He became aware of splitting as an important factor in psychosis and, encouraged by the unexpected success of this brief work, his interest in psychosis deepened (Rosenfeld 1987: ch. 1).

At the Tavistock, Rosenfeld's training was in ordinary adult psychotherapy. Particular problems would arise when patients thought to be neurotic turned out to be psychotic. With one patient he had to bring the work to an abrupt end when it was already well underway, after the patient was re-diagnosed as schizophrenic rather than obsessional. The patient's suicidal thoughts had become too detailed to be overlooked, and on advice from senior colleagues, Rosenfeld persuaded the patient to enter hospital. Both Rosenfeld and his patient found this very distressing and Rosenfeld determined that as soon as he was qualified to work on a private basis, he would do all he could to avoid sudden endings with any psychotic patients he took on. Even so, unforeseen difficulties could arise. For example, a transference interpretation aimed at clarifying the erotic feelings between the patient as a child and one of her parents was mistaken for a direct invitation for a sexual relationship with the analyst. The patient had a full breakdown following this interpretation and had to return to hospital. Rosenfeld felt 'very bad' about this, although he also learned from it to be aware of the tendency towards concrete thinking in such patients.

Klein and her work came to Rosenfeld's attention in 1942 and he started analysis with her during his subsequent training at the Institute of Psychoanalysis. He finished his training in 1945, and was accepted as a training analyst in 1949. He was deeply influenced by Klein, both through his analysis and her writings. It is not surprising that he not only made psychosis his particular area of interest but also rethought and extended some of Klein's key concepts, such as projective identification, destructiveness and narcissism. He worked and lived in London with his wife and children until he died suddenly of a stroke in 1986, while still actively engaged with his writing and practice. His main writings are gathered into his books *Psychotic States* (1985), containing papers from the 1960s, and *Impasse and Interpretation* (1987), which includes his papers on narcissism from the 1970s. We shall draw mainly from the latter in this section.

In refining the concept of projective identification, Rosenfeld introduces a new focus on confusional states, which he sees as a midway point between splitting and integration. Most importantly, he brings in a crucial division between libidinal and destructive narcissism. In the healthier kind of narcissism, the libidinal focus on the self is greater, as against that in which destructive impulses and structures predominate. Libidinal narcissism aims to increase self-love, whereas destructive narcissism aims to destroy the workings of love itself. These views of narcissism led up to his pioneering work on psychosis. We shall look particularly at his concepts of libidinal and destructive narcissism and the factors he saw as most important in aiding or hampering psychoanalytic work with psychotic patients.

Like his colleagues, Rosenfeld disagreed with Freud's view that narcissistic and psychotic patients could not be helped through psychoanalytic treatment and, together with Abraham, Klein and Bion, he built on Freud's clinical approach. Freud maintained that for most individuals, psychotic elements of the personality are kept out of awareness, as unconscious processes which may appear in dreams. With psychotic patients, conversely, it is reality-orientated aspects of the personality that are held in abeyance. Speaking of one of the 'rare' occasions when a patient recovers from 'hallucinatory confusion', Freud states that 'one learns from patients after their recovery that at the time in some corner of their mind (as they put it) there was a normal person hidden who, like a detached spectator, watched the hubbub of illness go past him' (S.E.23: 202). Kleinians, like

Freud, saw the whole variety of mental states as a continuum, from the normal/neurotic, through what came to be called the borderline states, to the psychotic. None of these modes is alien to any individual, although after infancy there is generally one which remains predominant.

Projective identification and splitting in psychotic states

Rosenfeld places considerable emphasis on the process of projective identification in his work on both psychosis and narcissism. He sees it as occurring together with splitting, which Freud had described as the division between those parts of the ego that are securely in touch with reality and those that are not.

Following Klein (1946), Rosenfeld describes projective identification as

> a splitting process of the early ego, where either good or bad parts of the self are [psychically] split off from the ego and are as a further step projected in love or hatred into external objects which leads to fusion and identification of the projected parts of the self with the external objects.
>
> (In Steiner 2008: 131)

Rosenfeld is saying that splitting is one of the earliest mental acts, followed by the projection of the threatening hate-filled or love-filled part of the self into another person. This involves identification of that aspect of the self with the external object, or other person. An infant or regressed patient who is terrified of his destructive hate will feel he is removing the dangerous part of himself and relocating it into a significant other (usually the parent or therapist) where, it seems to him, he will not have to deal with it. Alternatively, if he feels that his vulnerable, loving side is at risk of attack by his own destructiveness, it is this that he psychically exports.

This process is necessary in order for the infant to make use of the good aspect of the split maternal object: at first, he can take in the 'good' mother only if her 'bad' counterpart is kept well away. With increased maturity, however, the infant can attain an ambivalent viewpoint if he feels 'contained' – if he senses that his projections have been taken in by his significant object (mother) and received back in a manageable form. When containment is insecure, projective identification is used to excess, and the projector is left feeling empty and depleted, with insufficient substance to fill his sense of self. He ends up feeling dreadfully inferior to the 'perfect' people around him, and/or overwhelmed by a world that seems frighteningly oppressive and persecuting.

Projective identification is closely involved with psychosis, where the patient's relationship to reality is thoroughly distorted by the aspects of himself which he finds threatening and so locates in other people or objects. This begins with the people closest to him and potentially extends to include almost all aspects of reality – including computers, historical figures and other leading players in delusions. The patient does this less to communicate with others, as with normal projective identification, than to control others and keep himself safe, as explained by Bion. Rosenfeld, like Segal, maintains that the practitioner's task is to understand the patient, assuming that however bizarre his verbal and non-verbal expressions may appear, they can be reflected on and ultimately comprehended, both in the here-and-now of the transference relationship and beyond. If the patient can have an experience of being with someone who is less terrified or terrifying than he feels himself to be, he may gradually become able to join with her in attending to what is happening. For this kind of containing interaction to be possible, the psychotherapist has to access the details of her counter-transference, and this may be particularly challenging with psychotic patients. The work is slow and painstaking since the patient, in desperation, is resorting to wholesale projective identification in the aftermath of trauma, or at least in the wake of relationships going very badly wrong. Like neurotic symptoms, psychosis is an unconscious attempt to solve a problem which the patient cannot allow himself to be aware of. As Freud said, he holds whatever realistic self-awareness he has available in a split-off fragment of sanity that is always there.

One example that Rosenfeld gives is of a man diagnosed as schizophrenic, who did not suffer from delusions or hallucinations but who was nevertheless unable to maintain work or personal relationships of any kind. His condition was 'characterized by overwhelming panic, confusion and fears of complete disintegration' (Steiner 2008: 141). Even after two analyses, the second with Rosenfeld, the patient was still liable to feel as though he were totally 'inside' his analyst: he had projected so much of himself into the analyst that he could no longer feel that much of himself was outside him. If he emerged from this parasitical state he experienced intense envy of the analyst 'owning' the capacity to manage on his own; or he would project his envy into Rosenfeld, leaving himself in acute panic for fear that he had destroyed Rosenfeld's thinking capacity. We can imagine that Rosenfeld had to endure the unpleasant experience of emotionally containing this patient's persecutory and persecuted feelings, with all the greedy and envious features that went with them. Incrementally, however, by working through his dependence, inferiority and shame, the patient became able to experience himself as more separate from Rosenfeld (Steiner 2008: ch. 10).

As we saw in Bion's work, the capacity for symbol formation is severely affected by psychosis, making the experience of such patients concretely rather than symbolically structured. This patient of Rosenfeld's, for example, felt compelled to watch the Olympic Games late into the night in order to take on the strength and self-sufficiency of the athletes. This was not a harmless pleasure but a draining addiction. 'Why have I to be an athlete? Why can't I be myself?' he would ask (ibid. 142), adding that he felt engulfed by the world of the Games as it was mediated through the screen. Rosenfeld sums up:

> at first he felt he probably could control and possess these objects entirely when he got inside them, but very soon he felt enclosed and trapped and persecuted, which aroused his wish to destroy the bed and the television screen

> which had turned into persecuting objects. I thought that his fear of being trapped and his anger related also to the analysis and the analyst.
>
> (Ibid. 143)

As the patient began to feel more distinct from Rosenfeld he became 'overcome with impatience and envy' of Rosenfeld and other active men like him. He was trying to become such a man by the shortcut of identification rather than by the slow and steady route of self-development. Rosenfeld must have interpreted this with conviction and empathy, because the patient did not feel humiliated but agreed that this was so. This short summary of a much longer passage exemplifies the depth of understanding and detail of interpretation necessary in this kind of work.

Like other Kleinians, Rosenfeld sees splitting and projective identification as central to both normal and abnormal development. Splitting is necessary for experiences of the object world to be organised into benign and persecutory categories, giving the infant a start in an ordered experiential world and making unconscious communication possible in the form of projective identification. With adequate containment on the part of mother or therapist, a good internal object relation can form, and the infant or patient becomes able to integrate both positive and negative aspects of himself and others.

In pathological development, splitting is more complex. Threatening aspects of the self are split into smaller and smaller fragments in the vain hope of making them easier to cope with, demonstrating the divisive tendency of the death or destructive drive. These chaotic fragments of 'badness' may extend to the extreme of Bion's 'bizarre objects', and are pressed into the other person with such force that they may be all but impossible to resist. If this pattern is repeated, a spiral of negative development ensues, with divisions between self and other, thing and person becoming blurred and indistinct. This can result in psychosis, where the individual loses touch with much of both his internal and external realities.

However, as Freud points out, in every psychotic person there is also the normal person, quietly observing 'the hubbub of illness go past him.' (Freud S.E.23: 202) This is the healthier part of the patient with whom the analyst may be able to work. But even here, whether the hating or the loving aspects of the patient are projected into the therapist, the partial dissolution of personal boundaries results in an attitude that is effectively centred on the self, blocking the way to full relationship with others. Freud describes in detail how this state of mind comes about, calling it narcissism. Rosenfeld's work represents a major advance in both understanding and working with this kind of pathology.

Libidinal and destructive narcissism

While all individuals have narcissistic tendencies, these may veer more towards the libidinal or the destructive side. In Rosenfeld's terms, each kind of narcissism is one side of the same coin, with both acting as defences against the persecutory anxieties of the paranoid-schizoid position and the fear of one's own destructiveness of the depressive position. These positions together constitute the larger, overall structures of psychic life, with narcissism being one way of defending against the anxieties inherent to them. For Rosenfeld, libidinal narcissism constitutes an attempt to keep hold of the capacity to love, while destructive narcissism is an attempt to destroy it. In both cases, the ultimate aim is to safeguard the ego from vulnerability to the emotional power of other people, whether by taking control of the source of love (libidinal narcissism) or attacking love in all its manifestations (destructive narcissism). The libidinal type of narcissism has the aim of restoring the experience of love to the ego alone, while the destructive type aims to destroy all libidinal bonds.

Like other psychoanalytic dualities, libidinal and destructive narcissism do not operate in isolation; they always act together, but with one taking precedence. Rosenfeld sees the acceptance of dependence and vulnerability as the key to changing the emphasis in favour of the healthier libidinal type. It is this that enables a workable, quasi-infantile relationship to be gradually established between patient and therapist, which can then develop and deepen until the patient's inner life becomes more integrated. This long and difficult task entails the patient withdrawing his hateful and envious projections and accepting that he is separate from his therapist and other objects, and that they are separate from him. He can only do this by allowing himself to become thoroughly dependent on the psychotherapist, so that he can risk recognising her separateness; she can then take the place of the different significant figures in the patient's internal object relations. The earlier the situation he regresses to, the more his internal world can potentially develop.

Not all Kleinians agree with Rosenfeld's new clinical category. Segal, for example, rejects the concept of 'libidinal' narcissism since she sees all narcissism as involving a destructive turning-away from relations with others. She points out that because narcissism is driven by envy it leads to highly confusional states, making it difficult for the thoroughly envious person to judge what is good and what is bad (see Steiner 2008: ch. 4). Love may be felt as bad if it comes from the outside and renders one vulnerable to hurt and of course envy, while hate may feel good because it defends against this kind of pain. Some Kleinians agree with Rosenfeld, however, that there is a kind of narcissism in which envy is particularly virulent, with confusion becoming extreme. This has been named 'negative narcissism' or 'negativity' (Abraham 1924, in Abraham 1927), a 'Mafia-like organization' (Meltzer 1968) and in general, 'narcissistic object relations' or 'narcissistic states'. All are based on excessive projective and introjective identification.

Rosenfeld describes and discusses 'destructive narcissism' in detail and repeatedly. He begins by maintaining, with Klein, that narcissism is not a non-relational state – Kleinians believe there can be no human state without object relations. Rosenfeld's work with psychotic patients confirms this: such patients may appear psychically 'dead' to those around them, but beneath the surface there is an omnipotent relationship with the therapist going on, he argues, composed of overwhelming projective and introjective identifications and driven by aggression. The psychotherapist is felt to hold all the aspects of the patient which appear threatening to him. In the example described above, for example, the patient is bitterly aware of feeling weak and vulnerable, as he has projected his own strength and power into Rosenfeld, represented by the athletes he feels compelled to watch on television. Then, by identifying with the athletes/Rosenfeld and re-introjecting these qualities he experiences himself *as* an athlete, despite his conscious wishes – he wants to be 'himself'.

At the same time, the patient projects his own weakness and vulnerability into the 'Jews' who are being portrayed as such in Nazi Germany; this includes Rosenfeld, a German Jew (ibid. 144). The patient is terribly ashamed of this, but it is the only way he can maintain his feelings of both strength and safety. It is only the 'Jews' who are weak enough to need other people, he thinks, and only the 'athletes' who are strong enough to keep themselves safe. His shame demonstrates that he realises at some level that the 'Jew' also represents himself, as do the athletes. His introjective and projective forms of relating thus prevent him from feeling clearly separate from anyone else. And as Rosenfeld explains to him, these impulses are a protective reaction to the progress he was making, which faces him with feeling both more separate and more in contact; more self-aware, and therefore more envious.

The most extreme state of destructive narcissistic object relations is 'narcissistic omnipotent object relations' (Rosenfeld 1987: 20). Rosenfeld discovers this kind of narcissistic relationship to be the core of psychosis, where there is little true differentiation between the self and the non-self. In this state the main source of pleasure is gained from damaging or destroying anything good: libidinal ties are the prime targets for narcissism turned destructive. Rosenfeld studied the complex and contradictory nature of this form of relationship from the start of his work with psychotic patients. The concept of 'destructive narcissism', derived from this work, is his most significant contribution to psychoanalysis.

Rosenfeld says little about libidinal narcissism, except that it is in the service of restoring love to the deprived ego. This will normally occur when the patient's relationships with external objects have not gone well, so that instead of turning his love to other people he redirects it back to himself. With the feeling of being loved, even if only or mainly by himself, he feels better and can afford to be a little more generous in his attitude towards others. Libidinal narcissism is thus the milder form of narcissism which may naturally evolve into normal relating. It develops into 'destructive narcissism' only when it becomes controlling and destructive, blocking the patient's route towards loving relationships with himself or anyone else, while maintaining identification with others through virulent hatred.

'Thin-skinned' and 'thick-skinned' narcissism

Rosenfeld makes a further distinction between 'thin-skinned' and 'thick-skinned' narcissism. The thin-skinned narcissist is over-sensitive to any hint of criticism, while the thick-skinned narcissist is oblivious to anyone's views except his own.

In the first case, a precarious, idealised view of the self is built up through projective identification (to get rid of the less than ideal parts) and introjection (to bring in and identify with additional protective qualities). Even a small threat to his grandiose view of himself sends the individual into a dreadful state of fury, loss or confusion.

The thin-skinned narcissist has usually felt badly treated in childhood, so that he grows up with a sense of inferiority to all those around him. His symptoms are a compensation for this outcast state, with envy, as usual, playing a prime role. Humiliation and further rejection are constant, hovering dangers. This tendency to paranoid thinking means that the thin-skinned narcissist does not come across as particularly likeable and is therefore prone to have his fears at least partially confirmed. Rosenfeld recommends specific therapeutic approaches. First, the therapist should offer clear and unambiguous explanations of exactly what the patient is doing. Only later, and not too frequently, can she risk interpretations of envy, humiliation and other feelings that are difficult to acknowledge, so that the patient has the chance of developing increasing trust that these feelings and impulses can be accepted.

The thick-skinned narcissist, by contrast, requires firm and consistent treatment for anything at all to get through to him. His defences are such that he can scarcely conceive of feeling badly about himself, and it is the therapist's task to bring about a more balanced view – not through cruel humiliations, but through constant, detailed description of what he is doing in the transference relationship. If this is communicated with empathy and honesty, the patient may gradually bring himself to a greater degree of insight; but this can only happen when he recognises that the therapist is not out to destroy him but to show him the true state of affairs in order to help him develop a better life.

Thin-skinned and thick-skinned narcissism correspond broadly to the libidinal and the destructive forms, with the latter being more difficult to work with – but not impossibly so. Libidinal narcissism, Rosenfeld thinks, is largely defensive in nature and thus predominantly environmental in origin, while destructive narcissism is likely to have a more substantial constitutional root. However, we all live and grow within the parameters of what is given to us constitutionally and environmentally, and the majority of patients hold the capacity to have some effect on themselves if help is provided – as long as they can see enough to want it.

Conclusion

Rosenfeld was a natural clinician whose theoretical work flowed from his clinical work: 'I am no theoretician', he declared to his colleague Riccardo Steiner (Steiner 2008: 39). His personal friendliness and his ease with patients in even the most floridly psychotic states are often mentioned (ibid.). It was this that enabled him to make some of the earliest advances into understanding psychosis and working with psychotic patients.

Rosenfeld saw psychosis as an extreme form of disturbance in which the patient's personality develops almost entirely through projective and introjective identification – from psychically sending out and taking in threatening or desired parts of one's own or someone else's psyche. The patient has unconsciously put so much of himself into his objects that he may feel depleted, and has taken in so much from others that he feels unreal. Projective identification is typically triggered by envy, which necessarily adds to the confusion. Destructive narcissism is closely related to psychosis, with the patient making highly aggressive use of projective identification in an attempt to neutralise the vulnerable and loving aspects of himself or other people. The less severe libidinal narcissism, by contrast, Rosenfeld explains by the infant or patient feeling unloved and so attempting to redirect back to himself the love he was sending out to other people.

Rosenfeld is not the best known of the Kleinians we are discussing, but he is one of the most influential, with narcissism becoming the predominant psychopathology of modern times. We shall now examine the similarly lucid work of Paula Heimann and Betty Joseph. Together, these two analysts construct the framework for the characteristically Kleinian use of 'here-and-now' transference interpretation. While the Kleinian clinical approach is built around this, it also features widely in other psychotherapeutic approaches.

Paula Heimann and Betty Joseph: the transference/counter-transference dimension

Heimann and Joseph both became deeply interested in Klein's theories and approach. Heimann contributed to the 'Controversial Discussions' as a member of the Kleinian group and had a second analysis with Klein, while Joseph, a generation younger, had a further analysis with Heimann. Their particular area of interest came to prominence with Heimann's paper 'On Counter-Transference' (1949/1950). Although this concept has been associated with Kleinians ever since, it led to a rift between Heimann and Klein. Klein believed, like Freud, that counter-transference is made up of unanalysed parts of the psychotherapist's psyche, limiting her ability to perceive the patient clearly. However, in the same way that Freud came to see transference as an analytic tool rather than a hindrance, Heimann argues that the counter-transference can illuminate hidden aspects of the psychotherapist–patient relationship, making it invaluable in guiding therapeutic interventions; her concept of counter-transference is more clinically focused than Klein's. Joseph agrees with Heimann, and each wrote papers on technique, which accentuate the use of the counter-transference.

Paula Heimann (1899–1982)

Paula Heimann was born Paula Glatzko into a Russian Jewish family in Danzig, then a town in Germany. She qualified in medicine and became a psychoanalyst in Berlin, where her analyst was Theodor Reik. She married a fellow-doctor,

Franz-Anton Heimann, in 1924, and they had a daughter. By 1933, Jews were in increasing danger after Hitler's assumption of dictatorial powers following the Reichstag fire. Heimann's husband had to emigrate because of his political views and he went to Switzerland. Heimann and her daughter were not allowed to accompany him and they came to the UK instead; Heimann and her husband divorced. In common with other psychoanalytically trained doctors who came to Britain at that time, she had to re-qualify in medicine which, like Segal, she did in Edinburgh; she also joined the British Psychoanalytical Society soon after she arrived.

Highly impressed by Klein's work, from 1935 she underwent analysis with her intermittently for many years. However, Heimann left the Kleinian group in the wake of their disagreement over her paper on counter-transference, joining the Independents in 1955 and publishing further papers as an Independent analyst until her death in London in 1982.

'On counter-transference'

This is a short but crucial paper read by Heimann at the 16th International Psycho-Analytical Congress in Zurich in 1949. She starts with the observation that many students become nervous when they develop feelings of any kind towards their patients and therefore aim at 'becoming completely unfeeling and "detached"' (1949: 73). Like most analysts at that time, she is concerned not to appear to contradict Freud, and so suggests that this attempt at detachment arises from a 'misreading' of his work. She argues that Freud's evocations of the therapist acting with the precision of a surgeon's knife, or the accuracy of a well-polished mirror, should not be taken to mean that all feeling should be eschewed. Continuing to an opposite line of thought, she criticises Ferenczi and Michael and Alice Balint for disclosing their feelings freely, burdening the patient and taking him away from his own material.

Heimann contends that the patient's transference and the therapist's counter-transference are not exactly equivalent: 'For the purpose of this paper I am using the term "counter-transference" to cover all the feelings which the analyst experiences towards his patients' (ibid. 74). The psychotherapist's ability to register and think about the feelings stirred up in her by the patient should lead to a containing rather than a reactive response. This conception of counter-transference is less restrictive than seeing it merely as the psychotherapist's 'transference' onto the patient: the counter-transference is rather an 'instrument of research' into the patient's unconscious. Heimann links her version of counter-transference with Freud's 'freely aroused emotional sensibility'. Both refer to the state of mind which allows the psychotherapist to follow the less conscious strands of the patient's material without her own reactions intruding into it. Freud must have meant, she suggested, the capacity to experience emotions which are aroused by the patient and which have also been analysed. This enables her to differentiate her own emotional world from that of the patient and follow the patient's communications empathically while containing her own feelings.

It is this unspoken rapport which informs Heimann's version of counter-transference: it helps the therapist to understand the patient at a deeper level than would otherwise be possible, and in a more accurate way than if the therapist were to bring in her own response. 'Therefore', Heimann continues, 'the analyst's emotional sensitivity needs to be extensive rather than intensive, differentiating and mobile' (ibid. 75). Psychotherapy and psychoanalysis are hard emotional work for both parties. Heimann anticipates Bion's 'container–contained' as a mode of psychic development whereby the psychotherapist takes in feelings unconsciously communicated by the patient, transforms them through her 'reverie' and returns them to him in a state which he can accept.

The unconscious emotions that appear in the counter-transference are more sensitive and individual than rational thought, so focusing on the counter-transference enables elements to be noticed and considered where they might not otherwise have been evident. An unexpected emotional impulse, for example, can alert the therapist that there may be more going on in the patient than meets the eye (or ear). Of course, it is important that the therapist be sufficiently familiar with her own neurotic tendencies to tell the difference between her own and others' feelings. Often, however, a feeling or capacity 'put into' the therapist by projective identification may differ subtly from the same kind of feeling that arises within the therapist independently: it can seem to have a different quality or tone. It may also follow more meaningfully, if not more obviously, from the patient's than the therapist's thought processes. It may therefore be quite possible to distinguish one's own from the patient's feelings, although this is something that should never be taken for granted. As Heimann says:

> The analyst's immediate emotional response to his patient is a significant pointer to the patient's unconscious processes and guides him towards fuller understanding. It helps the analyst to focus his attention on the most urgent elements in the patient's associations and serves as a useful criterion for the selection of interpretations from material which, as we know, is always overdetermined.
>
> (Ibid. 77)

Heimann is saying that, far from being a hindrance, counter-transference, when properly used, is an essential tool of psychoanalysis. This radically new way of thinking about counter-transference has frequently been ascribed to Klein, although it led to a permanent rift between Klein and Heimann.

Betty Joseph (1917–2013)

Up to this point we have focused on practitioners who have introduced or extended a concept or clarified a theoretical point. The hallmark of Joseph's work, however, is the close attention she pays to technique. Her main interest is the continual interplay between therapist and patient in the nuances of words and the manner and actions of both patient and therapist (Feldman and Bott Spillius 2005: viii). Attention to the 'fine texture' of the interactions in the analytic setting is common in the Kleinian approach. Remembering John Hill's 1993 article, where he emphasises the marked differences between Kleinian practitioners, I think most therapists would agree that if anyone could be said to be a Kleinian, it would be Betty Joseph. Joseph herself vividly describes her professional background in an interview with analysts Daniel Pick and Jane Milton (Joseph 2006).

Joseph's central aim is for the psychotherapist to notice the way she is being led, nudged or pushed into a certain kind of response: 'Who is the patient turning me into at this moment?' she might reflect. 'How is he leading me to act? How am I acting on him?' In this way she can gradually discover, with the patient, the ways in which he continually moves away from his most pressing anxieties. This is no easy matter, because flattery and seduction are common but not necessarily conscious ways of avoiding anxiety on the part of the patient, and psychotherapists are not immune to these as they want to feel they are doing a good job. However, for a psychotherapist to succumb to such manoeuvres may be a sign that she is avoiding her own anxiety. It is only by being alert to the dynamics of positive and negative feelings and defences such as envy, denial and projective and introjective defences, that patients become able to tolerate a wider range of feelings and types of relationship, first within the therapeutic setting and subsequently outside it as well.

Although Joseph does not ignore the 'reconstruction' of the original situation which led to the emerging transference/counter-transference dynamics, she sees the ways in which these are played out as far more important. Her papers (all in Feldman and Spillius 1989) include: 'On understanding and not understanding: some technical issues' (1983); 'Envy in everyday life' (1986) and 'Object relations in clinical practice' (1988). This brief selection shows her concern with practice throughout her work, exploring the main Kleinian concepts – anxiety, projective identification, envy and transference/counter-transference – clinically more than theoretically.

Joseph was never an arrogant or particularly ambitious person, refusing the first offer of qualification by the Institute of Psychoanalysis, saying she knew she was not ready, and finally having to accept qualification against her own judgement. This gave her, she said, particular sympathy for those students who were late developers, or who for other reasons did not understand what the patient was saying, in contrast to such 'born analysts' as Hanna Segal, Herbert Rosenfeld and the ever-influential Wilfred Bion.

The main books in which her work appears were compiled by others. A late collection, Hargreaves and Varchevker (2004: introduction), describes a clinical seminar in which many of her students and colleagues participated over very many years. Perhaps the enduring success of such meetings was due to her combination of close attention to the progress of the session under discussion with clear and straightforward language, and a patient and sympathetic attitude towards all the participants – features which also appear in her writings.

'Transference: the total situation'

This paper revisits the issues Heimann had raised thirty years previously in 'On Counter-Transference'. In 'Transference: the Total Situation' (1985, in Feldman and Spillius 2005/1989), Joseph re-examines and develops the concept and use of the transference.

Those analysts immediately following Freud understood the transference through the patient's references to the psychotherapist, which could be taken as reflecting early relationships to significant others, generally parents and siblings. The psychotherapist would interpret and explore these comments but would assume that the rest of the patient's material lay outside the transference. Strachey (1934), like Klein, stresses that what is transferred is what the patient has internalised from his objects, rather than who they are in reality. By including associations and the effects of projection, splitting and other defences, much more could be understood in terms of the transference (Feldman and Spillius 1989: 156). This gradual broadening of the concept culminates in Joseph viewing everything the patient expresses in the session as an aspect of the transference: the analyst (or who and what she stands for) is the patient's 'object' in the therapeutic situation, so is necessarily referred to in his material – just as in Klein's view of the ego, there can be no subject without an object. Similarly, the patient brings a 'total situation', a conscious and unconscious world of object relationships, connections, experiences, rather than just the single strand of transference relationship within a setting which is 'real', or non-transferential, overall. For Joseph, the transference is 'a framework, in which something is always going on, where there is always movement and activity' (ibid.), transforming Kleinian practice.

Joseph does no more than mention the counter-transference in this paper, but does so in order to indicate that if the transference is to be seen in this way, then so must the counter-transference. Following Heimann, she takes counter-transference as the psychotherapist's responses to everything that comes from the patient, seen through the lens of its impact on the analyst: essentially, how the patient is unconsciously manoeuvring the analyst to play a particular role in relation to him. Joseph points us towards this understanding of the counter-transference through reference to the transference as a 'total situation':

> Much of our understanding of the transference comes through our understanding of how our patients act on us to feel things for many varied reasons; how they try to draw us into their defensive systems; how they unconsciously act out with us in the transference, trying to get us to act out with them; how they convey aspects of their inner world built up from infancy.
>
> (Ibid. 157)

The transference is thus understood as created by the predominantly unconscious attempt on the part of the patient to play out problematic object relationships deriving from the past, understood through the therapist's counter-transference, in an effort to resolve them. The transference is necessarily unique to each patient–therapist pairing, and the interpretation conveyed to the patient must be similarly personal, arising from the live situation rather than picked off the therapist's favourite theoretical shelf.

Interpretations and what is interpreted are more than just the spoken words, Joseph reminds us. Their significance lies in how the patient receives them:

> movement and change is [sic] an essential aspect of transference – so that no interpretation can be seen as a pure interpretation or explanation but must resonate in the patient in a way which is specific to him and his way of functioning ... Such points emerge more clearly if we are thinking of total situations being transferred.
>
> (Ibid.)

In Joseph's view, therefore, transference/counter-transference phenomena are a product of the patient's inner world. They are always part of an active process, as the individual continually readjusts to his changing experience of his inner and outer worlds.

This is why transference and counter-transference have come to play such a large part in psychotherapy. The 'here-and-now' transference is the central focus for interpretation by Kleinians, who use the details of the psychotherapist–patient interaction to understand as much as possible about the patient's unconscious functioning. What Joseph sees as mutative for the patient is experience in the current interaction with the therapist – not simply through his words, but also in subtler ways which can only be picked up in the psychotherapist's counter-transference (ibid. 167). Deducing how the patient came to be as he is – the 'reconstructive' work of analysis – is secondary to achieving understanding through the transference/counter-transference framework, she thinks, and emerges through it (ibid. 211).

The counter-transference dynamics can spread from the patient's psychotherapist to the supervisor and even beyond. Joseph gives an example from one of her clinical seminars when a participant was giving an account of a session with a patient which had left the psychotherapist particularly dissatisfied. The patient was not an easy person to work with: a young woman who was 'schizoid, angry, an unhappy childhood with probably emotionally unavailable parents' (ibid. 152). We can presume that her angry dissatisfaction was projected into the psychotherapist. The group could see that the therapist was doing her best, but that something was not being grasped.

Eventually the situation fell into place as a series of projective identifications, or transference responses:

> Slowly it dawned on us that probably this was the clue, that our problem in the seminar was reflecting the analyst's problem in the transference, and that what was probably going on in the transference was a projection of the

> patient's inner world, in which she, the patient, could not understand and, more, could not make sense of what was going on. She was demonstrating what it felt like to have a mother who could not tune into the child and, we suspected, could not make sense of the child's feelings either, but behaved as if she could, as we, the seminar, were doing.
>
> (Ibid. 158)

Finally, the participants understood that this very failure of understanding was the root of the patient's defences, rendering a difficult early situation a permanent state of affairs. This case demonstrates the value of clinical seminars, or supervision groups. Far more can be understood through a series of transference steps involving a number of people than through the therapist's counter-transference alone. The group acts as a stronger container for the difficult feelings of bewilderment, inadequacy and anxiety which started with the child, so greater intensity, confusion and other problematic dynamics can be tolerated.

Further examples are given in the later part of the paper where Joseph details clearly how the transference plays out in each situation. The patient begins by treating the therapist as she had the original object. Joseph, as therapist, takes the patient step-by-step to the point where he is able to perceive at least a minimal difference between the psychotherapist and the original object. From here, the gradual dissolution of the transference begins, as the patient's insights spread to his understanding of himself and his everyday relationships.

Thus Heimann and Joseph together brought a new stage to Kleinian practice, in which clinical work became more focused, more exact and more accountable. The task was now the unravelling and unlocking of the patient's transference, with the therapist's counter-transference as the key. This reveals the preconceptions the patient brings to each new relationship, together with his particular ways of manoeuvring those around him to take up the familiar though dysfunctional roles that were never resolved in his childhood. Additionally, the counter-transference is the clearest possible communication to the therapist of the patient's state of mind – so much so, that it can easily be missed. Working through the 'here-and-now' transference tests extends the therapist's capacity for empathy and for tolerating her own emotions, so that she can also manage the patient's: it is often said that the patient will unerringly find the therapist's weak spot, giving her continual opportunities to increase her self-awareness. Accuracy is of prime importance, but the Kleinians also consider the way in which interpretations are communicated to be crucial. Hard truths can be made palatable if spoken with warmth and understanding, which can only come from self-knowledge and self-acceptance.

Conclusion

The most striking feature of these 'Kleinians after Klein' is their intense focus on the disturbed, the difficult and the primitive in the patient – and, correspondingly, in the therapist. Perhaps this is the way that Kleinians have taken on

Klein's insistence on paying attention to, and interpreting, the area of greatest anxiety: there can be no anxiety greater than that located in narcissistic and especially psychotic states.

Rosenfeld, Heimann and Joseph brought new ways of thinking to theory and practice which continue to develop today. Rosenfeld's understanding of narcissism and psychosis arose through his natural bent for working with highly disturbed patients at a time when this was rarely done. His concept of 'destructive narcissism' is a way of understanding the core of severe disturbance in a form which is both object-related and yet essentially destructive. It illustrates Bion's concepts of 'attacks on linking' in which all attachments are the focus of attempted destruction: 'Feelings of hatred are … directed against all emotions including hate itself, and against external reality which stimulates them' (Bion 1959 in 1984: 107).

The work of Heimann and Joseph give the Kleinian practitioner a vision of the clinical field which is both wider and more focused. Although Klein herself disagreed with Heimann, the latter's new concept of the counter-transference has become a key part not only in Kleinian work but in all psychoanalytic approaches. However, it is only the Kleinians who use the 'here-and-now' transference/counter-transference as the principal focus of their work, the point at which they believe real change can take place. Joseph subsequently takes forward the concept of transference to bring it into alignment with the new idea of counter-transference. Instead of referring to specific references to the psychotherapist in the session, Joseph sees the transference as a 'total situation' which is transferred, rather than simply an aspect of the psychotherapist that reminds the patient of a former significant other.

The Kleinian contribution covers the formation, the nature and the process of thinking and feeling, from neurotic to narcissistic and psychotic functioning, and what it is that can lead to change in the psychoanalytic process. Taking the work of Bion, Rosenfeld, Heimann and Joseph together, we can see how much more detailed an understanding of the psychical worlds of both patient and therapist has been reached. New clinical attitudes have joined with fresh theoretical understanding to re-vivify the meticulous, in-depth psychoanalytic work that is typical of the Kleinian approach.

References

Abraham, K. (1924) 'A Short Study of the Development of the Libido, Viewed in the Light of Mental Disorders', in Abraham, 1927: 418–501.

——— (1927) *Selected Papers of Karl Abraham*, 303–311, trans. D. Bryan and A. Strachey, London: Hogarth Press.

Bick, E. (1964) 'Notes on Infant Observation in Psychoanalytic Training', in *The International Journal of Psycho-Analysis* 45: 558–566.

Feldman, M. and Bott Spillius, E., eds (2005/1989) *Psychic Equilibrium and Change: Selected Papers of Betty Joseph*, London and New York: Routledge.

Hargreaves, E. and Varchevker, A., eds (2004) *In Pursuit of Psychic Change: The Betty Joseph Workshop*, Hove, USA and Canada: Brunner-Routledge.

Heimann, P. (1949/1950) 'On Counter-Transference', in *International Journal of Psycho-Analysis* 31: 81–84.

Hill, J. (1993) 'Am I a Kleinian? Is Anyone?' *The British Journal of Psychotherapy* 9, no. 4: 463–475.

Joseph, B. (1985) 'Transference: The Total Situation', in M. Feldman and E. Bott Spillius (2005/1989): 156–167.

——— (2006) http://www.melanie-klein-trust.org.uk/domains/melanie-klein-trust.org.uk/local/media/downloads/Interview_with_Betty_Joseph.pdf, *The Melanie Klein Trust.*

Klein, M. (1946) 'Notes on Some Schizoid Mechanisms', in Klein, *Envy and Gratitude and Other Works*, London: Virago, 1988: 1–24.

Meltzer, D. (1968) *Sexual States of Mind*, Perthshire, Clunie Press.

Rosenfeld, H. (1985) *Psychotic States*, London: Hogarth.

——— (1987) *Impasse and Interpretation*, London: Tavistock Press.

Steiner, J., ed. (2008) *Rosenfeld in Retrospect*, London and New York: Routledge.

Strachey, J. (1934) The Nature of the Therapeutic Action of Psycho-Analysis', in *International Journal of Psycho-Analysis* 15: 27–159.

Chapter 6

Masud Khan and the British Psychoanalytical Society

We now turn from Kleinian to Independent developments in psychoanalysis. Fundamental disparities in their respective theories, practices and aims have already been noted. These centre on the relative influences of the state of the ego at birth[1] and what is provided later through the environment; and on the development of object relations and the place of destructiveness within it. In addition, Kleinian practitioners see themselves as part of a group with a shared theoretical inheritance, which each practitioner integrates in her own way. Independent practitioners, by contrast, identify themselves as autonomous practitioners who prioritise clinical experience over specific concepts, drawing flexibly from different approaches. In practice, Winnicott is their main formative influence, with his prioritising of external over constitutional influences – though neither Klein nor Winnicott disregard the other sphere.

Psychoanalytic autonomy, for good and for ill, is the essential characteristic of the first Independent practitioner we shall discuss, Masud Khan. Reaching a balanced understanding of Khan is a challenge, especially when his positive contributions are set alongside his extremely damaging actions. He contributed to all aspects of psychoanalysis, from editing, teaching and lecturing to developing innovative theoretical concepts and new clinical approaches. In his idiosyncratic therapeutic work he makes more direct use of his personal judgement and emotional style than any other psychoanalyst studied in this book – although he also advises consultation with colleagues when diverging markedly from the conventional psychoanalytic setting. Khan's brilliant yet catastrophic career gives us a rare insight into the functioning of the British Psychoanalytical Society (BPAS) at that time, and into the institution of reforms set in train by the problems he posed for it. For these reasons a complete chapter is given over to Khan and the BPAS, mirroring the chapter devoted to Bion.

Masud Khan (1924–1989)

Masud Khan's work embodies the characteristically Independent features of an emphasis on the therapeutic environment as the agent of change, and an optimistic view of human potential. Although at times critical of Winnicott he was also his first and staunchest disciple; he spelt out more clearly than did his mentor the conceptual roots of the Independent approach, its relation to Freud's work and their joint clinical innovations. Khan was often able to work successfully with patients whom other therapists had been unable to help and a number of his former patients attest to his skill, compassion and intuition (Hopkins 2006: 195–213). Little by little, however, a different picture emerged in psychoanalytic circles of widespread social, emotional and sexual exploitation of patients and supervisees, until eventually he was expelled from the BPAS. Khan became the skeleton in the cupboard of British psychoanalysis, his best papers seldom referenced and his pioneering clinical work developed without acknowledgement.[2] He exemplifies much of what is best in the Independent approach while offering a terrible example of the potential for harm in psychotherapy.

This most complex of psychoanalysts provoked conflicting responses from colleagues and patients, ex-patients and friends, all of them intense. These ranged from cherishing affection and adoring admiration to distrust, hostility and hatred. Those closest to him frequently held divergent attitudes towards him, both simultaneously and consecutively. Their responses were mitigated by his enduring charm and charisma and complicated by the scandals that erupted around him. Inevitably, as Britain's first non-white psychoanalyst, he was also the object of ambivalence.

Erudite and well-versed in Western culture, Khan was seen as one of the most promising of his generation of psychoanalysts. Much of Winnicott's work would never have been completed, it is said, without his support and guidance (ibid. 143). In his better clinical work he was perceptive, intuitive and kind, gaining a particular reputation for working with highly disturbed adults, adolescents and children. He worked with Winnicott to heighten the awareness and use of non-verbal aspects of communication. The two practitioners developed the 'management' of patients who were unable to support themselves or posed extreme difficulties for their family or carers. They saw little point in offering sessions to patients whose lives were empty or chaotic, and went about arranging and supervising a constructive and supported lifestyle for the patient, either in the place of individual sessions or alongside them. Throughout his work Khan consulted first and foremost his own beliefs and inclinations to an extent that few psychoanalysts, even of the Independent approach, have equalled. He made an international name for himself to an extent that few other British analysts did, speaking on psychoanalysis widely and particularly in the US. He took a leading role in collecting and organising the BPAS library as well as teaching its students and lecturing to its graduates. A close friend and colleague of Anna Freud and a valued associate of the leading French psychoanalysts, much had been expected of him as one of the generation following the pioneers of Object Relations.

Why allot so much space to a disgraced practitioner who has become little more than an occasional footnote to Independent psychoanalysis? It is inevitably curious to come across an Asian name in the post-war world of British psychoanalysis, and it is not difficult to identify with Khan's experiences of feeling excluded, or worse, an outcast; the darkly capricious nature of his life and career adds to the fascination. The clarity and verve of almost all Khan's published books and papers offer a striking complement to Winnicott's predominantly reassuring tone. A colleague describes Khan's overall approach as 'Winnicott with sex and violence added'. This is an apt description; yet in his best work these features are not gratuitous but arise within investigations into areas such as perversion (Khan 1989) where Winnicott barely ventured, and with a vigour that Winnicott did not, or could not, summon up.

It seems dishonest to respond to Khan's contradictory legacy by writing him out of psychoanalytic history. His positive contributions warrant consideration in their own right, while his wrongdoings throw light on issues which go beyond the personal. By extending the accepted limits of the normal psychoanalytic setting and then communicating them so clearly, Khan allows us to gain a more vivid sense of the essence of the Independent approach than would more orthodox contributions, and this is illustrated in the case study in Chapter 8. The 1993 biography of Khan by Judy Cooper, a former analysand, has been joined by two more recent studies by Roger Willoughby (2005) and Linda Hopkins (2006), and most of the biographical information for this chapter derives from these three books. Since the latter two were published recently and in quick succession, the time may now have arrived when it is possible to look at what Khan means for British psychoanalysis in a more direct and impartial way.

In describing Khan's life and career, we shall examine the part played by Winnicott and the BPAS in allowing his damaging behaviour to go unchecked for so long. There are sections on his early life in the Punjab, adult life here in the UK, his analyses and, most importantly, the long years of work with Winnicott. Khan's conflict with the British Psychoanalytical Society is of particular interest, together with the effect he had on the society's development and maturation. We shall also explore his own most important innovations: his theoretical concept of 'cumulative trauma', the 'schizoid personality' which leads up to it, and his new understanding of perversion. An example of his 'therapeutic care' is described at some length in Chapter 8. Overall, the aim is to provide enough balanced material for readers to make a preliminary assessment of what Khan contributed to psychoanalysis, and what he stole from it.

Life

Childhood

Even by the standards of his time and place, Khan's childhood was conflicted and extraordinary. Mohammed Masud Rasa Khan was born in 1924 in the Punjab, a state in Northern India which became part of Pakistan in 1947. Khan was the youngest son of a large extended family headed by a well-known and respected landowner, an ordinary peasant who had been generously rewarded for his services to the British Raj. The honorific titles 'Khan', 'Bahadur' and 'Raja' were added to his father's original name, Fazaldad, and money was provided, at least in part, by the farmers who lived and worked on the land given to him. Khan always maintained that this feudal tradition had a deep and permanent effect on him. Fazaldad was 76 when Khan was born to his much younger fourth wife, Khursheed Begum, said to be a courtesan, or high-class prostitute, whose illegitimate ten-year-old son lived with her family. Khursheed was illiterate, extremely beautiful, dreamy and distant; Khan claimed she had a long-term opium habit (Hopkins 2006: 6). Her lower social status must have reflected on Khan and his two surviving full-siblings, compared with the numerous, much older half-siblings born to Fazaldad and his other wives. These complex dynamics may have initiated the virulent arrogance, which was such a feature in Khan's personality.

Khan was born with a disfiguring 'cauliflower ear' which was not operated on until Winnicott insisted on him having it seen to before starting analysis. By the time Khan's older brother was born, Fazaldad's previous wives were no longer living in the family home, having divorced, died or decided to move away when the fourth marriage took place. The larger family strongly disapproved of Fazaldad's marriage to Khursheed, probably because of the difference in age and social standing: she, however, remained devoted to him for the rest of his life.

Khan grew up with his parents, his older brother Tahir and younger sister Mahmooda, together with other relatives and a number of servants; the household must have been the size of a small institution. He had been named 'Ibrahim' at birth, but this was changed to 'Mohammed Masud' by his father when Khan was four years old. This may have been a planned alteration since all but two of Fazaldad's sons bore the name 'Mohammed', but no reason is given for 'Masud' and the delay is curious. At that time Fazaldad scarcely knew Khan since, in customary fashion, he had been brought up by his mother and the servants.

Khan reports that he first came to Fazaldad's attention when he asked for a mere penny for his fourth birthday, after the women in the family had urged him to ask for a lesser amount than the 'four million rupees' he was planning! Charmed, his father took a special interest in him, citing this incident as the reason for handing a complete estate over to Khan when he was thirteen years old. This apparently included a private stash of money for the purpose of obtaining and providing his mother with opium. Khan 'learned the importance of gestures' (ibid. 8) or perhaps manipulation; it was dreadfully unfair to his siblings, of course, most immediately Tahir, his older full brother, and Khan's growing sense of superiority must have been bolstered. But he also had a kind and gentle side which he showed particularly towards Mahmooda – 'my first and model love' (ibid. 15) who, being younger and a girl, posed no threat to his position in the family. One wonders, however, if there is an earlier, deprived and impaired 'Ibrahim' as well as the glorified 'Masud' in Khan's complex personality, represented by his deformed ear – which might help explain why he left it unmodified for so long.

Khan tells us that he turned against his mother a few years later when, as he saw it, she failed to treat him and his father with due deference. She had arranged to visit her family for a month, as she did each year. Fazaldad suspected that she would not be back at the promised time and Khursheed persuaded Khan to convince him that she would. The day before her planned return a telegram arrived saying that she would be staying an extra fifteen days. 'My mammoth and majestic father raved in panic like a child. For fifteen days he made the whole estate a living hell … "I shall kill, kill, kill," he kept shouting and whimpering' (ibid. 7). Khan himself felt betrayed and humiliated.

The atmosphere on the family estate seems to have been brutal and violent. At the age of four, Fazaldad ordered that he witness his mother having some kind of fit after giving birth to a stillborn foetus or baby. Khan said this resulted in three years of mutism, but others disputed this (ibid.). Khan was the only son never beaten by his father but he was taunted about his ear, inside the family and out. Nothing is said about the consequences to family members, but when Khan told his father that his schoolmates were teasing him, Fazaldad sent a party of house servants to bugger the boys concerned in front of Khan (ibid. 10). There were similar events at home which led Khan to admire his father's strength and ruthlessness rather than abhor his cruelty. He boasted of his family philosophy to a friend: 'In my country, life is very cheap. I could have men disposed of for a mere five hundred rupees – that is how we deal with difficult situations' (ibid. 3). This is an interesting but not altogether promising axiom for a future psychoanalyst.

Khan was withdrawn from school after the teasing incident, and he and Tahir received an excellent British-style education from an Oxford graduate – explaining why he tended naturally towards the 'British' School of Object Relations. He was determined to live up to his father's expectations, and seems to have modelled himself on an intelligent, handsome and charming half-brother who had previously been his father's favoured son. This young man had died in a motorcycle accident when he was a student at Oxford University, shortly before Khan's birth.

In 1937, Fazaldad moved the family to another of his estates, partly, it seems, with the aim of providing Khan with a site of his own where his other sons would not interfere. It was very different from the rural surroundings Khan was used to, and he pined bitterly for his old home. At first, he and Tahir were left at the new house with only servants for company and care. Khan was panicked by this separation and pretended to be ill, forcing his father to take him back with him. To his astonishment, his mother faced him down, accusing him outright of faking illness and declaring tearfully that now he certainly would not inherit the estate – her main concern, it seemed. Fazaldad was planning to go against tradition by leaving the bulk of his estate to his youngest son instead of the eldest, and as women in this social group could not inherit anything, Khursheed would be financially dependent on him. Khan was so ashamed at being found out by his mother that he persuaded his reluctant father to take him back in a couple of days, and there he and Tahir stayed, unhappily, until the rest of the family joined them after a few months (ibid. 11–12). He was being trained to be materialistic and manipulative, in the midst of unhappiness and insecurity. Khan himself recorded in a self-written obituary that he had been 'nurtured by love and care, but apprenticed in cruelty and service' (Willoughby 2005: 246–247).

Khan's British-style education took place in their new home. One tutor impressed him particularly, and he developed a love for Shakespeare's works, which lasted the rest of his life. English literature showed him the possibility of internal self-knowledge and psychological reflection, and perhaps also how to relate to others. Prior to this, he had expressed his feelings in actions, not words, although he could speak five languages fluently – Urdu, Pashto, Punjabi, the Hindi that gathered them all together, and English (Hopkins 2006: 14).

Further losses were to come. In 1940, when he was studying at the local college, he fell in love with a Hindu girl; at seventeen, it was his first romantic relationship. Fazaldad would not tolerate him marrying a non-Muslim, and told him to break off the relationship, which he obediently did. Khan became depressed and anorexic to the extent that his father called in the local psychotherapist, which helped to some extent (ibid.). Khan said he felt unable to commit to any woman after this, a problem that endured throughout his adult life; no doubt, however, this trait was multiply determined from his earliest years.

Khan moved to the University of Punjab, joining his brother to study English Literature. He was awarded a BA and then an MA, for which he wrote a dissertation on James Joyce's *Ulysses*. Tragedy struck the family late in 1942 when Mahmooda died unexpectedly at the age of sixteen, and a few months later Fazaldad followed at ninety-six, having been bedridden for several years (ibid. 15). Despite Fazaldad's age, Khan counted this as the greatest of his bereavements, and it obviously came as a terrible shock; the lynchpin of his life was gone, and he withdrew into an isolation which made him appear arrogant and eccentric. He himself, however, felt utterly confused, lost and in a void. His tutor advised him to see a psychiatrist who had had some training with Anna Freud, and it was this which led him to seek personal analysis in London – and perhaps contributed to his lasting attachment to Anna Freud (ibid. 16).

Khan's ambivalence towards his father is evident in his account of his father's last message to him:

> As my father was dying, he reached out his feeble and trembling hand and said to me, 'Sudi, I have given you the title, the estates, and money you will gawp at.' [That is, the major part of his assets.] He died a few minutes later. What he had left me: the hatred of my half-brothers and sisters [surprisingly, he does not mention Tahir], and the deadly envy of my mother.
>
> (Ibid. 17)

Khursheed was left financially dependent on him.

Khan is said to have remained afraid of retaliation from his family all his life. He never seems to have given serious thought to sharing the money around, though he had no hesitation in arranging for the dying Tahir to be taken into a private hospital in the 1980s. He may have made similar gestures before, since it was control of the money which was most important to him, as well as keeping to the wishes of his father. However, he made thoughtless and extravagant use of much of the money left to him, spending it on endless trips and luxuries throughout his life. Although he worked hard in the psychoanalytic field, he never undertook any other kind of employment.

Khan thus grew to adulthood caught between two cultures, a sensitive, intelligent young man who was also grandiose, narcissistic and seriously confused. He studied Western thought, including psychoanalysis, while revering the Punjabi traditions embodied by his father, at a time when Pakistan was being violently carved out of India. Khan arrived in the UK with a veneration for all things upper-class and English, from a society still harking back to feudal ways. He spoke of his father 'as though he were God', a colleague reported, a terrifying and tyrannical presence. His mother could neither love him nor protect him, and his disfigurement was clearly visible. He was accustomed to being treated by household servants with a combination of servility, fear and envy, with the poisoned chalice amongst the family of being his father's favourite son. Periods of deep depression and acute anxiety assailed him throughout his life. Recently it has been suggested that, like Tahir, he suffered from bipolar disorder, then termed 'manic depression', at least in the last twenty years of his life (ibid. 261–262). Interestingly, both brothers also became alcoholic. This may have been in spite of or reinforced by the traditional Muslim abhorrence of alcohol – or, more likely, both.

Adult life

Khan sought psychoanalysis as soon as he arrived in London in 1946 at the age of twenty-two. The British Society had just emerged from the upheaval provoked by Klein's arrival in the UK, and was divided into the Freudian or Viennese members, the Kleinians and the unaffiliated remainder who hoped to mediate between them, and who later became the Independents. There was a shortage of work and rationing was still in force. Khan was appalled by the comparative poverty of even eminent analysts, while he himself thought nothing of hiring a Rolls-Royce, complete with driver, as his everyday mode of transport.

Through a blunder of misunderstandings Khan was taken on as a trainee instead of an ordinary patient, so his career as a psychoanalyst simply fell from the heavens. This may have been due partly to the impression he made on Bowlby and also on Ella Sharpe, his first analyst. As was habitual in the 1940s, Khan was offered an intellectually-slanted 'training analysis' rather than the thoroughly emotionally based 'therapeutic analysis' offered to patients. We may wonder how Khan, a very young man arriving in a new country, could possibly have been assessed as ready for training, but apart from his charm and erudition his pervasive air of entitlement may have influenced this decision. Additionally, his Asian origin must have provoked complicated responses in the senior members of the BPAS, while procedures at that time were a great deal less rigorous than they became later.

Khan recounts that he was both overjoyed and desolate at being accepted into training: he had no-one to celebrate with (ibid. 25). He marked his success alone by indulging his love of Shakespeare, watching Laurence Olivier play *King Lear* no less than twenty-seven times in the following month. The play must have had particular resonance for him at this time, not least in the lack of effective paternal functioning shown in his treatment by the BPAS.

Khan's aim in his new career was to qualify as soon as possible – he did not have to earn his living as did the other students, but associate membership in the BPAS meant he would be able charge fees. He succeeded in this in 1950, at the astonishingly early age of 26. He must have impressed the majority of his assessors greatly, although a full third did not support his entry. Going on to train as a child psychoanalyst, he was supervised by Winnicott, Marion Milner and Clifford Scott, for short periods by Melanie Klein, whom he disliked intensely, and by Anna Freud. She mentored him throughout his career, perhaps seeing him as a quasi-son; both were children of the leaders of their respective worlds and both had moved to new countries at a crucial point in their lives. They retained great affection for each other although, characteristically, he was not uncritical of her (ibid. 140).

Khan's analytic life, however, did not go smoothly. Ella Sharpe died after only seven months of the analysis, and he transferred to John Rickman, Bion's analyst and colleague. Neither Sharpe nor Rickman kept to the normal analytic boundaries, though Khan followed Rickman's advice on many matters, including reading the main psychoanalytic literature and living solely on his earnings as a practitioner. In 1951, Rickman died suddenly, and it was then that Khan entered into long-term work with Winnicott – a questionable decision on Winnicott's part, since he had also supervised Khan's early work with children. In Winnicott, Khan chose yet another psychoanalyst with heart problems, despite losing his two previous analysts to the same affliction. Although the analysis left much of Khan's personality problems unresolved, he for the first time gained the stability of long-term work. The two became close, breaking psychoanalytic boundaries by working, writing and socialising together from the start of the analysis until Winnicott's death twenty years later. Their relationship as a whole was complex and often troubled.

Khan quickly rose in his new profession and his new milieu. He immersed himself in the artistic world, buying original works and moving in ballet and acting circles. Together with psychoanalysis, the arts were becoming a focal point in his life (ibid. 44–45). In only a few years he had moved from being a strange and isolated figure on the periphery of the psychoanalytic world to taking a position far closer to the centre of London's psychoanalytic and artistic worlds.

Khan's first marriage was to the ballet dancer Jane Shore; their relationship was neither happy nor successful and ended in Shore having a breakdown after only a few years. It seemed that Khan valued those close to him as much for their social status as their personal qualities, and Shore's ballet career was declining. She found some of Khan's personal habits distasteful – his ravening attitudes to sex and food alike, and the Punjabi habit of bathing with scent rather than water (ibid. 39). He gradually changed his eating habits through contact with his Parisian friends, but that was all.

By 1956, Khan had started an affair with a leading ballerina, Svetlana Beriosova, and this Shore could not tolerate. Khan felt guilty enough to interrupt his analysis so that Shore could receive sessions with Winnicott that had been reserved for him, another dubious arrangement. After their divorce and, especially, treatment from Winnicott, Shore recovered, remarried and went on to have a successful life. The affair with Beriosova grew and improved, as did Khan's professional life. Immediately after graduating he rented a small, dark flat in South Kensington. Soon, however, he was being referred wealthy patients who were impressed at being treated by someone who was becoming well-known and well-respected. Khan and Beriosova were able to move to a small flat on Harley Street, which was a step up in social terms – but only just: there was no lift, and it could only be reached by climbing 89 stairs. But their next move was into an upmarket flat in Knightsbridge, in a building shared by the actor Corin Redgrave and his family. His happiest years were spent there with his wife, a secretary and a 'houseboy', developing his psychoanalytic and artistic knowledge and exploring the Parisian circles that were also becoming open to him.

As a Muslim, Khan had despised alcoholics, but he and Beriosova drank far too much during the remainder of the 1960s, and the 1970s became a disastrous decade for Khan. When Winnicott died in 1971, Khan was devastated, although his psychotherapeutic relationship with him had ended a few years previously. Winnicott had taken the place of a father, he declared; but of course, his own father had been far tougher and more aggressive than the generally sweet-natured Winnicott. 'Why do all my teachers accommodate to me?' Khan complained. 'I am yearning for teachers who would have the quiet authority that compels me to accommodate to them' (ibid. 170). Khan did not seem to realise how expert a manipulator he was, or that he chose for his 'teachers' those who would succumb to his talents and his seductive charms.

Khan had never got on with Clare, Winnicott's second wife, and he was outraged to discover that Winnicott had directed that she be the literary executor of his writings – a position he felt entitled to, since for many years he had helped Winnicott edit and re-order his writings. How could *his* Winnicott have betrayed him in this way? Khan also held Clare responsible for being debarred from editing a standard edition of Winnicott's works or writing an authorised biography. Personally, he found it more difficult to keep hold of his self-destructive tendencies without Winnicott's oversight, becoming increasingly self-destructive until the end of his life. The conflict between Clare Winnicott and Khan recalls the sibling-like rivalry between Khan and his mother over the attentions (and goods) of his father. Winnicott's death, moreover, came shortly before the death of Khan's mother, which came as another terrible blow. He had never resolved his combined contempt and adoration of Khursheed, any more than for his father.

His inability to fully mourn his parents was no doubt the precursor of similarly conflicted relationships with men and women alike.

Khan's marriage to Beriosova endured from the mid-1950s through the next decade, with each engrossed in an extravagant infatuation with the other. However, Khan's relationship with her was split between 'Beriosova', the sublime artist and 'Svetlana', the flawed person: 'With Beriosova, it was her art and not her I understood so profoundly. When it came to knowing Svetlana, I collapsed and let her down abominably' (ibid. 171) – unbeknownst to her, for example, he started an affair while she was away touring. Showing good sense for once, Khan refused Beriosova's plea for them to have a child, and as had happened with Jane Shore, his love and admiration for her waned in parallel with her professional star. When Margot Fonteyn returned to the Royal Ballet, Beriosova had been displaced as the prima ballerina, because she was too tall to partner Rudolf Nureyev, recently defected from the Soviet Union (ibid. 170, 189). Beriosova could not tolerate Khan's affairs, and their arguments grew uglier as both became increasingly dependent on alcohol. Most evenings they had screaming rows which eventually involved violence on both sides. Each felt attacked and undermined by the other.

Khan's deterioration spread into his work, at least with a proportion of his patients. Wynne Godley was a disturbed though successful civil servant who was referred for analysis with Khan in 1959 by Winnicott, then president of the BPAS. Godley's full account of his disastrous seven-year 'treatment' (Godley 2001) reveals the nature and extent of Khan's worst work. He describes an episode which sounds typical of this period. He was in the Khan household – outside his session time – and heard moaning from the hall, then his name being called. Khan was lying prostrate on the floor, murmuring weakly 'My wife has kicked me in the balls.' After helping Khan to his bedroom, he found Beriosova passed out, drunk, in the hall (Hopkins 2006: 196–200; Godley 2001). Eventually Khan realised that he was having a destructive effect not just on Beriosova as a person, but also as an artist. Her career disintegrated after she collapsed, inebriated, during a performance (Hopkins 2006: 189). She and Khan separated in 1971 and were divorced in 1974. All the same, she tells of a visit to Khan at the very end of his life, when he introduced her to a doctor: 'My one and only love' (ibid. 376).

Khan's affairs continued, often involving patients or ex-patients. He never saw this as either improper or wrong, writing to his friend Victor Smirnoff that he felt no obligation to live by psychoanalytic conventions: 'I do not regret any of the events in [my life] because I sense in them a deeper truer logic than I could have planned or programmed for myself' (ibid. 187). This 'logic' partakes of Khan's claims to feudal entitlement and implies disdain for the mores espoused by his middle-class European colleagues. His narcissism seems to have led him to believe that closeness to him could never be wrong for anyone. He easily elicited the adoration of women, but if he could not live without this, neither could he sustain such relationships. Khan's life revolved around the focal points of relationships with women, art, clinical work, lecturing and social and psychoanalytic matters in France and England. He made occasional visits to the Punjab where he had grown up in what had become Pakistan, the place where he felt more deeply at home than anywhere else, but he never resolved the conflicts between his Eastern heritage and the Western world in which he settled.

Despite episodes of sobriety, Khan's alcoholism increased, spiralling out of control after his diagnosis of lung cancer in 1976; he had been a long-term chain-smoker. He rewrote his will, with generosity and good sense, leaving the majority of his assets to Beriosova, his art works to the Victoria and Albert Museum and various objects to the friends who would most value them. Radical surgery gave him a prognosis of several months but, amazingly, he lived for twelve and a half more years. Additional surgery left him with almost no voice and with less and less energy, and possibly with a measure of brain damage as well. His Work Book (diary) shows that from about the time of his cancer diagnosis he started referring to himself in the third person – a striking illustration of his 'False Self':

> Of course his tape-recorder mind had registered every detail of the happenings, but as yet his psyche, sensibility, and his being could print little of it. Hence the acute and persistent passivity in him: he could neither read nor write; or see anyone but his closest friends.
>
> (Ibid. 293)

There is the sense of a depersonalised lost soul, portrayed with sensitivity and more than a hint of preciousness.

In Khan's last years he declined mentally, physically and behaviourally. Without Winnicott, he had no living father-figure to help him steady himself; and with his relationships to his parents so unresolved, there were no stable internal figures to act as guiding stars. Although he continued writing and seeing patients for as long as he possibly could, this important focus of his life inevitably ebbed away as colleagues ceased making referrals to him. An enquiry into his psychoanalytic transgressions led to an investigation by the BPAS in 1976, when he was treated very leniently as he was not expected to live for long. He felt outrage rather than gratitude, but had no justification for disputing the decision. His deterioration continued.

The flamboyant but attractive psychoanalytic celebrity now began to give the impression of decayed and depleted aristocracy, bizarre rather than merely eccentric. He started demanding to be addressed as 'Prince Masud Khan', with no basis other than his growing megalomania. Bullying aggression took the place of piquant charm and his last book, *When Spring Comes*, appears to be a deliberately offensive attack against the psychoanalytic establishment at large. Its anti-Semitic tirades may well have been directed towards the mainly Jewish colleagues by whom he felt betrayed and abandoned. It was this book which led to his final expulsion from the BPAS in 1988. This was a bitter blow – he could scarcely believe that it had come to this, and at last he gave up on life: 'If I had voice, I would fight back. Without voice I can do little' (Cooper 1993: 30).

Less than a year before his death, Khan asked a former analysand, Judy Cooper, to be his biographer. As a psychoanalyst herself, she was well aware of the context in which he worked, and being half-Indian, they also had shared cultural values and understandings. She visited him regularly to gather material, or rather, to listen to him talk, until after a couple of months he ejected her without explanation (ibid. xvii). Nonetheless, she carried out her task conscientiously and her book is the first biography on Khan. It has many strengths, but one feels it should never have been written. For an analyst to ask a former patient to undertake such a task is to destroy, distort or at least highly complicate the internal image of him retained from her analysis. Apart from his sexual liaisons, this appears to me to be the furthest that he went in his unprofessional – or anti-professional – actions.

When Khan died in June 1989, further acts of destruction were uncovered. It was found that he had destroyed his former quite reasonable will, replacing it with one in which all his material goods were left to the manager of his estate in Pakistan, apart from a desk which went to his solicitor. None of the bequests he had spoken of leaving to friends and colleagues were made, and Svetlana Beriosova, his ex-wife, received nothing whatsoever although she was in dire need of money. There is a question of whether he was himself manipulated by a supposed legal representative, but equally it could have been a final act of revenge on those left behind; by this time, he may well have been quite confused, and perhaps not fully cognisant of his actions (ibid. 383).

Khan was not just a waywardly gifted therapist who made significant contributions to psychoanalysis, nor simply a practitioner whose actions went well beyond the pale: it is due to him, albeit unwittingly, that psychoanalysis in the UK engaged in organisational reforms that were long overdue. Though no society can afford to be complacent, there is little possibility that transgressions like those perpetrated by Khan and Winnicott could now continue for so long (see Sandler and Godley: 2004).

Khan's analyses

Khan had come to England to seek treatment for a number of ailments. As well as intermittent episodes of terror, he suffered from feelings of emptiness and depression, insomnia and stress-related symptoms such as fever and back pain (Hopkins 2006: 149–150). There is no record of any of these improving through analysis. However, in his later years he spoke mostly of terror, anxiety and depression, so it is quite possible that his somatic symptoms abated. Psychoanalytically, he can be seen in a number of different ways: as living through a False Self, as a schizoid personality, with perverse features; particularly in his last twenty years he might be seen in psychiatric terms as suffering from bipolar disorder – acute depression alternating with manic episodes.

At the same time, however, reports of his clinical work by himself and others provide evidence that his general confidence, his access, at times, to a more authentic sense of himself and his ability to make contact with others all improved.

Nor was he entirely self-centred, as is shown by his commitment to a large proportion of his patients and by the unpaid editorial and librarianship work he undertook for the BPAS. Additionally, his ethnic identity may well have worked against him. While no analyst would have wanted to be thought to be acting in a biased way towards the British Society's first non-white trainee, a degree of patronising condescension to non-whites was commonplace, and their views of such individuals were routinely twisted. Winnicott, for example, commented of an Indian patient in 1948, 'Like many Indians he feels that he is such an interesting case that we should pay him for the privilege of seeing him' (Willoughby 2005: 42). This impression could easily fit Khan, but his analysts would have been most unlikely to have admitted to such attitudes in view of his Western education and lofty social status.[3] Instead of reflecting on whatever form their prejudice took, their discomfiture may have lurked underground where it could not be examined or its valid aspects considered. It is more likely that a tendency towards a wholesale avoidance of this uncomfortable area would be established, which would militate against confronting Khan with his arrogance. Thus, all the ingredients are present for a conflicted and confused relationship between Khan and the contemporary world of British psychoanalysis.

Whatever the reasons, it is remarkable how consistently Khan's analysts departed from their analytic role. Ella Sharpe, Khan's first analyst, was a well-known Kleinian who had moved towards an Independent stance. Like Winnicott, she was prepared to step outside the role of analyst when she thought it in her patients' interests, but was unlikely to have done so on a regular basis to the extent that she did with Khan. Finding her new patient a 'rare bird' who, like her, loved Shakespeare, she went out of her way to help him enter the higher echelons of artistic society in London, introducing him, for example, to the social circle surrounding the Stephens family, relatives of Virginia Woolf (ibid. 29). She also persuaded Khan to get on with his training without delay, despite his youth, a suggestion he was only too willing to take up but which could hardly have been helpful to him overall.

When Sharpe died, he wasted little time in transferring to John Rickman, whose fatal heart attack occurred only four years into the analysis. The Independent Harold Stewart remarked 'It's a great pity that John Rickman died. He would never have put up with Khan's nonsense' (ibid. 32). Nevertheless, Rickman acted outside the therapeutic boundaries even more than had Sharpe. He took Khan for coffee after sessions, even with the next patient looking on, and to psychoanalytic congresses as his guest – the only trainee attending (ibid.). Khan helped Rickman edit psychoanalytic journals, followed his direction to read the whole of the *International Journal of Psycho-Analysis* on the way to and from his sessions, and discussed Rickman's own papers with him. Although this may have had positive aspects, it would have been at the expense of normal analytic containment.

Khan tempted fate by choosing a third psychoanalyst who had already had a coronary. Although Winnicott went on to live another 20 years, he probably had neither the vigour nor the temperament to stand up to such a forceful, disturbed and manipulative patient. The therapeutic boundaries were porous from the beginning: when Khan asked Winnicott to take him into analysis, they had already worked together in the supervision of one of Khan's child cases. Winnicott appears never to have confronted Khan's narcissistic arrogance and outright rudeness (ibid. 42), making it impossible for the two of them to access the needy, deprived being underlying these unpleasant characteristics. In fact, their relationship became so multifaceted that its therapeutic potential must have been severely compromised. Throughout their work together, Khan and Winnicott engaged in frequent discussion of each other's patients, helped each other out with work dilemmas, discussed theoretical questions and accepted referrals from each other, as well as meeting frequently as friends and colleagues (ibid. 71, 95).

By 1952, only a year into the analysis, they had settled into a pattern of Khan having a session in the mornings and assisting Winnicott edit his papers in the afternoons, sometimes practically writing them himself (ibid. 143). Khan was quite sincere in wanting to gain as much psychoanalytic expertise as he possibly could, as well as advance his own reputation as Winnicott's protégé through promoting Winnicott's work. Many of Winnicott's major works include prefaces or introductions by Khan, such as the substantial 'Introduction' (1975) to the 1992 edition of *Through Paediatrics to Psychoanalysis*, in which Khan expresses his enduring admiration and affection for Winnicott in fulsome terms.

After the first four years of five-times-a-week analysis, Khan gave over his sessions to Jane Shore, apparently taking them up again after a year or so. At some point during the 1960s the work was reduced to what Khan called 'coverage', by which he meant intermittent support with flexible therapeutic boundaries on a long-term basis (ibid. 111–112). The therapeutic relationship between Khan and Winnicott 'ended in 1966 when DWW and I agreed spontaneously to opt out of our analytic contract with each other' (ibid. 168). The termination was bitter, and coincided with Winnicott's involvement in the ending of Khan's disastrous treatment of Wynne Godley; but they continued to work together on Winnicott's writings.

By now, Khan had developed a mix of highly contrasting feelings about Winnicott, relying on him more than he did on anyone else in the Western world while also blaming him for failing to confront his destructiveness: 'Winnicott, from envy and his need of me, was my most generous yet abominable exploiting accomplice' (ibid. 170). The praise that Winnicott lavished freely on Khan would have worked against him even beginning to attain that sense of ordinariness which Khan of all people needed to counter the narcissism fostered since infancy (ibid. 327).

Winnicott did indeed collude with Khan's defensive arrogance, and this perhaps reflects his own, with each acting as though the normal rules of psychoanalysis did not apply to him. However, they used this shared trait creatively in such clinical innovations as 'regression to dependence' (ibid. 114–120). It is a mode of treatment that can be particularly helpful for some patients, especially those with a 'False Self' pathology.[4] It seeks to enable the patient to regress as far as he needs to, for as long as he needs to, until he can relinquish his false persona and begin to live from his undeveloped, infantile 'True Self'. Because he would be unable to manage the adult responsibilities of everyday life during this period, arrangements would be made by the analyst in conjunction with the patient's significant others. Such deep regression is terrifying for the patient, highly demanding of the therapist and disastrous if it goes wrong. Most analysands are not in a position to take a break of unspecified length from their work or caring responsibilities: 'To have a major regression, you have to have money' as Khan remarked to an analysand (ibid. 115). Christopher Bollas, however, who was analysed by Khan as a young man, developed a modified version of this regime (2013) which would be suitable for some, if not all, patients without bankrupting either therapist or patient.

Despite both Winnicott's and Khan's gifts for taking analysands creatively through prolonged periods of regression to dependence, their own muddled modes of relating to each other prevented them from managing it in their work together. Khan's massive identification with his father meant he was too terrified of his own vulnerability to risk it, and this perhaps carried over into his relationship with Winnicott. Rather than developing sufficient trust in his analyst, the two of them inveigled each other into a far safer, and ultimately anti-therapeutic relationship based on intellectual concerns and mutual admiration. How could Khan allow himself to become dependent on someone he could manipulate so readily, and who even turned to him for help and advice?

However, Winnicott's analysis of Khan was by no means fruitless. Khan developed a successful and creative work life, in which he made valuable contributions to psychoanalytic thinking and practice. He held a number of responsible positions in the BPAS and became well known in the field of psychoanalytic publishing. Khan was ready to offer both help and criticism to colleagues embarked on their own works; he seems to have realised when people were capable of writing better and simply hadn't bothered, in which case he castigated them mercilessly, and when they genuinely needed support, which he offered generously (ibid. 136–137). The wide knowledge of new psychoanalytic writing that he developed through these activities served as a useful apprenticeship for his own writing, and informed his own clinical practice.

It was not until Winnicott's 'therapeutic coverage' was lost that the deterioration in his work and personality gathered pace and rumours about his sexual misdeeds began to surface. This mirrored Khan's self-confessed inability to cope when his father had died, leaving him with 'no expectancy of a traditioned discipline; I was instead impaled on the intensity of my own will and temperament' (ibid. 15). Khan had been able to use Winnicott as a benign superego figure, limiting the worst of his excesses; he suggests that Winnicott 'changed a catastrophic threat of loss of object [his father's death] into [mere] separation anxiety' (ibid. 36). The fleeting episodes of regressed dependence that Khan was able to experience with Winnicott may have been what helped him to respond so sensitively to those patients with whom he worked well:

> [I]n some 15 years of analytic relationship with Winnicott, I did succeed at three points … to sink into my Self, be silent, present in my person and related to him. All these three occasions were physical or rather psychosomatic. He was in his chair seated and I had got off the couch and buried my head into the side of his coat. I can still hear his heart and watch beating. All else was still and sentiently neutral and I was at peace. And DWW never interpreted those three occasions. He had enabled me to reach to that point, allowed it to actualise, and let it pass – without comment. And these three occasions were my only experience of the Self in me in analysis.
>
> (Ibid. 15)

Winnicott's response illustrates the elasticity of the normal psychoanalytic constraints that Independents believe to be necessary to fully live through this kind of regressed state. Khan was not on the couch, but sitting on the floor holding onto Winnicott who, rather than interpret what Khan was doing, simply allowed the experience to unfold. It is the experience itself that Independents see as therapeutic as opposed to how it is understood.

Winnicott seems to have seen in Khan the son he never had, while Khan took revenge on him as the 'representative on Earth' of his own father. A colleague of Khan's reports that at meetings chaired by Winnicott, 'Masud used to be quite rude to him, arrogant and challenging. Winnicott was always laid back, sometimes he would even go to sleep at those meetings' (ibid. 41). It sounds as though Khan was almost willing Winnicott to rise up and confront him, at the same time treating him in ways that he must have longed to do with his own father: 'DWW traumatised me by his public Christian masochistic humility: so phoney, and yet so him' (ibid.). Winnicott re-enacted the worst aspects of Fazaldad's relationship with Khan, treating him as the favoured son in whom overblown expectations were placed; Khan colluded with this willingly.

Khan and Winnicott were in some ways the two sides of the same coin. Winnicott presented himself as a wayward and unassuming maverick, though he was actually the master of his field, ambitious and determined. Khan, on the other hand, put himself forward with all the arrogance and superiority that Winnicott concealed, the egotistical student who knew better than the master but who could also act with a similar tenderness at times – as he had with his sister and did with some of his patients. He could appear either insufferable or magically attentive to those he saw as either his superiors or, like patients, dependent on him; but apart from the chosen few, he despaired of finding acceptance by his peers. Winnicott and Khan would have been mortified to be seen as like the other, but Khan reflected the best of his mentor as well as the worst. Khan shows unparalleled clinical acumen, as in his sensitive use of a playful and teasing manner to entice a reluctant patient into communication, or in offering him a totality of attention he had never experienced before (Hopkins 2006: 124–125, 172, 265). He was at home with confrontation and aggression where Winnicott was not – despite the insight and judgement shown in his early paper 'Hate in the Countertransference' (1947). It is also interesting to note that Winnicott, too, was anxious in relation to his father, leaving it to a friend, for example, to tell him that he planned to become a doctor rather than take his place in the family business (Goldman 1993: 51–52). There are thus many reasons why Winnicott and Khan might have unconsciously recognised each other as therapeutic collaborators. At his best, Khan could surpass Winnicott as a psychotherapist; at his worst, he was the absolute obverse.

In February 1977, following his cancer diagnosis and the limitations placed on his work after the first BPAS enquiry, Khan sought a further period of therapeutic help. He turned to the only figure in the psychoanalytic establishment he felt he could always rely on: Anna Freud. Her affection for Khan had continued since they first met in 1948, throughout the ups and downs of his career. She was still susceptible to his charms, and being now elderly, probably realised she could offer him little but support. On her suggestion, their work was described as 'supervision' rather than 'analysis' (Willoughby 2005: 200). Rather than providing Khan with some stability, it appears to have changed all too quickly into a collusion in which they saw themselves as joint victims of a Kleinian conspiracy. Khan's Work Book records that Anna Freud even compared the BPAS Committee to the Nazis:

> At the end of my session, where I had spelt out the way the Education Committee is persecuting me through terrorising my candidates, Miss Freud remarked, 'Now you have some idea of what my father and I had to cope with, with the Nazis.'
>
> (Hopkins 2006: 3)

Again, Khan had chosen the colleague least able to help him maintain some grounding in reality, and over whom he would always retain power.

Finally, in 1979, when Khan was turning increasingly to alcohol, his close friend Robert Stoller offered him a 'trial analysis', hoping for an improvement through transference. Stoller knew Khan intimately and could probably confront him more frankly than others had done. He focused on Khan's destructiveness and how it was played out in his relationships with women. Khan was touched, and did in fact turn away from alcohol for six months, until a relationship breakdown sent him back to it; but the work with Stoller may have been compromised through the usual confusion of boundaries. During the period of this work Khan was staying with the Stollers and going to social events with them. The limitations of all Khan's periods of therapeutic work, especially that with Winnicott, meant that when helplessness and dependence on others was forced on him during the long period of his final illness, he had few inner resources on which to draw. Towards the end, he finally exchanged the threat of vulnerability for the security of hatred. The publication of his last book, the hostile and clumsy *When Spring Comes* (Khan 1988), led to full and final expulsion from the BPAS, and he died in a state of loneliness and weakness, brazenly defiant in the face of the humiliation he had been unable to prevent. It was a sad end for a gifted and mercurial figure who was a true original, even amongst the unusual and creative world of twentieth-century psychoanalysis.

Khan and the BPAS

A first enquiry into Khan's conduct was carried out in 1976, while he was undergoing surgery for the lung cancer with which he had recently been diagnosed. Disquiet had arisen concerning a meeting of Khan's favourite supervisees, whom he called his 'villagers' and who frequented his flat as a social group. André Green had been a special guest at this meeting, together with a friend of Khan's who was in analysis with a Kleinian. As always, the meeting had been lively and fascinating, leading Khan's friend to complain to her analyst that her own analysis was far less exciting. This led to the BPAS setting up an enquiry led by Hanna Segal. There was no ethics committee as yet: the BPAS had had no experience of dealing with complaints about its members, and was not yet structured in a way which made oversight of their work possible. To maintain a separation between the investigation and its recommendations on the one hand and any action arising from these on the other, the Education Committee was given responsibility for the former and the BPAS council for the latter. The investigation focused on Khan's 'socializing with students' (Hopkins 2006: 281). Further concern emerged through Joseph Sandler, a member of the Education Committee. One of his analysands was the husband of a patient of Khan, who was currently developing a sexual relationship with her. Both the husband (Sandler's patient) and wife (Khan's patient) were training at the Institute. When Sandler brought this up at a committee meeting Segal initially dismissed it, presuming it to be a product of Sandler's patient's imagination. There was in any event no case to answer since information had come through third parties alone.

Eventually, however, Sandler's patient made a formal complaint which the committee went on to investigate with care and thoroughness, discovering that Khan and his now ex-patient were widely known to be living together. They also found that Khan had held a meeting to try to resolve the conflicting feelings of all concerned, including himself and his lover, her husband and her parents, together with Barrington Cooper, Khan's close friend and physician, and two of the 'villagers'. It is not clear why these last three were invited – perhaps to dilute and contain the anger likely to arise. The committee's report expressed disquiet at students witnessing such a meeting, revolving as it did around one of their peers who was also in analysis with their supervisor. One of the committee, Eric Rayner, remarks on 'how decent and fair everyone was to Masud' (ibid. 297). The committee went on to say that Khan had a 'past history of instability, mood lability and an inability to stop hurting himself' but that none of the complaints about him had been made official (ibid. 298). Eventually the committee made three recommendations: that Khan should be barred from using the title of 'psychoanalyst'; that he be excluded from the BPAS; and that those of his current patients and supervisees who were training with the Institute should move to a different analyst (ibid. 298–299). The committee members were aware that if these recommendations were carried through, Khan would no longer be able to continue with any clinical work: unlike many other members, he did not have an additional qualification, such as psychiatrist, which would allow him to treat patients.

Since Khan was in hospital having surgery at the time, others heard about the decision before he did. After pressure from his friend and physician, Barrington Cooper, the committee was prevailed upon to soften its recommendations: Khan could remain a member of the BPAS and thus continue to work, but not with Institute candidates. Segal explained this: 'Being the soft marks that we always are, we decided not to act against a dying man' (ibid.), or at least not to act so strongly. It seems not to have been apparent to them that this was a rather ignoble compromise in which they appeared to value candidates above ordinary patients.

Khan was predictably bitter, protesting to his colleague Nina Coltart, who remained a positive figure for him, that he had 'behaved totally honourably' throughout, and that it was only his inborn graciousness that stopped him from taking legal action against the Institute. The BPAS did allow him to formally 'retire' from teaching and training, thus avoiding the humiliation of expulsion. Barrington Cooper, however, considered it an act of treachery to act against Khan when he was suffering so much, whereas Adam Limentani, the chair of the council and president of the BPAS, was more sensitive to its professional obligations (ibid. 298).

Any lingering misgivings were laid to rest, however, with the publication of *When Spring Comes* in 1988. Five complaints were made about the book, protesting that it contained anti-Semitic passages and reports of unprofessional clinical work, and that as a whole the book brought the profession into disrepute. Written during the 1980s, it comprises seven case studies and an afterword, purporting to explore the 'awakening' which accompanies the acknowledgement and acceptance of 'transgressions' – behaviour or thinking which goes against deeply held principles. These are inevitable, Khan maintains, in meeting personal needs and desires. The patients described include two homosexual patients and one whose Westernised behaviour diverged from her cultural traditions. Ironically, she deeply offended Khan by smoking in front of him, an older man.

Khan does not mention his own persistent 'transgressions' against psychoanalytic principles but depicts his mode of 'psychotherapeutic care', seeking to distinguish it from psychoanalysis as such: 'The former [psychotherapeutic care] I learned from my father from the age of nine to nineteen' he states. 'The "care" was of our peasants, and it was total care … [a]ugmented by Dr Winnicott's teachings in particular … From Miss Anna Freud I learned, without dogmas or strictures, Freud's psycho-analytic method' (ibid. 64). Khan may well have learned much that was positive about the care of others from his father, but this would have included cruelty and sexual exploitation being combined with nurture. We might doubt whether love and hate were ever properly differentiated in his mind, with psychological versions of his father's mixed attentions towards social inferiors inflicted on his patients. Khan was compelled to gain and maintain the more powerful position, both in social and clinical settings.

Khan makes clear that he uses conventional methods in his clinical work when he thinks it in his patient's best interests, and indeed he could not have taken on more than one patient at a time needing the kind of care he depicts. However, he describes Freud's use of transference as 'a rather sick programme' (Khan 1988: 196), and this throws into question just how conventional his more classical work was. He preferred a 'spontaneous' relationship, which he saw as 'real' and authentic, to a reflective one. In *When Spring Comes* he portrays himself readily responding to a patient's hostility, active or passive, with aggression designed to render him compliant to Khan's own agenda; and he discloses far more about himself than even the most liberal psychotherapist would normally do. The 'total care' he offers includes bluntly-worded insults, frequent advice, money, home visits and meals laid on for the patient's whole family. He often interferes with decisions made by relatives and medical professionals, with or without the wishes of the patient being taken into account. Khan genuinely believes that he knows best, and of course the case studies he chooses to publish appear to have turned out well, with the patients indeed being helped to live more fully and authentically.

Khan does to some extent seek to justify his departure from normal practice. He defends his extensive self-disclosure as a means of '[neutralising] the situation in a positive way', portraying conventional psychoanalytic approaches as provoking 'unnecessary infantile attachments and attitudes in the patient which analysts then interpret as the patient's transference'. His own clinical approach, he says, 'creates its own demands for analyst and patient', but also 'facilitates that mutual sharing which is fundamental to my way of working' (ibid. 200). Presumably he counts his sexualised and aggressive ripostes as authentic 'sharing' – his personal way of conveying that he would not put up with any form or degree of competition.

Khan is not always on the attack – he can also invite the strongest of positive transference feelings. He often finds a way of unsettling the patient; and this glides easily into his very effective use of humour – using play with words as Winnicott describes play with children. For example, Khan reports suggesting to a food-refusing young woman, who had told him she has meals brought to her room, 'Oh, so you *don't eat* with yourself alone' (ibid. 29). In various ways, Khan promotes an image of himself as the powerful, benign magician-father. When combined with the focused and deep attention described by many of his patients, the hope would arise in them that he could cope with any disclosure, however shameful or extreme. Most of the studies in *When Spring Comes* make clear that the relationships continued long after the 'therapeutic care' had ended, and all include strong links being built up with the patient's immediate circle. This looks like a way of creating surrogate families, in which Khan always played a dominant role. We can see that he could have been an effective clinician for those patients he did not insult or exploit, but with those that he did, he would easily have invited a toxic dependency. The complex relationship between Khan and his father seems always to be hovering in the background, to be played out in one of its many forms.

While not as well written as his previous books, the earlier case studies still show his hallmark lively story-telling style and his winning manner. Some of the work is interesting and creative, describing how the patient's family members are helpfully involved in their treatment. The case from which the title of the book was taken, 'When Spring Comes' (ibid. 26–51), contains rare details about how Khan worked with Winnicott, conveying a sense of a gifted pair of professionals improvising their own approach to treating 'problem' patients. Khan could be thoughtful as well as impulsive, castigating a patient considering suicide, for example, by telling him 'fathers do not often realise that, during their adolescence, their children *need* them to be there, and available *on demand*, as urgently and constantly as infants do their mothers' (ibid. 124). Khan is making the interesting suggestion that the father sustains the adolescent in leaving the family and entering into the outside world in the same way that the mother brings the child out of the womb and into the family.

The brunt of the provocation is in the chapter entitled 'A Dismaying Homosexual' (ibid. 87–116). It seems likely that the subject is made up from a compilation of patients (Hopkins 2006: 373). As written, it is concerned with the long treatment of a somewhat perverse American homosexual from a background of poverty and sexual abuse. After describing his sordid and despairing past, 'Mr Luis' sets Khan a challenge: 'I made a New Year's resolution that I would end my life this year, on my fiftieth birthday' (Khan 1988: 88). Khan responds that he probably could help 'Mr Luis', as he referred to him, but that he does not want to. 'You are not ill or sick or neurotic, or my sort of patient. I shall learn little from you … You are not a true pervert either' (ibid. 90). They trade increasingly sexualised insults, until Khan produces the deliberately offensive rant which so incensed the BPAS:

> Yes, I am anti-Semitic. You know why, Mr Luis? Because I am an Aryan and had thought all of you Jews had perished when Jesus, from sheer dismay – and he was one of you – had flown up to Heaven, leaving you in the scorching care of Hitler, Himmler and the crematoriums.
>
> (Ibid. 92–93)

Nor does he overlook Mr Luis' homosexuality: 'Poofs, especially the gilded ageing ones, do fill me with instant disgust and disdain' (ibid. 91). Since a number of such speeches are included, it is not surprising that the BPAS accused him of 'gross misconduct', specifically explicit anti-Semitism. His close friend Stoller raged against him, comparing the book to '[watching] a kamikaze pilot in his final plunge ... [Masud's] damnable book, with its gross, gauche, nasty-little-boy-piss-on-you scurrility, is a joke out of control' (Hopkins 2006: 366).

Stoller's reaction is readily understandable; but Khan's shock and outrage at the sanctions delivered by the BPAS suggest that he was not, at least consciously, pursuing professional suicide. It could easily be assumed that the writer of such objectionable material must be a blindly prejudiced bigot; and his intelligence, together with an extra measure of hatred, makes his attitude appear more dangerous than that of an ordinarily intolerant man in the street. However, Khan's biographies show that he could direct insults against social groups without being set against them more than briefly. Otherwise many more groups would have to be included – 'Americans, the British, Hindus, feminists, and psychoanalysts in general' (ibid. 367, fn. 20). Khan did not in general act in a prejudiced manner towards anyone Jewish, American, homosexual, either in his everyday life or his work life. The American Robert Stoller was arguably his closest friend, and as an adult he depended on him more than on anyone except Winnicott; other close friends were homosexual, and elsewhere, Khan speaks highly of Jewish contributions to culture, and of, course, to psychoanalysis. Khan's colleagues suggested that he was explicitly anti-Semitic only after the BPAS acted to limit his work (ibid. 367–369).

The more disturbing passages in the case studies frequently result from Khan's concern to establish himself in the more powerful position. This may have had legitimate therapeutic purposes – in the case of 'Mr Luis', for example, to jolt the patient out of his passive-aggressive stance into something more authentic, by confronting him with the virulent self-hatred embodied in internalised homophobic and anti-Semitic attacks. Mr Luis does not appear shocked at Khan's abuse, since it may have been little different from what he was already telling himself. His masochistic streak might even have led him to feel excited at the closeness intimated, and he may have been reassured that Khan was not someone he could easily dominate. Unfortunately, that does not preclude the possibility that there was unconscious collusion between the two of them in prolonged sado-masochistic verbal intercourse. At any rate, Khan's work overall does not convey entrenched prejudice: his relationship with 'Mr Luis' could be regarded as one of increasing respect and affection. Khan continued to visit him in the US for the next fourteen years.

Important differences can be seen between Khan's and Winnicott's style of offering management, or therapeutic care. Winnicott describes the therapeutic relationship with his most disturbed patients as being 'almost-but-not-quite' real (Hopkins 2006: 432, fn. 35): most essentially it is a professional relationship, though deeply personal at the same time. Khan did not maintain the fundamental boundary between the social and the professional; his patients were in a relationship with him which he seemed to see as equally 'real' and therefore reciprocal as those he had with his friends. With Winnicott the intimacy went one way only: it is possible that he might have disclosed something about himself to his patients, but it would have started from the therapeutic situation rather than his own needs – and ended there as well, at least in his intentions. Khan's own accounts, by contrast, describe his patients becoming companions and friends, and he never denied that some became his lovers. It is therefore very likely that, from the start, there was a critical boundary missing. As Khan repeated frequently, he saw them as he thought his father saw his tenant farmers, who were being looked after ultimately so that they could provide for his father. In the same way, Khan's own needs may have been set alongside the patient's wellbeing to a greater degree than is usual.

Khan's final book has limited but real strengths alongside its weaknesses. Although undeniably provocative, the most extreme passages can be read as using a wish to shock for therapeutic ends. The substance and tone of the highly offensive rants made to 'Mr Luis' (Khan 1988: 92–93) are not congruent with Khan's lifestyle in general, or even with that piece of work taken as a whole. He was quite capable of judging others as individuals rather than as members of a group, and usually did so. It is also possible that such 'rants' were written or at least edited for effect, presenting himself as an imposing and intimidating 'prince' wielding unconditional power over his adoring subjects, supposedly for their own benefit.

Thus Khan's work appears as dazzling and ambiguous as his personality. The most consistent feature appears to be his attempts to trigger emotionally intense responses from others – in effect, to elicit the very transference he speaks against: the worst possible reaction for him would have been indifference. However, his 'therapeutic care' may have been helpful on some occasions, especially if he did indeed consult with colleagues over such work, as he advised other practitioners to do.

The final question is how the BPAS decisions should be assessed. Khan lived far longer than had been expected in 1976, but when his final book was published in 1988 the end of his life was clearly approaching fast. If there was ever a time for leniency, this was it; the action against him can be seen as wantonly cruel, especially when a closer look is taken at the supposedly 'anti-Semitic' passages. The BPAS seems to have acted to some extent from a long history of finding itself impotent in the face of Khan's patients persistently refusing to see things straight and make a formal complaint about him. This was due almost as much to problems in the society's structure as it was to Khan's infractions, and it was not until 2001 that the society was forced to face up to its own limitations.

When Wynne Godley published his devastating account, Donald Campbell, then president of the BPAS, immediately called a meeting to discuss the implications for the profession. The main topic discussed was 'the severe institutional difficulties and limitation we face … in tackling perverse and psychopathic behaviours in our membership' (Boynton 2002). What emerged most strongly were the historical weaknesses in the admissions and qualifications procedures at the time when Khan applied for training, was admitted and finally qualified. We have seen that Khan had not realised he was applying to be admitted as a student: Khan had no more than a single interview with John Bowlby, held over lunch and a walk in Regent's Park. It emerged in the meeting, however, that even by the standards of the time, Khan met with unusually positive responses throughout his training, and that his misdeeds were well known to a number of senior analysts, all of whom failed to act (Willoughby 2005, 242). The suggestion was that senior society members were under the spell of a group counter-transference which was difficult to resist, perhaps arising from a reaction formation against the general prejudice held towards ethnic minorities. When referring prospective patients to Khan, for example, Winnicott normally asked if they had an objection to working with a Pakistani analyst – implying that they had every right to do so (Hopkins 2006: 197, 273).

Khan's private income meant he was able to apply for qualification as a psychoanalyst unusually early, but his progress was not entirely smooth. His first supervised case remained unfinished, but he was nonetheless let through. Qualification as a child psychoanalyst came soon after, and in 1959 he was accepted as a training analyst – but only on his fourth attempt. He had previously been repeatedly rejected 'for unspecified reasons' (Boynton 2002) which may have had to do with his age or his obnoxious personality, together with the ambivalent attitude held towards him by BPAS members. From the time of his qualification, however, there was no official oversight of his work. Only a formal complaint could trigger an investigation, and none was made until 1976. At this point the society found itself unprepared to deal with such a situation, with no Ethics Committee and no ethical codes. This was why it fell to the Education Committee to examine the substance of the complaint and offer recommendations on what should be done.

Winnicott is the only analyst who could realistically have raised questions about Khan's work but, as we have seen, Winnicott was deeply enmeshed with Khan, promoting him rather than examining the disquiet he must at times have felt. Godley expresses almost as much outrage towards Winnicott as he does towards Khan, but it was only with the publication of his paper that Winnicott's part in the whole debacle became known. The meeting became focused on the question of whether psychoanalysis necessarily requires adherence to traditional boundaries, or whether the relaxation of such boundaries is needed to create the authentic relationship that the patient needs if he is to make progress. 'Was Khan's behaviour anomalous, or are there ideas within certain traditions of psychoanalysis that unwittingly encourage such flagrant boundary violations?' (ibid.). The answer is clear – Winnicott's technique of 'regression to dependence' and 'management' can be misused by being taken to an extreme, and especially by the blurring of the boundary between therapeutic and social or personal relationships. So too, however, can the traditional approach of the 'blank screen analyst', which Ferenczi had described as a misuse of the analyst's power. The overall conclusion must be that all psychoanalytic practice carries with it the dual risks of excessive detachment on the one hand and collusive enmeshment on the other, and this dichotomy has to be negotiated by all practitioners with the support of their professional framework. It mirrors the central focus of this book – the similarities and differences between a more classical or Kleinian approach as against a more flexible Independent approach to practising Object Relations.

The discussion in the BPAS concluded by raising further questions for consideration, which still remain important. First, there is the need for psychoanalysts (and psychotherapists) to acknowledge the 'perverse and psychotic areas in ourselves while concurrently trying to analyze such areas of the personalities in our patients'; second, 'Where does our first loyalty lie? To patients or to colleagues?' (ibid.). It might seem obvious that the Society's first loyalty must be towards patients – to the public – but the complexities of relationships within psychotherapeutic institutions, as in other areas of public service, make this difficult to carry through. Finally, the Society concluded, all concerned must recognise that psychoanalysis is not a panacea but has its own limitations; these can be easily overlooked by practitioners who have invested so much, practically, emotionally and financially, in their training, which may not have included much critical examination of its teachings.

This meeting was followed by a paper by the respected analyst Anne-Marie Sandler with a response from Wynne Godley (Sandler and Godley 2004). This article does not add much to our understanding of the destructive Khan–Winnicott interaction, but focuses on the particular difficulties psychotherapeutic societies have in managing the misdeeds of their own members, especially when the member concerned shows neither awareness nor remorse. Sandler emphasises the special danger of 'transgenerational transmission', where violation of boundaries gets passed on from analyst to candidate analysand, and thence to the candidate's future patients – as we see with Winnicott and Khan. Sandler also details the safeguards that have now been set up in the BPAS to reduce the likelihood of further patients suffering harm at the hands of those who are supposed to be helping them.

Most societies did not introduce an ethical code specifically prohibiting sexual involvement between analyst (or therapist) and patient until the 1980s, and a heady atmosphere of sexual liberation was at its height in the late 1960s to the 1970s. It is not surprising that several senior analysts fell from grace during this period. Some were leading contributors to the teaching and training of psychotherapists, with the charismatic style that is often a feature of narcissistic personalities. It was therefore almost inevitable that such episodes led to damaging divisions within their societies, with many of their peers or ex-students unwilling to accept that their gifts should be permanently lost.

Sandler paints a very different picture of the BPAS in 2004 from that in which Khan's unprofessional behaviour originated. Any association concerned with human suffering is likely to have its own internal difficulties, playing out aspects of the dynamics with which it is engaged on a daily basis. It will therefore always be necessary to retain oversight of the workings of the psychotherapeutic institutions as well as their individual members, but we have seen that progress in this area can clearly be achieved. As a result, Masud Khan can be remembered not solely as the Janus-faced 'fallen angel' (Boynton 2003) who brought both valuable innovations and pervasive damage to psychoanalysis, but also as the catalyst for the ethical maturation of the BPAS.

Khan's contributions to psychoanalysis

Khan contributed much to the development of psychoanalysis. He assisted Rickman in his editorial work and commented on his writing, taking this very much further with his main analyst, Winnicott. Khan helped Winnicott turn muddled tangles of words into eloquent and beautiful papers (Hopkins 2006: 142–144). In addition, he was honorary librarian for the Institute of Psychoanalysis, book review editor and then associate editor. He was generous in offering help to the colleagues, having difficulty in writing, who turned to him (ibid. 136).

Khan must have spent thousands of hours in tedious editorial tasks with no direct reward other than taking forward his own knowledge of psychoanalysis and his reputation amongst his peers and seniors; but there was also the transferential satisfaction of assisting his own analysts – and gaining power over them. He made himself extraordinarily knowledgeable about almost everything that was published in the British psychoanalytic world, justifying his view that it was a valuable form of apprenticeship. He also became sufficiently fluent linguistically to take a full part in psychoanalytic conversations with his close French friends. The most important of these were Victor Smirnoff and Wladimir Granoff, but they also included André Green, whose work we shall explore in the next chapter, and Jean-Bertrand Pontalis, the co-author of the essential *The Language of Psychoanalysis* (Laplanche and Pontalis 1985). Khan wrote the Editorial Preface for the English version, and but for Khan, Winnicott would never have become known in France. Green was particularly impressed with Winnicott's work, but when he began developing the concept of transitional space in his own way, Khan's competitiveness led to outbreaks of insulting behaviour in conferences and their friendship soured.

Khan wrote a number of remarkable papers, some of them in French, and his first three books are thoughtful, vivid and innovatory. *The Privacy of the Self*, first published in 1974, recounts the development of his theoretical and clinical outlook, including a detailed examination of Fairbairn's idea of the schizoid personality, from which he developed his own concept of 'cumulative trauma'. Khan also explains and justifies his clinical approach, in which he engages with the patient at an unusually personal level. His second book, *Alienation in Perversions*, first published in 1979, lays out his own understanding of perversion. This is a valuable contribution in which he presents this pathology as an attempt to resolve 'cumulative trauma' by enticing another person into a private, make-believe world sustained by shared perverted acts. *Hidden Selves* (1989b), which first came out in 1983, moves between clinical accounts and the thinking that informs them. All are engaging and informative books in which the patients he describes come alive, as does his unique way of making deep contact with them from very early in the work.

In developing his own approach, Khan looks mainly to the work of Freud and Winnicott. From Freud, he takes the basic tenets of psychoanalytic theory and practice; following Winnicott, he rejects the death drive and accepts the idea of primary narcissism, together with a new emphasis on the role of the environment. Khan and Winnicott maintain that the mother, or mothering person, plays a far more direct part in disturbed psychological development than previous theorists, such as Klein, had supposed. Where Winnicott remains vague about the initial structure of the infant psyche, Khan explicitly rejects Klein's tenet that 'the ego is present at birth'. He states plainly that 'the human individual at the beginning is not a *subject* but an *object*. The human infant exists and experiences itself only through the mother's idolizing attention, hence he is the *object* of the maternal care' (1989a: 11). It is only with the development of the infant's own psychological functions that distinct and disparate episodes of experience gradually become linked together with the infant's own developing psychological functions: 'as the maturational processes release the various ego and id apparatuses, the infant will begin to assemble self-representations that can then be described as the subjective self' (ibid.). He maintains, however, that the infant's 'biological givens' do not develop properly without responsive care. Correspondingly, the main agent of therapeutic change is placed in the environment – in the atmosphere of the clinical setting rather than the patient's insight into his inner world.

The schizoid personality

Khan's theoretical framework is founded on the subject of his first paper, 'Clinical Aspects of the Schizoid Personality' (1960, in 1986: 13–26). The concepts of the schizoid state and personality had recently been developed by Fairbairn (1952) and Khan no doubt recognised schizoid tendencies in himself. Both Fairbairn and Khan suggest the schizoid personality to be the most prominent form of disturbance in the mid-twentieth century, especially in Western societies; the dominant 'Truby King' childcare method meant infants spending long periods alone, with quiet and convenient behaviour valued over happiness. Khan concurred with Fairbairn, Winnicott and Klein that splitting is the most primitive psychical defence, with intolerable experiences being separated from the main body of the infant's experience and ego to allow the basic psychic organisation to form. The most fundamental pathological state is therefore a schizoid or split state; all human beings develop this to a certain extent, but the 'schizoid personality' is dominated by splits, leaving much of his psychic world out of reach.

The schizoid personality is allied to Winnicott's 'False Self', with similar characteristics coming from a different account of early life; it also bears similarities to the Kleinian account of narcissism. Fairbairn describes the schizoid state as arising from the reaction of the infant to one or both of what he defines as the primary traumata: doubt whether his mother loves him for who he actually is, and whether his own love is accepted as authentic. The child may experience the mother as either indifferent to him or over-possessive, indicating that she values him mainly as an extension of herself, one that reflects the qualities she cherishes.

All mothers (or parents) inevitably fail their children at times, especially since it is the child's subjective sense of his relationship with his mother that is crucial. However, when the mother–child relationship normally works well, he can recover from intermittent episodes when it does not. There will still be parts of the ego which are split off because some experiences will always be too painful or contradictory to be tolerated, but the major 'central ego' will develop as an integrated whole. In the 'schizoid personality', however, the main part of the ego comprises split-off, disparate segments. There is little left to constitute the integrated central ego, leaving an overall sense of futility and emptiness. The main aim becomes to defend against further pain rather than to develop loving relationships, and the infant experiences himself as a lesser being, unable to love or be loved.

The infant remains fixated on the simplest and most primitive relation with mother as breast-mother, fearing more mature and separate modes of relationship. Internal reality is privileged over an external reality that has proved unmanageable. A narcissistic sense of grandiosity develops to defend against the underlying extreme dependence and sense of inferiority. Mother and child may then develop a special, secret bond in which they are superior to all. Other relationships can only be tolerated if they conform to this pattern, reinforcing the schizoid avoidance of intimacy and inability to recognise others as equal beings. The ego becomes a collection of disparate pieces, the legacy of repeated trauma. Khan points to Deutsch's 'as-if' personality, as well as to Winnicott's 'False Self', as further examples.

Khan emphasises the fragility of such patients, their inability to tolerate anxiety and their need for the analyst to complete their psychic experiences, as it were: 'the patients compel the analyst into the role of the primary environment. They utterly depend upon his ability to empathize and crystallize this into an affective ego-experience' (ibid. 24). In other words, the analyst has to enter into the patient's ego development by taking on the roles that the mother, or carer, normally adopts in early infancy. Khan emphasises, however, that he is not recommending that the analyst 'become' a better mother, in a version of 'corrective emotional experience' suggested as a follow-up to Ferenczi's work (Alexander and French: 1980: 66). In 1960, when Khan's paper was written, he was still holding to the customary psychoanalytic parameters, maintaining that the aim of enabling 'primary affective integration' through the healing of some of the splits in the ego could be facilitated within the normal analytic situation. Not long after, however, he began to recommend that the 'primary environment' of a closely attuned mothering person is provided not solely or even mainly through accurate understanding, but through the 'real' and authentic relationship with the analyst. Those aspects of the original maternal care that the patient had missed out on could be drawn from the therapeutic relationship, or the therapeutic atmosphere, but without the therapist trying to change the patient's history by replacing his own mother. The 'authentic relationship' is the defining feature of Khan's clinical approach.

Cumulative trauma

Khan goes on to examine the early relational state which gives rise to the schizoid personality, and in doing so introduces his most important theoretical contribution to psychoanalysis, the concept of 'cumulative trauma'. He explains and explores this idea in two papers, written in 1963 and 1964 (ibid. 42–58, 59–68), in which he establishes trauma as another central concept in his thinking. In the first of these papers, 'The Concept of Cumulative Trauma', Khan starts with a careful and accurate summary of Freud's concept of trauma and its subsequent development. He clarifies the conventional psychoanalytic understanding of trauma, defining it as a sudden shock, coming from inside or outside the individual, which is strong enough or disturbing enough to prevent assimilation and integration. An example might be Khan, aged four, having to watch his mother suffering a fit following the birth of a stillborn child and becoming mute as a result.

He uses the contemporary ideas of 'shock' trauma and 'strain' trauma to explain the cumulative trauma. While the example above is clearly a 'shock' trauma, Khan defines cumulative trauma as a 'strain' trauma, the consequence of numerous minor experiences of a similar kind, starting in infancy and potentially continuing into adolescence. This promotes a pathological twist in the parent–child relationship, without there ever being an obviously traumatic event: the trauma is only recognizable in retrospect. Khan thus extends the concept of trauma beyond a single event.[5]

The development of 'cumulative trauma' begins with the inability of the mother or carer to fulfil consistently the role of 'protective shield' to compensate for the child's psychic immaturity. Khan takes this idea of the mother's role from Freud's physicalistic account of the cortex, the receptor of stimuli which eventually develops into the 'system conscious'. Freud (1920) proposes that the constant bombardment of external stimuli on the outermost layers of the cortex causes a 'crust' to develop, and then a 'protective shield', which prevents the sensitive inner layers from being damaged or overwhelmed by excessively strong stimuli. Internal stimuli, when they present a similar danger, are typically projected outside the organism and treated as external stimuli. In Khan's view, the 'good-enough' mother acts to prevent the child from being overwhelmed, whether by his own feelings and sensations or by stimuli from the outside world: in other words, by acting as a protective shield (Khan 1986: 44–46).

In the development of cumulative trauma, the mother or carer fails the infant by expecting him to manage more than he is capable of, or by treating him in a cold or distant manner, which does not meet his need for love and responsiveness. It is not the child's instinctual needs that are left unsatisfied – his needs for food and warmth, for example: 'the breaches I have in mind are in the nature of maladaptation to the infant's anaclitic needs' (ibid. 47), by which Khan means his dependency needs. The child's development is distorted, although his progress through the libidinal stages (oral, anal, phallic, and even the Oedipus Complex) remains, in principle, unaffected. He thus becomes unable to encompass easily the usual tasks faced by the ego, of mediating between the pressures of reality and the super-ego in the service of gratifying instinctual or drive needs. In particular, it is relationships with others that he is ill-equipped to negotiate.

As we have seen in the section on the development of the schizoid patient, a pattern of interaction builds up and becomes established in which the child feels impelled to meet the needs of the mother before his own. He finds trust and intimacy difficult and threatening. It is only when these failures of the mother as protective shield are significantly frequent and take on a specific pattern that they set up a nucleus of pathogenic reactions. Cumulative trauma, therefore, builds up silently and invisibly throughout childhood right up to adolescence, and leaves its mark on all crucial phases of psycho-sexual development, which become clinically observable later on in ego-pathology and schizoid type of character formation.

A compliant 'False Self' develops in the place of, or alongside, the 'True Self':

> The mother who is not good enough is not able to implement the infant's omnipotence, and so she repeatedly fails to meet the infant gesture; instead, she substitutes her own gesture which is to be given sense by the compliance of the infant. This compliance on the part of the infant is the earliest stage of the False Self, and belongs to the mother's inability to sense her infant's needs.
> (Winnicott 1982: 145)

That is, the mother (or main carer) does not meet the infant's needs in a way which is sufficiently appropriate and unobtrusive for him to delay having to recognise that his needs are met from outside himself until he is naturally ready to do so. The infant's 'gesture' is the first sign he makes of an emerging need which, if met, heralds the brief 'experience of omnipotence' that Winnicott believes the very young infant to require for a secure start in life. As a visible sign of an internal state, it marks the beginning of the integration of external and internal reality. It is this integration which is the basis for 'True Self' living – living that is both authentic and relational. When the 'False Self' or cumulative trauma is developing, however, the mother's need takes precedence: it is her 'gesture', her needs, that the infant has to comply with.

In his best clinical work, Khan's main aim was to help the patient reach and develop his 'authentic self', even if this meant an increase in suffering. His 1964 paper, his second on cumulative trauma, considers how to treat such patients. Where the ego is dominated by cumulative trauma, the analyst's attention should be focused on how the patient reacts to the actual situation offered to him: 'The patient repeats with acute finesse and in minute detail all the elements of the primary infantile situation. This indeed is repetition in the concrete, as it were.' (1986: 66) Typically, the patient 'twists and distorts the situation in order to avoid those areas of stress with which his ego-defect cannot cope' (ibid.). His techniques of avoidance will include his own way of 'acting out', which Khan casts as part of the repetition, rather than simple avoidance of conflict or guilt. All the elements of the patient's encounter with the analytic setting can be used to reconstruct a picture of the original situation, which formed the template for the patient's cumulative trauma. By combining authenticity with a flexible sensitivity, the therapist may then provide a response or clarification, which will enable development to proceed.

Thus Khan's original concept brings together the main tenets of his psychoanalytic thinking: the priority of relationship over gratification in psychic development and the impact of the environment, or the object, on the subject. Despite lapses in his clinical work, which cannot be overlooked, Khan was capable of work that was flexible and rigorous, authentic and responsive. This allowed the patient to direct the path of his own treatment, consciously or unconsciously, with the therapist remaining both attuned to the patient and also firmly and genuinely himself.

Perversion

Khan's second book, *Alienation in Perversions*, dates from 1979. He brings compassion and empathy to an unpopular subject as he seeks new ways of understanding this pathology. As the title suggests, the 'pervert'[6] is divided within himself and against himself. He constructs an identity which is limited to sexual identity, and this in turn is rendered only partly personal:

> the pervert puts an impersonal object between his desire and his accomplice: this object can be a stereotype fantasy, a gadget or a pornographic image. All three alienate the pervert from himself, as, alas, from the object of his desire.
>
> (1989a: 9)

The pervert may try to pass himself off as engaged in an idiosyncratic but legitimate sexual liaison, but a fearful craving takes the place of desire; the impersonal adjunct stands in for a personal way of loving. As in normal use of the term in criminal conspiracies, the accomplice is connected with the pervert not by reciprocal loving but by their shared inability to commit to society's norms.

Khan understands perversion as one way of resolving the false and compliant way of living that comes with a particular kind of 'cumulative trauma'. He describes the early life of the future pervert as very similar to that of the person who will become schizoid, but with additional features. In both cases the infant's world is focused on a close and special relationship with the mother who, typically, does not see her child as a person, let alone as the person he is. He is her 'thing-creation' (ibid. 11) – a special, admired object of her own making on whom she bestows continual physical attention and gratification. The child identifies with his mother's view of himself as very special and the bodily focus of their connection acts as a 'fast track' to the formation of psychical structure. The child's identification with his mother's 'thing-creation' is imprinted on him at a somatic level, more primitive than the emerging psychical level.

Both mother and child devote themselves to their thrilling special relationship, with the child becoming adept at maintaining and developing those aspects of himself that his mother most values. Each is highly invested in this gratifying yet illusory connection and they become, in effect, accomplices for their shared perverse scenarios. But when oedipal processes rise to their height (ages 3–5) the mother often realises how inappropriately fixated she is on her child, especially in a bodily sense, and withdraws from him. The child, feeling abandoned and panicky, consolidates his internal view of himself as centred on, yet divided from, the 'thing-creation'; he turns to a secret relationship with this superior but arid sense of himself as a source of comfort. In the same way as the markedly schizoid person prioritises internal reality over the external reality he has been unable to engage with, the future pervert withdraws to this internal narcissistic relation. It carries overtones of his mother's care and adulation, but does not allow more mature and separate relationships to evolve. The child does not have the resources to develop his own personality and imagination through unplanned play. He remains caught in a solipsistic, masturbatory fixation, which involves a basic alienation from himself, while seeming to reflect a core sense of his identity. The developing pervert's life becomes a prolonged and anxious acting out of a striving to recreate the sense he once had of being loved, albeit not for who he truly was.

At puberty the pressure to push into real life experience and object relations becomes overwhelming: 'It is in … an inner climate of strangulated affectivity and instinctual tension that an opportunity or encounter with someone would provide them with an opening into life' (ibid. 14). The future 'accomplice' is unconsciously selected as someone who also feels himself to be a 'thing-person', with a particular penchant for 'body language' and who is unlikely to demand real intimacy. The pervert treats this other as a 'sacred fetish', with only those aspects of himself realised which were originally valued. There is no room for the separateness of each participant to be recognised, but the link with an accomplice forms the training-ground for the development of the full perverse scenario. This will be structured closely on the original situation from which the mother–child relationship began to take a pathological turn, transferred to the area of sexuality to cover intense anxiety. The pervert draws on his mother's seductiveness to entice the 'accomplice' into an apparently gratifying 'play-world' of his own without risking any kind of true relating. Instead of interaction between two subjects, the pervert and his accomplice both remain inside the pervert's distorted fantasy.

For analyst and patient, the meaning of the original scenario is hidden within an enactment of the perversion, but it can also be discovered through close attention to the way the patient comports himself in the therapeutic setting. The pervert, more than any other kind of patient, will be hampered by shame and bewilderment, which may be overt or hidden behind a false bravado. As with the schizoid personality, he has developed an ego dominated by splits, gaps and jagged edges, with only his unique creation, the act of perversion, appearing to hold out any hope of integration, satisfaction or completion of his unresolved relational structures.

The perversion is a kind of corrupt transitional object. It is similarly individually created and located in a position that is subjective yet objective: its object exists, concretely or abstractly, in the external world. Unlike the true transitional object, however, the pervert's creation brings only a tantalizing promise of fulfilment, which is never realised. The pervert is too engaged in setting the stage for its enactment and coaching his accomplice in his role to be able to lose himself in sexual surrender. It is only the accomplice who, without these responsibilities, appears free to let go into what, for the pervert, would be the sole context for true satisfaction. The accomplice, however, is not the creator of this perversion, although he may have one of his own which is very similar, and therefore full satisfaction will not come his way, either.

Khan was particularly interested in how the pervert uses a highly developed way of persuading, enticing and seducing his accomplices into taking part in acts likely to appear degrading and repulsive, or at least distasteful. The urgency of his craving leads him to reconstruct or rediscover a world in which shame does not exist. Khan terms the pervert's method 'the technique of intimacy': a pseudo-closeness by which he draws the accomplice into his subjective world almost as powerfully as he was originally drawn in by his mother. Bringing together a 'technique', which can be practised and improved, with the very personal quality of 'intimacy' gives the pervert consummate powers to draw the other in. The absolute necessity for an accomplice to bring this world into being enables him to pass his conviction of its reality on to or into him. The pervert creates the parody of a close and trusting relationship where shame can be bypassed and innermost secrets shared without fear. This is, of course, a corrosive reflection of early infancy; for the pervert the mother only *seemed* to enter into the experiential world of the child, and likewise, he only seems to be attuned to the experience of his accomplice. All that exists is the pervert's subjective world, containing nothing but the idealised version of himself.

Conclusion

Unusually, Khan's contributions to psychoanalysis are neither primarily theoretical nor primarily clinical. We have considered both the strengths and the weaknesses of his work: the originality of mind and therapeutic independence which led to bold innovations, as well as the destructive self-indulgence which raises questions about some of his clinical practice.

Khan's main theoretical contributions include the development of the concepts of the schizoid personality and cumulative trauma, his account of perversion and the elucidation of the Independent theoretical position. While Winnicott clearly disagrees with Klein's belief that the ego is present at birth, Khan spells out that the newborn infant is 'not a subject but an *object* ... of the maternal care' (1989a: 11, and see 103 above, where Khan goes into more detail on this point).

The 'maternal care' does not build on, draw out from or elaborate a kernel of individuality, but is part of what creates this individuality.

Khan's most significant clinical innovation is the 'therapeutic care' he introduced, together with Winnicott, for patients who seemed unable to use the conventional therapeutic situation. Their 'regression to dependence' is an extreme version of this. In an orthodox psychoanalytic approach, the setting remains consistent and may act as a container for the patient's changing emotions and experiences. In therapeutic care, the analyst adapts the setting according to his view of the patient's needs, with containment being a function of the therapeutic atmosphere and relationship. For Khan, the therapist's role replicates good-enough mothering through interpreting the patient's impulses and acting as a 'protective shield' to prevent the patient from being overwhelmed by the external world or the intensity of his own feelings. Importantly, the therapist does not 'become' a second mother to the patient – a collusion that Khan sees as a sign of 'magical thinking' which makes the patient the therapist's 'project', rather than an independent person (see Khan 1986: 67–68).

How can the phenomenon of Khan be understood? Are we looking at a psychiatric condition? We know that his brother Tahir suffered from bipolar disorder. What happened to Khan in psychological terms and how far can he be considered to have been wilfully destructive? How important were cultural conflicts, both within himself and in his relationships with the artistic and intellectual milieux he inhabited? Khan's closest friends and colleagues were left to ponder these questions after his death.

Victor Smirnoff, one of the closest of his French friends, wrote that he was 'gifted, beautiful, rich, intelligent' but also 'cunning, boastful, narcissistic, stingy, prejudiced and cruel.' He concluded, however, that he was a 'faithful friend' (Hopkins 2006: 380). Robert Stoller, another of his intimates, rejoined, 'I disagree that he was a faithful friend. I think he was, in the end, faithless to himself, to the goddamn tradition he was always hooting about, and to the rest of us' (ibid.). He conceded later, however, that Khan was also lovable, 'something that I cannot yet make sense of but know is true' (ibid.). André Green, who had fallen out with Khan some years before, describes Khan's divided personality in terms of

> at least three Masuds. The first one was the brilliant psychoanalyst … an original thinker, sharp, intuitive, with a very quick mind. The second Masud was an eccentric personality who lived by his own standards, spending his nights reading and painting, interested in meeting distinguished people … Finally, there was a third Masud, the psychopathic one, deeply disturbed, envious, cynical, full of resentment, needing to harm his rivals, to debase them and to use every possible way to fulfil his aim.
>
> (Ibid. 381)

All these views of Khan highlight the destructive streak competing with, but seemingly not eclipsing, his attractive traits.

When Khan was not allowing his pathology to leak – or flood – into his clinical work and his everyday life, he was capable of considerable insight. He writes, with the perceptiveness born of personal turmoil, of his own understanding of 'madness', which he saw as arising from a particularly disturbed mother–infant relationship. The term 'technique of intimacy' which Khan adopted for the *modus operandi* of the pervert seems peculiarly appropriate to his own interpersonal style: a sensitive and warped individual feels compelled to develop an unusually effective means of seduction into a corrupt and corrupting scenario. Are we to understand this as compulsion or choice? Khan knew of his own destructiveness without being able to control it. Close to the end of his life, turning against Winnicott as well as himself, he declares: 'I am false to my back teeth. This works better for me than my True Self à la DWW' (ibid. 319). Yet he also had an 'authentic self' which drew his close friends to him. Whichever 'self' was dominant at any given moment may have been the one that felt most real at the time.

Khan can certainly be seen as narcissistic: he often, though not always, related to others through his own needs. In terms of Independent theory, he seems to have incorporated a number of selves, mostly 'False' but also 'True'. The former are easy to find in his destructiveness and self-destructiveness, his arrogance and his boastfulness: 'Prince' Masud Khan is a consummate example. Yet there was also the genuinely lovable side that Stoller speaks of. He must have received responsive as well as inadequate maternal care for such a strong loving inner object relationship to become established – even alongside those that take self-obsessed and alienated forms.

It has often been suggested that despite his success in the Western world, his Eastern heritage remained fundamental to his sense of identity: 'My people do not feel Judaeo-Christian guilt. My people feel vengeance', he declared (ibid: 3). It is also doubtful whether Khan ever fully adopted the psychoanalytic principles he was trained in. At one point he even boasted that the tradition of care he was born into meant that psychoanalysis had little to teach him: 'I come from some 600 years of taking care' (ibid. 299). Towards the end of his life, his whole personality disintegrated: apart from his alcoholism, there may have been a degree of brain damage from his cancer surgery. He asserted to André Green that he had 'never lapsed from a total belief in [this tradition] … I have never believed in psychoanalysis … for some two decades I exercised a "willing suspension of disbelief" – but now I disown it totally' (ibid. 358).

However one understands this statement, there is no doubt that Khan increasingly came to ignore the most fundamental of psychoanalytic rules: the prohibition of sexual activity between therapist and patient. Khan did not go so far as to advocate liaisons between analyst and patient, but stated that he regretted nothing he had done (ibid. 187). His insistence that he is identifying with his forefathers in providing all-encompassing care in a feudal tradition is suspect, however. Khan's father did not come from generations of 'seigneurs', but from peasant farming stock; his wealth derived from being rewarded for his services to the British Raj (ibid. 4).

The poorest of peasants can dream of being the lord of his environment, but this is not the same as being born into an aristocracy. So even Khan's oft-repeated claim that he came from a tradition of care-giving reflects what Khan wishes had been the case, rather than what was. It is very likely that Khan did identify strongly with his father's view of his own superiority, and that the status conferred by material goods was felt to carry with it a right to sexual possession. In his sexual relationships Khan seems only to have felt a sense of responsibility to his two wives which, paradoxically, he showed by leaving them. Thus he told Jane Shore that she would ultimately be grateful that he was rejecting her, and he left Svetlana Beriosova, for whom he still retained deep feeling, because he realised he was damaging not just her but her art.

Khan's complex identity, with its cultural dimensions, included 'selves' that were based on phantasy rather than reality. This makes Winnicott's concepts of 'True' and 'False' self questionable when used in relation to Khan, or for that matter his preferred terms, 'authentic' and 'reactive'. In Winnicott's definition, the 'True Self' is simply the 'experience of aliveness'; yet it is hard to believe that Khan had no inkling that the ancestral tradition he parades was more wish than reality.[7] We might say, therefore, that Khan's personality was made up of a collection of authentic and reactive selves, with the reactive selves taking precedence over the authentic, and demarcated from each other more than is usual.

His various analyses were incomplete or unsuccessful; perhaps he would have gained more insight if he had bitten the bullet and gone for analysis to Melanie Klein who, it is generally agreed, would have been the only psychoanalyst working at that time who could have met his forceful manipulativeness (ibid. 155). By the time Khan died, however, he seemed quite aware that he was leaving a poisoned legacy for friends, colleagues and the psychoanalytic world as a whole.

It is to be hoped that the time has come when the psychoanalytic world can go beyond the negative heritage of Khan's final book and his lack of professionalism to appreciate his valuable innovations, clinical and theoretical, while continuing to learn from his mistakes and transgressions. A more fitting legacy than the neglect with which his work is generally treated would be a better understanding of what can be brought to the profession from members of minority groups, or those who become severely disturbed after qualification. In the case of Khan, both forms of understanding were sadly lacking.

Notes

1 That is, what is given constitutionally and by the environment at birth, which make up the ego and its most basic tendencies. See Chapter 3.

2 Christopher Bollas developed the 'therapeutic care' of Winnicott and especially Khan into an organised and thought-through method, practical for both therapist and client, where selected patients in breakdown are offered intensive psychotherapy and care for short periods as an alternative to hospitalisation. As a young man, Bollas was analysed by Khan. His method is described fully in *Catch Them Before They Fall* (2013). Laing and the Anti-Psychiatry movement also experimented with provision

for those in breakdown or with long-term psychiatric conditions. These continue through the Arbours Association and the Philadelphia Association, which have therapeutic households for such individuals.

3 When Bowlby asked for personal references in his initial interview, Khan reports that he put forward the Governor General of India and the Governor of Punjab – assuring Bowlby that he knew both of them well, as his family probably did (Hopkins 2006: 23).

4 See section on Khan's clinical work in Chapter 8.

5 A related conception of retrospective trauma ('nachträglichkeit') can be seen in Freud's early hypothesis that neurosis was caused by sexual abuse in early childhood. This was not necessarily traumatic at the time it occurred, because the child would be too young to understand its significance, but would become traumatic at puberty, when the advent of genital sexuality brought with it the realisation that the previous sexual interaction was shocking and abnormal (Freud 1895).

6 The quotation marks indicate that the usual revulsion accompanying this term is suspended. However, having made the point I shall not continue with them.

7 See Freud's *Family Romances* (1909) S.E.8.

References

Alexander, F., French, T., et al. (1980/1946) *Psychoanalytic Therapy: Principles and Application*, Nebraska: University of Nebraska Press, first published in New York: Ronald Press.

Bollas, C. (2013) *Catch Them Before They Fall*, London and New York: Routledge.

Boynton, R. (2002) 'The Return of the Repressed', in *Boston Review*, December.

——— (2003) 'The Return of the Repressed: Psychoanalysis's Fallen Angel', in *Boston Review*, January.

Cooper, J. (1993) *Speak of Me as I Am: The Life and Work of Masud Khan*, London: Karnac.

Fairbairn, R. (1952) *Psychoanalytic Studies of the Personality*, London: Routledge and Kegan Paul.

Freud, S. (1895) *Project for a Scientific Psychology*, S.E.1: 281–397.

——— (1909) *Family Romances*, S.E.9: 237–241.

——— (1920) *Beyond the Pleasure Principle*, S.E.18: 1–65.

Godley, W. (2001) 'Saving Masud Khan', in *The London Review of Books*, February, 23: 3–7.

Goldman, D. (1993) *In Search of the Real: The Origins and Originality of D.W. Winnicott*, Northvale, NJ: Jason Aronson.

Hopkins, L. (2006) *False Self: The Life of Masud Khan*, New York: Other Press.

Khan, M. (1960) 'Clinical Aspects of the Schizoid Personality', in 1986: 13–26.

——— (1963) 'The Concept of Cumulative Trauma', in 1986: 42–58.

——— (1964) 'Ego-distortion, Cumulative Trauma and the Role of Reconstruction in the Analytic Situation', in 1986: 59–68.

——— (1975) 'Introduction', in Winnicott, 1992: xi–1.

——— (1986) *The Privacy of the Self*, London: Hogarth. First published 1974, London: Hogarth.

——— (1988) When *Spring Comes: Awakenings in Clinical Psychoanalysis,* London: Chatto and Windus. Also published 1989 as *The Long Wait*, New York: Summit Press.

——— (1989a) *Alienation in Perversions*, London: Karnac. First published 1979, London: Hogarth.

——— (1989b) *Hidden Selves*, London: Karnac. First published 1983, London: Hogarth.
Laplanche, J. and Pontalis, J-B. (1985) *The Language of Psychoanalysis*, London: Hogarth.
Sandler, A.M. and Godley, W. (2004) 'Institutional responses to boundary violations: the case of Masud Khan', in *The International Journal of Psychoanalysis* 85: 27–43.
Willoughby, R. (2005) *Masud Khan: The Myth and the Reality*, London: Free Association Books.
Winnicott, D. (1947) 'Hate in the Countertransference', in Winnicott, 1992: 194–203.
——— (1982) *The Maturational Processes and the Facilitating Environment*, London: Hogarth.
——— (1992) *Through Paediatrics to Psycho-Analysis*, London: Karnac. First published 1958, London: Hogarth.

Chapter 7

Further Independent developments

Although Winnicott is more popular than Klein has ever been, the Independent group is less prominent than their Kleinian counterparts. In this chapter we shall explore concepts from the work of two influential members of this group: André Green, who develops some of Winnicott's central concepts as the core of borderline processes, and Thomas Ogden, who proposes the concepts of the 'Autistic-Contiguous position' and the 'Analytic Third'. Both these theorists exhibit the cross-fertilisation that was beginning in Object Relations during the second half of the twentieth century. While being set within the Independent viewpoint, Green's work on the 'borderline' concept rests on the Kleinian introduction of the term, while Ogden puts forward his Autistic-Contiguous position as a precursor of Klein's paranoid-schizoid position.

André Green (1927–2012)

André Green was born in Cairo, the fourth child of a French Jewish family. He lived much of his life in Paris, where the family began to visit during his childhood to seek medical treatment for his seriously ill sister. Green's father died when he was fourteen and his mother when he was twenty-two.

Green married Litza Guttieres-Green, a training analyst of the Parisian and Swiss psychoanalytic societies, and took pleasure in their large extended family. He held prominent positions internationally: he was president of the Paris Psychoanalytic Society, 1986–1989, vice president of the International Psychoanalytical Association, 1975–1977, and professor at University College London, 1979–1980. He died in Paris early in 2012.

Green was fluent in English, and much of his work, first written in French, soon became available in English. He describes his writing as 'a fairly representative sample, a derivative, of the French psychoanalytic movement of the second half of the twentieth century. And this is what I would like to impart to the Anglo-Saxon reader on the threshold of this translation' (1986: 3). He hoped his writings would act as a bridge between French and British psychoanalytic traditions.

Green studied medicine and psychiatry in Paris before training in psychoanalysis. It is a mark of his independence that he did not follow a Lacanian path, as did many of his contemporaries. He studied Lacan's work closely, attending many of his seminars and conferences, but decided that the Object Relations viewpoint matched his experience of his patients more closely (personal remark, *Confer* supervision masterclass, February 2003). His decision arose from a lecture on Object Relations given by the French psychoanalyst Maurice Bouvet, whom Green then chose as his training analyst. Green, like Bouvet, took issue theoretically with the Lacanian view that psychoanalysis should attend to the patient's language, understood in the widest sense, arguing that the unconscious is structured not by language but by object relations (1986: 6). Nevertheless, he valued the characteristically French intellectual rigour, with psychoanalysis being linked to literature and philosophy rather than pragmatism and science. He positioned himself as an Object Relations psychoanalyst with special connections to the French tradition.

Green maintained that Bion and Winnicott influenced his thinking most deeply (ibid.). In Bion, he found 'an author who could measure up to Lacan' (1986: 11) and in Winnicott, despite his shortcomings, 'a richly alive experiencing rather than an erudite schematizing' (ibid. 286), whose theory always stayed in touch with practice. Nevertheless, this double loyalty put him in an unusual position with regard to the death instinct, in particular. He adhered to it 'completely', he maintains (ibid. 118), yet what he adhered to is hardly what anyone else might understand as the death instinct, or death or destructive drive. It is what he calls the 'disobjectualizing function', a move towards emptiness and nothingness (Kohon 1999).

Green's style is abstract, following the French tradition of making use of complex interlinking concepts in the place of illustrative vignettes. He gives several reasons for avoiding clinical examples: many of his patients read his work; case material can be presented in such a way as to fit any theoretical point under discussion; and the most valuable illustrations are those evoked in the mind of the reader (Green 1986: 4–5).

Green's work is comprehensive and wide-ranging and we can only begin to explore a facet of it in this chapter. We shall look at two of his best known papers as exemplars of his contribution to Independent theory.

Green's concept of the borderline

'The Borderline Concept' was first published in 1977 (Green 1986: ch. 3). Green opens his paper with a quotation from the 1950s: 'Just as the hysteric was the typical patient of Freud's time, so the 'borderline' is the problem patient of our time' (ibid. 60). Nevertheless, the terms 'borderline' state or borderline patient are used frequently but in different ways; patients may settle, psychically, in either of these ways of being. First, there is the border area between the psychotic and neurotic, where the person is neither mad nor sane, yet both; and second, there is the position between the paranoid-schizoid and the depressive positions. Here, the individual develops far enough to begin to move from the paranoid-schizoid to the depressive mode, but cannot tolerate the loss, guilt and remorse that go with it and reverts back to a paranoid-schizoid state. A healthy ambivalent attitude is only attainable in the non-pathological part of the ego.

Green reviews contributions to the borderline concept from the work of Freud, Klein, Bion and others, after which he focuses on developing some of Winnicott's main ideas. This may strike us as odd, since Winnicott barely mentions borderline issues as such. Nevertheless, his work on the 'False Self', transitional phenomena, potential space and the like, implicitly addresses relevant issues: 'it is Winnicott', Green maintains, '... who is specifically, in my opinion, *the analyst of the borderline*' (ibid. 68; italics in the original). He points out that while Winnicott's work on 'the area of the intermediate' is frequently discussed, far less attention has been given to the negative of these, such as 'non-communication', 'void', and 'emptiness' (ibid.). It is these states which are characteristic of the borderline, and Green brings together different aspects of Winnicott's main themes under a concept which is usually seen as Kleinian.

Green believes that the counter-transference is the therapist's primary tool for looking into the 'negative side of relationships', that aspect of the borderline patient where 'a sense of lack and a feeling of nothingness predominate' (ibid.). The borderline patient cannot trust himself or others: neither internal nor external reality is secure enough to be relied on. Since there is no positive way of talking about what is not there, or what by definition cannot be talked or thought about, the therapist's counter-transference is the only way of tuning into the 'missing links, which are not hidden but experienced as gaps, the only things that are real for the borderline patient' (ibid.)

In describing clinical work with these patients, Green turns to Freud's concept of primary-process thinking: in the unconscious, logic, time and contradiction do not exist. As Green puts it, 'in borderline thinking we have the result of a destructive perversion of primary-process thinking, rather than a genuine expression of what primary process is supposed to be in infancy' (ibid. 69). Borderline processes are not regressions to what has gone before, but a pathological detour leading away from healthy psychic development.

Green describes the 'border-line' as a '*moving and fluctuating* frontier' between two parts of the mind (ibid. 73), with continual communication between them in a healthy psychic life. Maintaining this connection is, for Green, 'the work of symbolization, which requires the splitting of two elements and their conjunction in order to make a third element, which is composed of the two split-off elements, each of them remaining the same and yet becoming in reunion a different one' (ibid.). Unless the symbolic object and what is left of the real object are experienced as simultaneously the same and distinct, they will not have the relation of object and symbol: they will be experienced instead as duplicate psychic objects. This primitive precursor of the symbol is what Segal (1957, in Segal 1986) terms the 'symbolic equation'.

Green goes on to define the borderline as a 'no-man's-land, an entire field whose borders are vague' (Green 1986: 74). This recalls Winnicott's fascination with uncertainty, paradox and fluidity in psychic processes. Winnicott develops the idea of a 'third area' of psychic functioning which is intermediate, between the subjective and the objective. Green goes on to explain what happens when this area does not develop or does not do so properly. We then have a space which, instead of holding transitional phenomena, is experienced as an unbridgeable gap, a form of splitting which does not pre-empt the creation of a whole object and hampers the development of thinking, logic and the linking of inside and outside, the real and the imagined, me and you. The primitive defence of splitting does not develop into the more mature defence of repression, because links between symbol (imagined object/thought) and perceived object are not maintained.

We can normally give the answer 'yes' or 'no' when asked whether an object is internal, or whether it is external. In Winnicott's transitional sense or 'third position', however, the answer is an imaginative 'either yes or no', or an inclusive 'both yes and no'. There is no 'right' answer to the question as to whether the child's transitional object is internal or external: the answer lies where subjectivity and objectivity overlap. The same applies to a child's imaginative game, or an adult's favourite piece of music or literature. In the borderline mode, however, this inclusive ambiguity is not available: there is only an inability or refusal to choose. In this way we get '*neither "Yes" nor "No"*' (ibid. 82) instead of its creative alternatives; this brings psychic development to a halt.

Green is thus treating the borderline state as the negative of Winnicott's transitional state, characterising it as a perversion of an earlier state rather than a return to it. In borderline functioning, the ego itself is split, resulting in 'islands' of ego functioning not connected by meaning, time or space. Instead of areas of openness between these islands which could act as a connecting transitional area, the islands are divided by borderline 'gaps' between which there can be no mode of communication: the connections between them have been cut through. These gaps are more important than the islands, or partial areas of functioning, since it is they that hold the sense of blankness and nothingness which defines the borderline state. Their psychic mode is represented in consciousness in the same way as in unconscious functioning, without logic, time, negation or differentiation between thinking and feeling. Typically, the borderline mode of thinking is discerned as feeling, since it makes no sense and does so in a very intense way. It is as though the borderline aspect of the individual lives solely through disconnected affects such as senseless fear and rage, leading to ever more confusion.

In the normal mode of dreaming the links with meaning are retained in the unconscious dream thoughts, enabling the latent content of the dream to be reached through the manifest content. But borderline dreaming leads nowhere: there is no meaning to be reached, since the connections between unconscious and conscious have been split, abandoned or cut off. This both leads to, and comes from, the problem that 'borderline patients' dreams do not express wish-fulfilment but rather serve a 'function of evacuation' (ibid. 80). In this way they are more like actions than dreams, a way of getting rid of what is not wanted in the psyche. Just as borderline gaps constitute failed thoughts, borderline dreams are failed dreams.

Similarly, in the normal oedipal process the child reaches ambivalent relationships with each parent: both are good and both are bad, with plenty in between. In the borderline state, however, this depressive functioning cannot exist, and typically one parent is idealised while the other is demonised by the psychic splitting. The starting point for mature relationships is the realistic ambivalent mode, neither impossibly bad nor unrealistically good, so this lack of ambivalence plays havoc with relationships of all kinds.

Thus thinking and feeling, relating and understanding, are all compromised in the borderline mode, a development which must follow from inadequate containment in the early months. The ground of the ego does not develop fully, or as fully as is usual, or in a normal way. There is almost no mode of functioning that is not affected; the individual endures the misery of blank meaninglessness in himself and in the world.

This is a brief summary of one aspect only of Green's paper. It says more than we have been able to survey here. Essentially, however, Green explicitly brings out his admiration of Winnicott, and his view of the borderline mode as the transitional state gone wrong – and of course a greater understanding of the borderline mode itself.

The dead mother

Mother below is weeping
weeping
weeping
Thus I knew her

Once, stretched out on her lap
as now on dead tree
I learned to make her smile
to stem her tears
to undo her guilt
to cure her inward death
To enliven her was my living.

(Winnicott 1966, in Phillips 2007: 29)

'The Dead Mother' is Green's best-known paper. We can place his concept of the 'dead mother complex' in the context of different kinds of separation from the mother-figure. In the poem above, which Winnicott wrote as an ageing man, he, like Green, explores the effects on the child of the psychical as opposed to the physical death of the mother. Winnicott's mother, though 'inwardly dead', is weeping: she is open to her grief, and can therefore receive comfort, not least from her child. He, meanwhile, feels compelled to dedicate himself to the endless task of 'enlivening' her, bringing her out of despair to life and love. Maladaptive as this is, it is preferable to having no way of restoring his image of her to what it was before. In addition, taking on this role gives him a sense of 'specialness': the main resonance in the poem is with the figure of Christ on the cross.

The 'psychic death' which Green discusses in his paper is different in important respects. The mother appears to her infant as blank, empty, unable to meet him, however conscientiously she may care for him in practical terms. The infant experiences her unconsciously as 'dead' and finds himself totally unable to 'enliven' her. After a period of intense anxiety he enters into what may be a lifelong process of quasi-mourning for a mother who is physically present but emotionally absent.

In *Playing and Reality* (1986: 114–5) Winnicott writes of the effects of the temporary but real loss of the mother. If she is missing for 'x' minutes he can cope with it, and greets her cheerfully on her return: the inner figure of the mother is not seriously threatened by a gap of this length. If her absence extends to 'x + y' minutes this is difficult for him. He is distressed on her return, but recovers under her reliable and loving care – the child's inner figure of her has wobbled but remained intact. But if she is gone for 'x + y + z' minutes he cannot recover: he is traumatised. The inner figure has now fallen into pieces, and the baby feels that he has too. The mother's absence has become more 'real' than her presence, or at least more to be relied on, so that unless the child comes to terms with the loss he cannot find what was there before. Devastating as it is, this picture at least makes sense to the child: his mother was there, and then she was gone, and that becomes her most important attribute. He may enter into a depressed state, either heavy and guilt-filled, where he is continually caught up with an attacking inner object, or flat and empty, identified with a lost inner object. In either case, however, internal reality and external reality match up: the mother is gone.

The kind of mourning that Green describes as the 'dead mother complex' has echoes of this flat and empty depression, but is more complicated: '*the essential characteristic of this depression is that it takes place in the presence of the object, which is itself absorbed by a bereavement*' (Green 1986: 149; italics in original.). As in Winnicott's poem, this infant has lost his object. She is still present, however, preoccupied with a loss she herself has suffered, and this leaves him unable to make any sense of his own loss. At a point where there is not yet a distinct sense of self and other, what was most intensely alive for him goes missing. This includes not only an embryonic sense of his object, but also of his own relational capacities. The consequent emptiness continues into all his future relationships. It is as though the infant has become possessed of or by the ghost of someone both living and lost. This is why the 'dead mother complex' is difficult to grasp.

Once he had become aware of this state of mind, Green found it sufficiently common to realise its importance in what his patients brought to their analysis. Nothing had been written specifically about it, presumably because of its near-invisibility. While actual bereavement, if unresolved, leads to depression, the mother's 'psychic death' leads to the more insidious narcissistic symptomology – the defensive withdrawal from what has proved to be a dangerous dependence into a pathological preoccupation with the self. The catastrophe happened before the infant was able to separate out his mother from himself, or love from hate: he is left to identify with a bereaved and therefore absent object who is also mystifyingly present. There is confusion between what is there and what is not there, between different kinds of impulses, and between self and other. Because the infant cannot identify the origin of the hole, or gap, his pathology can only show itself in the transference: 'when the analysis is underway, the transference will reveal, sometimes quite rapidly but more often after long years of analysis, a singular depression' (ibid. 148).

But what kind of depression? Green emphasises that all the patients in whom he became aware of this condition presented with narcissistic rather than depressive symptoms; the transference depression is thus unforeseen. Green differentiates between two kinds of depression, identifying them by the two traditional colours of mourning. There is 'black' depression which is motivated by the hatred directed at the abandoning object, and the 'blank' or 'white' ('*blanc*') depressive state of mind which presents as flatness and emptiness: this stems from a narcissistic loss, which is felt as a gap in the self rather than the loss of an object (ibid. 146, footnote 1). In the 'dead mother complex', while signs of a 'black' depression may hover at the edges, the main experience the therapist receives from the patient is rather a picture of negation – 'a "blank" anxiety which expresses a loss which has been experienced at a narcissistic level' (ibid. 146). The infant has lost what feels like a part or an aspect of himself. The patient he goes on to become then relates to the therapist as though the therapist were the mother who is no longer there – or who might as well not be there, since she is herself absorbed by loss. The real object of bereavement goes back from the infant to the mother and beyond into the realms of the unknowable. No wonder he is confused by his anxiety, since it is literally 'nothing' which is making him afraid; and this nothing extends to himself.

The 'dead mother complex' is initiated early in infancy, before the mother has become registered as a being who is clearly separate from the infant, yet not so early that he has never experienced a responsive, live mother who is to some extent 'other'. In an attempt to put matters right, the infant reverts to an earlier state of affairs. But instead of the usual primary narcissism where love and the tendency to unity predominate under the aegis of the Eros drives, the reverse happens: Green's version of the Death Drive appears to differ from Freud's in that it is not concerned with death, and is not a drive. It is more like a 'negative hallucination', where the object becomes emptiness and attachment, decathexis. He is no longer able to relate fully to others: the only possible explanation for his confusing bereavement is that his own relational capacities have destroyed not only his mother, but also the 'him' that she was part of. His emotional aliveness is itself so destructive, he feels, that all he can do is try to destroy it. Of course, no pathological state is total, and the infant continues to develop around this state of negation; but it is always there, a 'cold core' of meaninglessness and lack of feeling at the centre of himself and his relationships.

The infant is left in the grip of an all-consuming passivity, with elements of love and hate, neither of which is fully formed, each blocking the development of the other. For example, we can see that Winnicott's psychic life was influenced by such a mother, but one who had straightforwardly loving aspects which enabled him to empathise with her guilt and to want to repair her – to 'enliven her' with his 'living'.

The child of the absent mother, the mother who suddenly distances herself from her baby, not only faces complications as he reaches Winnicott's stage of concern (the depressive position) but also in his oedipal development. Normally, the relative and temporary turning-away of the mother is explained by whatever comes between himself and his mother's love: typically, the father. This gives rise to the unconscious phantasy of the primal scene, and usually the infant feels himself, indistinctly, to be the product of his parents' love. This mitigates the loss and simultaneously enables the psyche to take its mature form, able to attach to more than one figure, and eventually to accept that there are relationships and situations in which he has no place. This 'triangulation' means he can gain different perspectives on aspects of his world, and come to realise that other people have their own, different, subjectivities. The capacity for symbol formation and with it, meaning, flourishes.

In this case, however, instead of the erotic union with mother being lost to a hateful, frightening interloper, there are a number of different consequences that can occur when the infant is ready to recognise rivals for his mother's love, to whatever extent he has it. Residual traces of the lost mother, and with it his own capacity for passion, make their way up from the depths of his being. They may reconfigure as the phantasy of the primal scene, but this bestows not the sense of being created out of the love between his two objects but a threatened destruction of the whole complex, which is now incompatible with the emerging traces of a live mother.

> The fantasy of the primal scene will not only recathect these vestiges, but will confer to them, through a new cathexis, new effects which constitute a real *conflagration*, that sets fire to the structure which gives the complex of the dead mother retrospective significance.
>
> (Ibid. 159)

The child attempts to soften the destruction of his psychic organisation by fiercely projecting onto the actual mother, or other significant object, the available elements of having lost both his mother and himself. The gap between himself and his mother is heightened and he feels anew his utter impotence. The stage is set for a violent and sadistic interpretation of the parents' relationship, and sexuality in particular. There are various alternatives to this outcome, the main one being wholesale repression, which increases the negation through which the infant lives.

Green continues on to how one might approach the analysis of a patient in this situation. It is clear that eventually, what has happened to the patient as an infant will be relived in the transference, if the therapist is able to refrain from interfering in the unfolding of the puzzling precursors. He describes how long it takes in psychotherapy to go through the extent of the negation again and again, until the patient's violent or apathetic oedipal dynamics draw into view and eventually his hidden hate and possessiveness appear. Eventually, it becomes possible for the patient to sense the original good relation to the mother; but it is likely to be tinged with the looming catastrophe. Instead of a happy resolution, there is the feeling of 'a *false breast* (or mother), carried within a *false self*, nourishing a *false baby*' (ibid. 160). The patient may then undergo what turns out to be a false mourning, before the reality of the original situation can be faced. The patient is likely to become very attached not to the analyst but to the analysis: if he treats the analyst as the absent mother, he treats the analysis as that which maintains the familiar status quo, and behind this, that which holds the promise of a reunion with the live mother. Either way, he is unable to give it up. We can see that treating a patient with the 'dead mother complex' may well encompass the whole range of emotionality from endless blankness to impotent rage, from a feeling of artificiality to real passion both for the lost and the regained mother.

It is clear that the Freudian approach in which the analyst remains predominantly silent, in order to leave space for the projections of the patient, is likely to merely prolong the blank, empty relationship which is at the root of the problem. More useful is the Kleinian approach of focusing on the immediate anxieties and the inner drives of love and hate that they represent. Yet unless the work leaves more than adequate space for the environmental as well as the constitutional factors, this will not reach to the foundations of the pathology, which lie more with the mother than the child, and the absence of a presence rather than the presence of an absence. Not surprisingly, Green prefers a Winnicottian approach, in which the analytic setting takes the role of a transitional space, with the therapist remaining neutral yet alive. She can show this through her interest in the patient and the ideas sparked off by him. Yet she has to be ready for the repeated and essential disillusionment, which must be gone through in all analyses, and this kind in particular. One can imagine how difficult this would be with a patient who evinces a flat and empty determination to hang on like grim death to a therapy which seems useless. 'It is essential', Green states, 'that the latter [the analyst] remains constantly awake to what the patient is saying, without falling into intrusive interpretation' (ibid. 163). Eventually, the common loss of mother and child may be relived as the transference is finally relinquished: 'The blank mourning for the dead mother will be the common body of their deceased loves' (ibid.). With that, a real relation may be garnered from the scraps of unconscious memory of the mother loving a responsive child.

It is apparent that this paper was enormously influential, clarifying clinical situations which were simply baffling before. Part of the difficulty is that such complex problems take a long time to work through, so the therapist has to keep faith with the analytic situation, without much indication that she is on the right track. It must have been a great relief to many to come across this paper. We can also see the parallels with his paper 'The Borderline Concept', exploring a kind of pathology which may at times overlap with the dead mother complex. The same emphasis on negation, blankness, the 'hole', which is the most real element in the psychic structure, is revisited here. It is the movement towards these elements that makes up Green's idea of the 'death instinct' or 'destructive drive'.

Green's work brings Object Relations to a new level, with extended exposition, detailed argument and deep thought, rather than focusing on clinical description. He has had a considerable influence on Independent and non-Independent practitioners alike, and acts in many ways as a unifying figure, bringing Kleinian exactitude to an Independent flexibility of thought, and a new concept of the destructive drive to both.

Thomas Ogden

Unlike the other psychoanalysts this book is concerned with, Ogden is still working. He practises in San Francisco and has been granted a number of positions and awards for his outstanding work in psychoanalysis and literary criticism. He makes regular contributions to subjects such as reverie, containment, supervision and technique. His writing conveys his openness to unconscious communication.

It is unusual for an American psychoanalyst to position himself in the Object Relations tradition. Ego psychology dominated psychoanalysis in America for much of the twentieth century, with the ideas of Kohut (1984) and Kernberg (1975), more closely related to Object Relations, emerging later. Ogden's work is influenced by all the main Object Relations pioneers, but especially Klein, Winnicott and Bion. He values Klein's concepts of the paranoid-schizoid and depressive positions, and indeed the theoretical idea of a position as a 'dimension of experience' rather than a stage to be worked through (Ogden 1992: 11, fn. 2). By differentiating himself from the Kleinian group, however, he implicitly disagrees with her views of the death drive and the technique of 'here-and-now' transference interpretation (ibid. 10, fn.1).

Ogden's fluid writing is far more reminiscent of Winnicott than of Klein, and indeed he prizes Winnicott's style of writing as a way of evoking the experience described rather than articulating specific ideas. He draws our attention to the way in which Freud discovers what he means as he writes 'Mourning and Melancholia' in the same way that we are invited to share the experience of a poet such as Robert Frost as we read his poems (Ogden 1997). The effect of Ogden's own writing depends as much on texture and rhythm as on the clinical precision of its meaning.

Ogden explicitly compares Winnicott's well-known quote that '"there is no such thing as a baby" [without the maternal provision]' (Winnicott 1960: 39 in Ogden 1994a: 63) with the analytic situation – that 'there is no such thing as an analysand apart from the relationship with the analyst, and no such thing as an analyst apart from the relationship with the analysand' (ibid.). He considers that

> the analytic task most fundamentally involves the effort of the analytic pair to help the analysand become human in a fuller sense than he has been able to achieve to this point ... The effort to become human is among the very few things in a person's life that may over time come to feel more important to him than his personal survival.
>
> (Ogden 1999a: 15)

He does not define in any tight sense what he means by 'being human', since he relies on the writer's and the readers' ability to communicate and understand these ideas intuitively. 'Words and sentences, like people', he comments, 'must be allowed a certain slippage' (ibid. 3). As in writing, so in life meaning is always in flux and in motion, depending as much on its context as on its history and established definition. If it is good writing, different shades and inflections will come over to each individual reader, while remaining comprehensible in a meaningfully similar way to all.

In the coming section we shall examine one concept which forms a building block in Ogden's theoretical outlook, the concept of the autistic-contiguous position; in the next, one which is central to his clinical work, the analytic third.

The autistic-contiguous position

This paper (1992: 47–81) makes use of the Kleinian concept of position; Ogden maintains that his 'autistic-contiguous position' is more primitive than Klein's paranoid-schizoid position, and lies outside Winnicott's concept of earliest infancy – fusion with a mother who adapts as closely as possible to her newborn infant's needs and expectations. Nevertheless, he frequently uses Winnicott's terms to describe what the autistic-contiguous position is *not* – there is no sense of 'potential space' and nowhere for a 'transitional object' to be found, although presumably the initial layers of 'going-on-being' are being laid down at the most primitive level. Ogden draws from authors such as Meltzer, Tustin and Bick, all of whom used Kleinian perspectives in working with autistic patients and thinking about autistic states. Although they are related, Ogden differentiates clearly between the pathological state of autism and the normal autistic-contiguous position. The autistic-contiguous mode tends to predominate over the others at the very start of psychic development, as Klein's two later positions do in their turn. All three positions remain configurations structuring the way the individual perceives and understands his experience: they are not stages which can be grown out of.

As in pathological autism, the infant in the autistic-contiguous position does not perceive another person as a person, but in terms of their effector imprint on the infant's body and therefore on his mind. It is for this reason that the term includes the adjective 'autistic', while 'contiguous' brings in the sense of the touching of two surfaces. Thus the infant orients himself through sensations – raw sensory messages that do not as yet have an associated complex of meanings. They are registered in the form of 'bounded surfaces' – finite planes – on which the ego gradually comes to cohere, carrying attributes which will later come to be recognised as self and other, inside and outside. The infant is never without some surface on which his sense of self can evolve: even in the womb there is the amniotic fluid, the pulsing placenta, the umbilical cord and an enveloping wrap-around of sound. After birth, the phenomena he meets up with are more tangible, clearly-bounded surfaces with different qualities – the face which he is hard-wired to respond to with eyes which give him the sense of a meeting-point, the rhythmicity of feeding, the hard edge of the nipple or object he is biting on.

Although the infant does not perceive the 'bounded surface' he is in contact with as separate from himself, it is not entirely identical with himself either: minor shades of difference allow him to begin to develop a sense of himself as a distinct being, with experiences on the edge of becoming emotional as well as physical. The shades of emotion which the baby experiences from being held roughly or sensitively, looked at deeply or coldly, could be seen as constituting part of the autistic-contiguous position or hints of paranoid-schizoid or even depressive functioning that can exist alongside: there must be some admixture of more organised functioning for the infant to be able to progress through the more primitive positions.

Ogden describes how, as adults, we can locate the autistic-contiguous experience by focusing solely on the sensations given by the chair we are sitting on or the bed we are lying on. 'This primitive psychological organization under normal circumstances contributes the barely perceptible background of sensory boundedness of all subsequent subjective states' (Ogden 1992: 50). It is possible to imagine excluding everything we know about the world except these immediate sensations, the forerunners of what will come to be known as objects and which endure beneath all later psychological experience. Rather than recognizing that 'I' am 'sitting' on a 'chair' or 'lying' on a 'couch', we know only the comforting or empty shifting softness in conjunction with another surface. There is an entire world of different emotionally-coloured sensations which Ogden introduces as the autistic-contiguous position.

The notion of the autistic child is a fairly recent one, distinguished from other kinds of mental functioning by Leo Kanner in the 1940s (Kanner 1943). Autism was first explained psychoanalytically as deriving from an extreme lack of containment: a cold and unresponsive 'refrigerator mother' leads to the enclosed state of the autistic child, who turns away from other people and seems not to have a sense of himself or others as persons. Understanding has developed considerably and inadequate mothering is no longer seen as its cause, nor is it seen purely as an impairment. Although the aetiology of autism remains unclear, it is mostly regarded in constitutional terms today, which is not to say that there is no experiential 'story' taking place at a psychological level. The work of Frances

Tustin with very young autistic children (2013/1981) is particularly interesting in this respect.

Ogden explains that the difference between an autistic person's functioning and the autistic-contiguous position corresponds to that between paranoid schizophrenia and the paranoid-schizoid position or clinical depression and the depressive position. Patterns of functioning that occur early in neurotypical development become lifelines for autistic individuals, with the difference lying in use and degree. Where anxiety is particularly intense and enduring, some elements of the autistic-contiguous position are clung to so fiercely by the child who is becoming autistic that development is blocked or even reversed. Normal infants, in Ogden's view, experience the shape sensation provided by emotionally-tinged contact with his body without becoming dependent on it. A mildly insecure child may use the sense of hardness derived from clutching a solid object as a kind of armour, protecting him from chaos; as he gains in security, he has less need of this defence. The autistic child, whose anxiety is more intense or even overwhelming, may become fixated on the continuous 'hard' shape sensation given to his hand by holding a specific hard object such as a metal car or spoon. The child feels reassured that he exists in as concrete a way as the object and, like it, cannot be seen through or walked through (Ogden 1992: 129). The shape sensations that are impressed on the infant's body surface are termed 'autistic shapes', while the external objects that the autistic person uses in the same way are known as 'autistic objects'.

A primitive sense of self, of being a distinct entity, can also be drawn from other sensations: head-banging brings power and rhythmicity, while twirling a piece of string, or twiddling a strand of hair, can give the same sense of control and predictability as sensations derived from softer objects. Most objects can give the sense of a boundary, while familiar actions, like spinning around or lining up toy cars, are used systematically by autistic individuals to create a sense of order. Milder versions, such as stroking one's chin or tapping one's foot, can provide reassurance to any of us in an anxious moment.

While there are clear connections between Kleinian concepts such as 'adhesive identification'[1] (Bick 1964) and Ogden's autistic-contiguous position, we can also see its relation to Winnicott's 'going-on-being', or rather the negative of it. The fears defended against are reminiscent of Winnicott's 'primitive agonies' of coming apart, falling for ever or having no orientation (Winnicott 1962). Ogden emphasises that we build our most primitive sense of being around basic sensation, together with the emotional tinge it carries. It is only when this is established that the infant can go on to develop the split world of the paranoid-schizoid position, or blissful fusion with Winnicott's 'environmental mother'. These uses of the body and objects are also, therefore, the first step towards symbol formation.

This paper offers help to the psychoanalytic practitioner in two ways. First, it enables understanding of what would otherwise be puzzling symptoms, such as strange intensifications of certain sensations arousing fear and anxiety, or the compulsion to grip hold of an object to bring a sense of safety and comfort.

These are symptoms resulting from fixation when the autistic-contiguous position was dominant. Second, it enables the practitioner to understand the workings of the autistic mind, whether this appears in isolated patches in an otherwise neurotic personality, or in someone whose functioning is more clearly on the autistic spectrum. Both are being encountered in the consulting room more often, making it important for all practitioners to have a sense of the meaning and implications of their symptoms.

Ogden is one of the key figures to bring together Kleinian and Independent ideas, and especially to conceptualise a new psychic position. Theory is generally less to the fore among Independents than Kleinians, and like Green, Ogden manages to link his own clearly Independent approach with Kleinian concepts.

The analytic third

The 'analytic third' (Ogden 1994a, ch. 5) is another of Ogden's most important formulations, developed mainly through the 1990s. As a concept it has much in common with the work of all the main Object Relations theorists – in particular, Winnicott's ideas of the development of the self, its dependence on communication and on conscious and unconscious intersubjectivity. Ogden gives the term 'the analytic third' to what he sees as the purely intersubjective element created from the conjunction of the therapist's and the patient's interactions. He treats the therapeutic process, once established, as having a life of its own, influencing and structuring the sessions in a way comparable to the two other subjects, psychotherapist and patient: 'the sense of aliveness and deadness of a given moment of an analytic hour [or session] is perhaps the most important gauge of the analytic process' (Ogden 1999a: 4).

Therapist and patient will each experience the 'analytic third' differently and, since the patient contributes the major part of the input to the therapeutic process, the components of the analytic third will always derive more from the patient's material than from the therapist's. It is not an easy process to distinguish or decipher, given the different and sometimes subtle roles the therapist and patient hold in relation to it. The patient supplies the majority of the material through his presence – his free associations, styles of talking and behaving, what he projects onto and into the therapist. She, meanwhile, has her own part to supply through her own way of being. The background sense she makes of these and the patient's contribution subtly affect the atmosphere of the session and how the patient perceives it. It is the therapist's task to gather together as much of the patient's and her own background material as she can and by reflecting on it, bring it to a state where it can be given words, in her own thoughts or in communication with the patient.

In this way the analytic third gradually emerges, 'co-created' by both parties. The therapist's 'reverie' enables a conscious sense of it to become available, rather than simply an unconscious or subconscious background. This is a continuous and lengthy process, since it may take a number of sessions for a niggling sense of doubt, or irritation, or forgetfulness to begin to make sense to the therapist, and when it finally does it may differ considerably from her own or the patient's expectations. This is one of the reasons why it is so important for the therapist to be able to tolerate lengthy periods of doubt, inadequacy, feeling lost and having little confidence in her own current thoughts – all are needed for the analytic third to develop and begin to make conscious sense to her, even if barely noticed by the patient.

In his earlier paper on this subject (1994b), Ogden gives two lengthy descriptions of the ways in which components of the 'analytic third' can be picked up, gradually connected and finally used. In each case he describes an analysis that has arrived at an atmosphere which is deadening, boring, without specificity or vivacity. In the first example he 'focuses on the importance of the most mundane, everyday aspects of the workings of the mind (which appear to be entirely unrelated to the patient) in the service of recognizing and addressing the transference–counter-transference' (ibid. 4–5), and through this, the 'analytic third'. He elucidates the 'analytic third' of the second case mainly through bodily sensations and somatic fantasies, in each case picking out what could easily go unnoticed, fail to be connected or made sense of.

The first instance occurs in an analysis of about three years' duration with 'Mr. L' (ibid. 5). Ogden describes remembering fleeting images, perceptions, emotions and thoughts from the edge of the counter-transference; at first sight, he says, they seemed to bear little connection with the patient or what he had just said, and he did not immediately see how these odds and ends might help the analysis along. Reflecting on the first session he writes of, he remembered noticing an envelope by his chair which he had been using over the past few weeks to jot down thoughts or telephone messages. For the first time, apparently, he saw that it had marks on it which suggested it had been sent to him as part of a 'bulk mailing'. This brought a sense of disappointment: he had assumed that the letter inside the envelope had been written to him alone, since the subject matter was delicate and personal. He dragged himself back to the session to try to connect this with what the patient had been saying, without much success. It felt like the familiar ground of impersonality and disappointment which they had already been over several times. Associations to letters and other relevant elements led him to remember a childhood book he had read several times during a period of intense loneliness. Again, however, he could make little sense of his association apart from the superficial and obvious interpretations which had already been covered – that the therapy itself felt impersonal and mechanical, and that both he and the patient felt lonely in it. There seemed little point in interpreting along these lines yet again so he kept quiet and kept listening and thinking.

Shortly afterwards Ogden remembered how often the patient dreamed of paralysed, mute and otherwise powerless people, and realised, similarly, that he was picking up the patient's feelings of being overlooked and powerless through a continual process of projective identification. In a recent dream, however, the atmosphere had changed to one of hope and joy as the patient found a stone with carvings on it; however, these turned out to be hieroglyphics which the patient could make no sense of, leaving him tantalised and in the same familiar sense of 'deep despair' (ibid. 6).

At this point Ogden recalled that he would have to finish this last session of the day very promptly to get to the garage where his car was waiting to be collected before the garage shut. In his mind's eye he imagined getting there too late and being confronted with the impersonality of the garage's closed doors, the gritty pavement and the roar of traffic as he stood outside it, with a profound sense of rage and impotence. This seemed like more of the same, except that it offered the clue of the rage which must underlie the flatness of the interaction. Later in the session, he remembered that someone had phoned earlier in the session, leaving a message for him. He did not know who it was, but found himself looking forward to listening to a focused, vivid voice on the answering machine rather than the droning on of the patient's voice in the session. He then returned to the envelope, by chance it seems, and noticed that it had in fact been personally typed on a typewriter, with an idiosyncratically misshapen letter 't', and that the colours of the stamps were bright and clear. This immediately changed his sense of the envelope into something far more personal. Ogden was able to offer an interpretation along the lines of his thoughts, and the atmosphere of the session became alive and connected. A long, relaxed silence followed – a rare occurrence with this patient – and the next session began with Mr L recounting a dream which seemed more hopeful and trusting than his usual dreams. A step had been made through that particular block in the therapy.

The portion of the session Ogden describes could have been taken from the work of any conscientious psychotherapist with a blocked patient. However, it would have been easy for the therapist to miss what does not seem to be connected with the patient in any way, at least at the outset – the appearance of the envelope, or remembering he had to hurry to the garage at the end of his working day. How many of us would bother to include details of this kind in discussing a session in supervision? By following these small points he finds he is able to connect them, at least partially, with the patient's communications, to form the fragmentary but decipherable voice of the 'analytic third'.

Ogden reveals how certain psychic objects become 'analytic objects' or 'analytic events' by being recognised as 'carrier[s] of psychological meaning' (ibid. 9) and coming alive as such. The envelope, for example, had been by his chair for weeks, but it was only in this session that it shifted from being the carrier of 'impersonal' to 'personal' features; was only now that he remembered about his car, with the garage carrying impressions of flatness and impotence, underpinned by rage and despair. What facilitated these changes was not, Ogden suggests, the lifting of his repression or the lowering of a defence, but linking together his own with the patient's supposed subjective experiences in a way which lit up the communications of the 'analytic third'. From that point, neither the envelope nor the patient's dreams could exist in the same way as they had before.

We can see projective identification going both ways in this section of the work. Ogden received the emotions that the patient no doubt wanted to be rid of: the flat, powerless, boring sense which he brought in with him at the beginning of the session. Conversely, through reflecting on what was being conveyed to him, Ogden was able to find a new sense of life and energy underlying these communications, regained as Ogden allowed the therapeutic process to continue unhindered and unblocked. This aspect of the projective identification must then have been returned to the patient.

What then is the 'analytic third'? It has been difficult to define, and particularly to get a sense of as something coherent, since it is made up of continually shifting combinations of the therapist's and patient's subjectivities. It resonates with his intersubjective emphasis on dream, reverie and of course projective identification, all conscious and unconscious processes which involve people in communication with each other. In another paper (Ogden 1999b), he defines the analytic third not merely as a merging or overlapping of subjectivities, but as both supporting and pulling against each other to prevent each other from collapsing into one, while being always 'on the move'. We can see in the example above, how the balance of vividness and deadness continually shifted until Ogden was able to glimpse the backdrop of rage behind it – a lively and definite feeling – and then the work took a step forward with both Ogden and his patient feeling more of a sense of trust and authenticity.

A final consideration: what conditions are necessary for the analytic third to be activated? Ogden makes clear that it is always latent in the analytic situation, and I think this can be extended beyond psychoanalysis as such to psychotherapy with sessions of any frequency. If the psychotherapist gives the kind of attention to her work that we have seen Ogden do, the therapy can seem to take off on its own, leading both parties down sometimes unexpected routes. We can see in this an example of Freud's contention that the ego naturally moves towards further integration, unless it is blocked: this appears to apply to two or more egos in the therapeutic situation.

Ogden's descriptions and explanations demonstrate his ability to listen to his patient's communications as he would a poem or piece of literature. He shows a delicate sensitivity to tone and rhythm, juxtaposition and inflection, without which he would not have been able to discern the primitive, pre-verbal mode of experience which he conceptualises as the autistic-contiguous position; nor would he have been able to find the right words to express its significance, connecting normal early experience to later forms of pathology, as Klein did with the paranoid-schizoid and depressive positions. Similarly, in his paper on the 'Analytic Third', Ogden himself describes the painstaking way in which he came to understand the material of a patient whose analysis had become blocked, and who he was finding it difficult to attend to. His new concept potentially enables practitioners of all psychoanalytic approaches to bring an added dimension to their clinical work, through a term which could become as familiar as Winnicott's 'transitional object' or Klein's 'projective identification'. Ogden brings together the emotional and the logical, the clinical and the theoretical, combining the perspectives of the main Object Relations theorists in a way which particularly illustrates the imaginative potential of Independent thinking.

Conclusion

We have looked at the work of Khan, Green and Ogden as exponents of Independent psychoanalysis. Their work and thinking are more diverse than those of the Kleinians, reflecting the Independent championing of individuality and plurality. On the whole, Independent practitioners follow Winnicott's lead in eschewing the death drive, though Green places negativity, blankness and emptiness at the heart of pathology, still seeing it as a death drive, though not primary. Independents also give a greater role to the effects of the environment than Kleinians; this is also illustrated in Green's 'dead mother complex'. Ogden acts as a significant mediator between Kleinian and Independent approaches, while Khan spreads his wings wide with innovations in both theory and practice. All three of our contributors illustrate the depth and range of the Independent imagination.

Note

1 Identification not through introjection but through 'sticking' to the object, usually when introjection fails, or there is insufficient internal space.

References

Bick, E. (1964) 'Notes on Infant Observation in Psycho-Analytic Training', in *International Journal of Psycho-Analysis* 45: 558–566.

Green, A. (1986) *On Private Madness*, London: Hogarth Press; (1997 and 2005) London: Karnac.

Kanner, L. (1943) 'Autistic Disturbances of Affective Contact', in *Nervous Child* 2: 217–250.

Kernberg, O. (1975) *Borderline Conditions and Pathological Narcissism*, New York: Aronson.

Kohon, G., ed. (1999) *The Dead Mother: The Work of André Green*, London, New York and Canada: Routledge.

Kohut, O. (1984) *How Does Analysis Cure?* Chicago: University of Chicago Press.

Ogden, T. (1992), *The Primitive Edge of Experience*, London: Karnac. First published (1989), New Jersey: Jason Aronson.

——— (1994a) *Subjects of Analysis*, London: Karnac, by arrangement with Jason Aronson.

——— (1994b) 'The Analytic Third: Working with Intersubjective Clinical Facts', in *International Journal of Psychoanalysis* 75: 3–19.

——— (1997) 'Listening: Three Frost Poems', in *Psychoanalytic Dialogues* 7, no. 5.

——— (1999a) *Reverie and Interpretation: Sensing Something Human*, London: Karnac, by arrangement with Jason Aronson.

——— (1999b) 'The Analytic Third: An Overview', in S.A. Mitchell and L. Aron, eds., *Relational Psychoanalysis: The Emergence of a Tradition*, New York: Routledge.

Phillips, A. (2007) *Winnicott*, London, Penguin Books.

Segal, H. (1957) 'Notes on Symbol Formation', in Segal 1986: 49–65.

——— (1986) *The Work of Hanna Segal*, London: Free Association Books.

Tustin, F. (2013) *Autistic States in Children*, London and New York: Routledge. First published 1981.

Winnicott, D. (1960) 'The Theory of the Parent–Infant Relationship' in *The Maturational Processes and the Facilitating Environment*, London: Hogarth, 1982: 37–55.

——— (1962) 'Ego Integration in Child Development', in *The Maturational Processes and the Facilitating Environment*, London: Hogarth, 1982: 56–63.

——— (1986) *Playing and Reality*, London: Tavistock.

Chapter 8

Kleinian and Independent approaches to practice

Having focused mainly on theoretical areas up to now, this final chapter explores the clinical application of Object Relations. In the first section we turn to leading Kleinians and Independents of the later twentieth century and investigate how they themselves defined their own approaches, and what they thought of the other's. We finish with accounts of psychoanalytic treatment by Bion and Khan, respectively. These two innovative psychoanalysts provide striking illustrations of the features discussed in the first part of the chapter, and throughout the book more generally.

Clinical approaches

By the latter half of the twentieth century, the Kleinian and Independent approaches had become distinct. Broadly speaking, there was an emphasis by Kleinians on precise and accurate theoretical understanding, and by Independents on intuition and authenticity, based broadly on Winnicottian thinking. Many Independent psychotherapists made use of particular Kleinian concepts, as we saw with Green and Ogden; it was far less common for Kleinian practitioners to take up Independent ideas, though this has increased in more recent years. This may be because the Kleinian focus on the transference highlights the state of the object relations in the patient's internal world, while the Independent emphasis on the self and its experience encourages a wider focus.

There is in any case a limit to how far the two approaches can be brought together. Every Object Relations practitioner has to decide where she stands with regard to the crucial points on which these approaches diverge. Clinically, these include at least three points which directly affect what happens in sessions. First, how far does containment rest on the consistency of the setting and the accuracy of interpretations, and how far on the therapist's personality as opposed to their mere presence: who the therapist is, as against the experience of being with a responsive figure? Second, how far may a state of merging reflect regression to a point before object-relating began, or alternatively a defence against separateness? And thirdly, how far are hate and envy intrinsic aspects of human nature, and how far reactions to frustration or attack?

These three considerations reflect corresponding theoretical standpoints: the overall weight allotted in the development of the human psyche to later environmental factors as against internal and external conditions at birth; whether the primitive psyche has a subject–object structure or consists of an undifferentiated unity; and the existence or otherwise of a destructive drive.

Freud stated the aim of psychoanalysis as to '[transform] what is unconscious into what is conscious' (1917: 280) – to become aware of what had previously been repressed. This was reworded in Kleinian thinking as the development of insight, expressed particularly clearly by Hanna Segal (1918–2011):

> When we offer a patient analysis, we undertake to provide the conditions in which it can be conducted. The analytical setting has been often described. I want to mention here, however, that the *analyst's attitude* is an essential part of this setting. If we accept that insight is by itself the main curative factor, we undertake as part of the setting which we have to provide that the analyst shall do nothing to blur the development of the transference, that he shall be there as a person whose sole function is to understand sympathetically and to communicate to the patient such relevant knowledge as he has acquired at the moment when the analysand is most ready to understand it. This is a part of the setting.
>
> (Segal 1986/1962: 70–71)

Segal's emphasis is entirely on the 'development of the transference' as the means whereby the patient becomes able to recognise his internal world in action, directly and immediately. The facilitation of the development of the transference is seen as a 'part of the setting', a non-negotiable component of the approach. This endorses Klein's assertion that it is the 'consistent analysis of the transference' that can bring about the 'deep-reaching revision of the earliest object-relations' (Klein 1952b: 56) on which psychoanalytic effectiveness depends, particularly with more disturbed patients.

We may note that Segal counts sympathetic understanding as equally important in gaining awareness of the inner world as communicating knowledge at the right time. However, she repeatedly lays out her disagreement with the Independent approach, sometimes in uncompromising terms. She traces their approach back to Ferenczi's 'experiments', asserting that he and his followers 'focused on various notions of cure and change that did not rest on attaining truth and that considered the personal influences of the analyst – e.g., his support, advice, and comfort – to be integral to the analytic process' (Segal in *American Imago* 2006: 289). This was something she could not accept: 'Here the changes in technique were of a kind that made them essentially non-analytic. They went against the psychoanalytic effort to bring about change through the search for truth' (ibid.). She went so far as to insist, in the first publication of the paper: 'When the analyst actively takes upon himself the parental role, he invites the patient to live in a lie. This in turn promotes concrete functioning rather than symbolization and psychic growth' (ibid.). Segal is saying that the growth of insight is impeded if the analyst's interventions embrace tasks proper to a parent. Instead of the patient assimilating aspects of the analyst's emotional presence at a symbolic level, he is encouraged to do so concretely; the analyst presents herself literally as a second and better parent, whose superior care can replace the perceived deficiencies of the original internal parent – the 'cure' which Segal believes the Independents claimed, as opposed to simply 'analysis'.

Not surprisingly, a number of her colleagues – more than fifty in all, including André Green, Pearl King and other eminent psychoanalysts – complained, in a jointly signed response to the editor, that this was not a fair or accurate criticism: 'her comments are simply unsubstantiated defamation of the work of a particular, named, group of her colleagues.' Moreover, 'we disagree', they asserted, 'with the idea that being supportive, or offering advice or comfort to patients, is necessarily anti-analytic and necessarily a hindrance to attaining "truth" about psychic reality' (Segal et al., 2007b: 121–124). Segal felt obliged to apologise, acknowledging: 'All analysts of every theoretical persuasion have to grapple with the need to help their patients lead a more satisfying life', but added 'and I believe that a contact with reality is essential to achieve this' (ibid.).

It is both unusual and useful to have the essential difference between the clinical stances of the Kleinian and Independent approaches set out so clearly. If we temporarily set aside the question of 'cure', the issue is whether support, advice, comfort and the like *necessarily* impede insight –Independents do not dispute that insight is a key psychoanalytic aim. Segal endorses 'sympathetic understanding' and so, by implication, the offering of support and relief by the analyst. Betty Joseph also comments on the importance of the attunement of the analyst's interventions: 'no interpretation can be seen as a pure interpretation or explanation but must resonate in the patient in a way which is specific to him and his way of functioning' (Joseph 1985). Thus analysts from both approaches believe that for psychotherapy to best help the patient, the therapist must foster emotional development through sensitivity to his current state, as well as promote insight through understanding the transference.

This is a revisiting of a psychoanalytic controversy from before the 'Controversial Discussions': the disagreement between Freud and Ferenczi as to whether the main therapeutic factor in psychoanalysis is the patient's insight or the therapist's 'love'.[1] On closer examination, however, we find that the two schools seem to mean something different by 'love'. Segal, for the Kleinians, distinguishes firmly between how love is shown in different situations: 'It is inappropriate for a parent to express sexual love. It is inappropriate for the analyst to manifest sexual or parental love. The appropriate expression of love by the analyst is understanding' (Segal 1986: 80). Although Independent psychotherapists would agree broadly with this, they would come closer to a parental type of love than the Kleinians, as they include active interventions in their work. This is seen as providing the patient with the qualities or responses which were lacking in his early care – so it could be seen as a form of 'reparenting', an aim which undoubtedly bears risks.

Khan took on the idea of 'therapeutic care' from Winnicott, but Winnicott stayed closer to the conventional psychoanalytic setting. For example, where a patient seemed unable to settle into the usual fifty-minute sessions, Winnicott offered longer sessions (Winnicott 1971: 31–43). At most, he would arrange for a patient in breakdown to be taken in by a hospital of his choice for full care during his breaks (Little 1985). Thus, Winnicott extended conventional boundaries, whereas Khan recast them dramatically to fit what he saw as the patient's needs. His alterations to the frame varied from the minor, such as actively refraining from interpreting at a crucial point in a patient's regression (Hopkins 2006: 108–109) to the major, as in the case described in the later part of this chapter, where he arranged alternative living situations for his patient for the major part of their work together (Khan 1989: 59–87). For the reason Segal has given, all such interventions would be judged inadmissible by orthodox Kleinians. For them, it would be for the patient's family, rather than the psychotherapist, to arrange entry into hospital, for example, should this be needed; the therapist might advise, but should not act.

The waters were muddied by a suggestion by Franz Alexander (1891–1964), who proposed that at least one purpose of psychoanalysis was to provide a 'corrective emotional experience suitable to repair the traumatic influence of previous experiences' (Alexander, French et al., 1980: 66). This amounts to the shortcut of practitioners offering themselves as better parents to their damaged patients – hoping for the 'cure' that Segal refers to. The more sober alternatives are to rely on the painstaking working-through of pathological internal object relations in the transference, or on the patient unconsciously assimilating into his own psychic structures aspects of the therapist's presence and responses. Khan himself rejected Alexander's suggestion as a useless and omnipotent attempt on the part of the therapist to rewrite the patient's history:

> The analyst's task is not to *be* or *become* the mother ... We can persuade ourselves only through an act of magical thinking that we can do so. What we do provide are some of the functions of the mother as a protective shield and auxiliary ego ... Those who *become* (or so they believe) the original object (mother) inevitably introduce an element of exaggerated cathexis of the patient as a person ... whereas those who make themselves available only as an auxiliary ego ... are thereby capable of that psychic distance which alone enables them to register, perceive and report (reconstruct) what is happening.
>
> (Khan 1986: 67–68)

It is regrettable that Khan did not take more notice of what he sets out so clearly in this passage: as he observes, such an approach is geared towards the wishes of the therapist rather than the needs of the patient, who becomes in effect the therapist's 'project'. Yet psychotherapists often feel tempted to avoid appearing a 'bad' parent: being potentially perceived as critical, for example, or bringing up ways in which the patient makes himself 'unlikeable'.

Alexander makes more extreme suggestions, such as examining and altering counter-transference feelings, and intentionally acting in an opposite way to the patient's expectations (1957: 93, in Segal 2007b: 159); he really does seem to think that a therapeutic 'cure' is possible by replacing 'bad' experiences with 'good' ones. Therapists who hold such beliefs are more likely to fall into the trap that Khan describes; this is less of a risk if the focus remains on the patient and his needs. Of course, the personality and pathology of the patient are also relevant: some patients are searching, perhaps even consciously, for a replacement parent with whom to relive their childhood. These patients[2] could easily interpret 'therapeutic care' as an implicit confirmation that it is the therapist's responsibility to take care of the patient as if he were the child he feels or wishes himself to be. For both therapist and patient, the focus would tend to remain on the therapist's gratifying or frustrating actions rather than on the patient's understanding of himself and his use of his own experience and resources. Needless to say, such patients would do better with the standard psychoanalytic setting – with sessions increased to the maximum five a week, if necessary.

Segal does state, however, that 'analysis is a corrective experience' (1986: 79), in that the gradual working-through of one's ways of being and relating leads to increased emotional understanding and improved functioning. She describes the difficulties with approaches such as Alexander's as arising when the therapist *tries* to be a 'good object' to the patient, rather than the patient simply experiencing her as such, as she helps him understand why he feels and acts the way he does. Clearly, this aim would be hampered if the therapist were needlessly cold or attacking, but so it would be if she indulged her own need to be liked, veering towards emotional seduction. The presumed sadism of the rigorous Kleinian analyst may be largely a myth, but it is not without foundation. Nor, moreover, is the corresponding notion of the Independent analyst as woolly-minded and averse to the negative transference.

Kleinians believe that the main burden of the therapeutic work takes place when the negative transference is active. Dysfunctional patterns from past relationships can then be modified and perhaps even transformed through reworking them in the transference. The essential final phase is the dissolution of the transference, when the patient relinquishes the image of the analyst overblown through transference, leaving him with the insight gained and development achieved. Independents, meanwhile, see the effects of the therapeutic setting as the main therapeutic agent, and do not place the same emphasis on the negative transference. In both Object Relations traditions, practitioners and patients may go on to become colleagues and perhaps also friends, though perhaps less often now than at the time we are considering. Any sexual involvement, of course, whether during the treatment or long after it has finished has always been viewed as destructive to the psychotherapeutic process and any gains made through it. The transference makes such actions a form of incest, with the psychotherapist embodying the exploitative parent.

We have already noted Winnicott's mixed views of Klein. She was his first and most important mentor in the British psychoanalytic world, and he strongly supported her taking emotional disturbance back to infancy (Winnicott 1962c). Having upheld her work, he was very disappointed when she rejected his – she excluded him from the Kleinian group rather than him leaving it (ibid. 176–177). She had little choice, however: he went against some of her first principles, such as the concept of the death instinct, including envy, which he regarded as too structurally complex for a young infant mind (Winnicott 1959: 444). Nevertheless, Winnicott agreed with much of Klein's thinking, leading him to emphasise, like Segal, the central role of the transference interpretation: he described the aim of psychoanalytic treatment as 'to verbalize the nascent conscious in terms of the transference' (1962b: 170).

Making the same point more fully, he writes that as an analyst he should also communicate with the patient 'from the position in which the transference neurosis (or psychosis) puts me' (ibid. 166). These are technical definitions of exactly what the analyst must do, rather than everyday descriptions of what it is like to practise psychoanalysis. He adds that the therapist has to combine communicating from the transference position with standing in objective reality ('it is I who must keep an eye on the clock'), making the therapist akin to a transitional object. Like any transitional object, the therapist matches the subject's needs, yet is not infinitely malleable: her separateness makes her more than a hallucination. The therapist has to attune herself to the disturbed patient's internal world, sometimes very closely, as does the mother to the newborn infant; only then can the patient 'find' her in the subjective area of external reality, a separate object who is nevertheless consonant with his needs and expectations.

Winnicott explains: 'I do adapt quite a little to individual expectations at the beginning. It is inhuman not to do so. Yet all the time I am manoeuvring into the position for standard analysis' (ibid.). In practice, many Kleinians probably do something similar, though they might be less concerned about appearing 'inhuman' than an Independent practitioner. A more substantial problem arises with those more disturbed patients who Winnicott, Khan and their colleagues felt were less able to benefit from 'standard psychoanalysis'. Winnicott discusses this issue in 'The Aims of Psycho-Analytical Treatment' (1962b: 168–169), where he lists those criteria which suggest patients who are likely to get stuck in treating him as either solely internal or solely external; most useful is when the patient can 'play' with his presence in the intermediate transitional space. Provided the aim is to interpret what is nearly conscious, he counts the treatment as psychoanalysis. Otherwise, it would presumably be seen as the 'management' or 'therapeutic care' which Winnicott and Khan introduced, conducted more through the provision of a carefully thought-out environment than explanations of the transference. In deciding which form of treatment to offer, the psychotherapist should note whether the patient has reached whole-object, 'unit status', or whether he requires ego-support more than interpretations:

> In treatment of schizoid persons, the analyst needs to know all about the interpretations that might be made ... but he must be able to refrain from being side-tracked into doing this work that is inappropriate because the main need is for an unclever ego-support, or a holding. This 'holding', like the task of the mother in infant-care, acknowledges tacitly the tendency of the patient to disintegrate, to cease to exist, to fall forever.
>
> (Winnicott 1963b: 241)

Returning to Object Relations as a whole, we can say that the common clinical aim is to facilitate the patient's access to the deeper aspects of himself. The Kleinian approach lays more emphasis on knowledge, though without neglecting the emotional. Their objective is for the patient to increase his understanding of his inner reality through reflecting on his emotional experience, primarily in relation to his therapist, working towards achieving a fuller acceptance of himself and a better adjustment to outer reality – including taking responsibility for his own part in engendering negative responses from others. The Independent approach is more concerned with the quality of experience, measured more by the degree of authenticity. Feeling deeply in tune with oneself is the overall aim, but the social nature of human beings means that this involves the ability to relate readily and non-defensively with others. Khan describes this as finding the 'hidden self': 'One learns to tolerate unknowing, so as to facilitate converse (*sic*) and thus engender that unpredictable growth which, if it actualizes, is called "cure"' (1982: 'Preface', in 1989). This is one of the few times in which any of the theorists discussed in this book speaks of 'cure'.

The Kleinian and Independent approaches are not in absolute opposition to each other. Object Relations work can of course include theoretical exactitude as well as imaginative improvisation on the part of the therapist, and enhanced self-knowledge as well as deep authenticity on the part of the patient. Kleinian theory recognises the importance of maternal care in the development of the psyche, and Independents, the importance of realistic knowledge of the self. Each approach, additionally, risks its own form of misuse – the Kleinians, by depriving the patient of the supportive contact he needs to face shameful aspects of himself, and the Independents by enticing the patient to believe that his wellbeing is in the therapist's gift, rather than being largely the product of psychical work.

The following accounts show Kleinian and Independent approaches in practice, highlighting their differences in presentation as well as substance. Bion's work leaves us with a detailed knowledge of the patient's inner world, but comparatively little of the effect of the work on Bion himself. Khan's, by contrast, keeps the relational dynamics between patient and analyst at the centre.

It would be most regrettable if the stereotypes of the cold and hostile Kleinian analyst and the warm but unboundaried Independent psychotherapist are perpetuated. The most important point is that each approach works effectively when its risks are managed well, and with a similar population of patients: borderline and psychotic as well as neurotic patients, adults, adolescents and children – even babies. So far, each approach has also led to promising further developments, such as Fisher's elaboration of Bion's theory of 'K' and Bollas' rethinking of Khan's 'therapeutic care'. Both could co-operate more to address areas which are neglected throughout psychoanalysis, including work with patients from minority groups ranging from the disabled to ethnic minorities; and both could work to link psychoanalysis with other perspectives on the human mind, such as neurophysiology or philosophy, to the benefit of all involved.

Clinical accounts

Bion's and Khan's accounts of their work spell out much of the thinking that underpins it. Especially with Bion's account, it is advisable to go carefully through the paper itself, using this section for clarification. Bion's writing is dense and can be obscure, yet it repays the study it demands. Like many Kleinian papers, it is weighted towards theoretical detail, while Khan's emphasis is on how the patient's therapeutic progress developed – especially through her use of the changing therapeutic settings. Bion's and Khan's papers show divergent clinical practice and contrasting theoretical approaches, but both demonstrate the sensitivity and intelligent self-reflection that all psychotherapeutic work requires if it is to reach the patient emotionally and assist in the development of authenticity, autonomy and insight.

Bion: The Imaginary Twin

'The Imaginary Twin' was presented to the British Psychoanalytical Society in 1950 and published in *Second Thoughts* (1984a: 3–22), a collection of papers, which Bion continued to regard as important years after they were published. This paper is also referred to in the first part of the 'Commentary' (1984b: 120–166), another paper included in *Second Thoughts* in which, seventeen years later, Bion reflects on all the papers in the volume. He discusses a number of issues but only the most significant are considered here. The main purpose of 'The Imaginary Twin' is to put forward a new theoretical proposal: the correlation of psychological and physiological developments.[3] Bion suggests that as the infant gains mastery of binocular vision – the ability to see things in perspective – a clearer mental vision is also gained; he realises that his significant figures are whole, separate beings in their own right and, therefore, that he must be as well.

After introducing the patient's background and presentation, we focus on Bion's discussion of the therapeutic work in two parts. Each is built around a central interpretation which leads to the patient developing his understanding of crucial details of his internal world, and so becoming more able to dismantle his defensive structures. The first main insight arises from Bion listening to the patient with particular attentiveness, in an example of what he called 'reverie' and Freud, 'free-floating attention'. The figure of the 'imaginary twin' comes to Bion's attention, not through the content of the patient's material but through the way in which he talked. The second section introduces the paper's key theoretical proposal, the correlation of mental and physical development. Here, Bion illustrates how his patient's material suggests to him a link between the development of binocular vision, the co-ordination of the eyes, and the ability to 'see' a whole person rather than a collection of parts. This in turn led to recognition of the oedipal context of whole persons and a more mature and profound working-through of the patient's material. Bion's writing is meticulously detailed, reflecting the precision of his thinking and his attention to non-verbal aspects of the patient's material, such as punning and rhythm. The Kleinian focus on the individual's internal world is prominent: minimal consideration is given to the effects of external factors, in line with the Kleinian belief that the therapeutic process occurs primarily within the transference, and can only be understood fully from that perspective.

Bion's account is written in numbered points, in the manner of a geometric theorem. He begins: '1. The patient from whose analysis I draw most of my material had had many years of psycho-therapy which ended when the therapist advised leucotomy' (Bion 1984a: 3). He goes on to refer to a 'shocking family history' that, together with the equally alarming proposal of brain surgery, suggested to the referring doctor that the outlook was 'bad'. Our attention is drawn to the patient's troubled and traumatic history, with the recent treatment apparently ending in the psychotherapist giving up in frustration or despair.

Bion continues with information about the patient's family history. There had been a sister, eighteen months older, who had died when the patient was a year old, the cause being a disease from which the patient had also suffered; the only symptom we are told of is 'severe diarrhoea'. Until he was ten, the patient's sole 'playmates' were two girls who lived next door, two and seven years younger. Bion implies that the influence of these children was problematic: 'The younger died in an asylum before the war; the other still survives but in a state of incurable insanity, supposedly schizophrenia' (ibid. 3).

The patient is given no name, not even the commonly used 'Mr A', until, later in the paper, Bion starts referring to him as 'A' to differentiate him from two more patients, 'B' and 'C'. Despite the abstract presentation, these few stark details are sufficient to arouse our interest in this unpromising-sounding patient and how the work is going to proceed. The impression given is of mess and illness, loss and confusion, in a context of insecurity and general isolation.

We then learn, to our surprise, that the patient had been an active and intelligent child, gifted in sport and academic work, living outside the UK in a country where sport, in particular, was being developed. There was therefore every reason to expect him to do well, but by the age of thirteen his family situation had deteriorated economically and domestically: the 'complication' of 'disunited parents' led to a breakdown from which he had never fully recovered. The patient's mother died four years later, after 'years of chronic and painful illness', and his father when the patient was an adult. Circumstances we are not told of prompted a move to the UK when he was seventeen to 'start afresh'. Clearly, this had not brought the hoped-for results.

A brief pen-portrait describes the patient as he presented to Bion: a teacher in his mid-forties, tall and wiry, with a 'sallow complexion and dull expressionless features' (ibid.). His difficulties emerged in a discussion to which the patient contributed with 'monosyllabic listlessness', leading to the discouraging 'He agreed without enthusiasm to give analysis a trial' (ibid. 3–4).

The patient's problems clustered vaguely around contamination: 'he felt that he contaminated his bath on which he relied to give him a feeling of cleanliness and that it contaminated him back again' (ibid. 4). He also suffered anxieties about his level of drinking and his sexuality. He 'could not bear' someone sitting behind him, but sitting behind them was no better. Unsure whether or not his penis was erect, sexual feelings for his students left him feeling 'unclean'. The patient's associations frequently involved 'phantasied therapeutic injections' given by him, using a needle which he feared he had not sterilised properly.

As readers, we do not know whether this collection of worries emerged quickly or slowly, but it reflects anxieties of an infantile kind. Although his unease about his drinking indicates an oral fixation, his anxieties were of a predominantly anal nature – he disliked people sitting behind each other, and sexuality felt 'unclean'. We are reminded of the 'severe diarrhoea' of his and his sister's early illness, connecting directly with his sister's early death, at an age when his libidinal focus was changing from oral to anal. All in all, Bion's description suggests a patient suffering in the wake of continual infantile and childhood trauma, his severe disturbance covered over by a mask of normality, probably deriving from a relatively positive first year.

First interpretation

After an initial two years of tedious and unrewarding sessions, Bion reached a significant insight – the existence and functions of the 'imaginary twin' in the patient's internal world. Bion picked up this feature through listening to the flow of the patient's speech rather than through its content, and conveyed his understanding through several explanatory comments which link together to make the first main interpretation.

In general, Bion found it difficult to understand the import of what the patient was saying, because of the flatness of his intonation and the ambiguity of his statements; they 'admitted of different meanings if one considered them now with one emotional content, now with another' (ibid.). Bion felt little confidence in his understanding of the patient in any depth, or in the accuracy of his interpretations. 'There was plenty of oedipal material, produced on a most superficial level, which I duly interpreted to meet with a perfunctory response or none at all' (ibid.). This was worrying since, as a Kleinian, he saw interpretations as the main therapeutic vehicle, judging their accuracy by how far they succeeded in enabling the patient to bring further material.

Nonetheless, on two different occasions over the first period of analysis he heard from outside sources that 'the patient was said to be greatly improved' (ibid.). Bion himself saw no sign of this, but the patient's responses to interpretations began to intensify from being at most 'perfunctory' to demonstrating 'more than usually stubborn indifference'. This was followed by more open resistance, 'as if I was a parent who was issuing ineffectual exhortations and warnings to a refractory child' (ibid. 4–5). It sounds as though the patient was becoming less able or willing to ignore Bion: he was now pressing home to his analyst that he would take no notice of his pronouncements, acknowledging his presence in a negative manner, like a sulky teenager. Drawing the patient's attentions to this change brought further developments. Bion now realised that the patient's communications expressed simultaneous contrasting emotional states, conveyed through the rhythm of the speech more than the meaning of the words.

> It was as if two quite separate co-existent scansions of his material were possible. One imparted an overpowering sense of boredom and depression; the other, dependent on the fact that he introduced regularly spaced pauses in the stream of his associations, an almost jocular effect as if he were saying 'Go on; it's your turn'.
>
> (Ibid. 5)

Bion must have been listening to the patient in a different way to hear this unusual effect, changing from a position of duty and conscientiousness to 'negative capability'[4] – listening to the 'music' of the communications rather than sticking stalwartly to their content. He believed that this non-specific attentiveness heightens openness to unconscious processes, terming it 'reverie'; he saw it as the way in which emotional communication develops, through the psychotherapist relating in this way with the patient, or the mother with the infant.

Bion first detected the figure of the 'imaginary twin' in the rhythmic structure of his patient's words. One twin seemed to be allotted the state of 'boredom and depression', the other, jocularity and playfulness. It sounds like a children's playground game that Bion was implicitly being invited to join in with. He seems to have changed, in the patient's eyes, from being an irritation to ignore (at the outset of therapy), to an authority figure to challenge (as his resistance became more open), and eventually to a partner to co-operate with, work with, play with.

Bion realised, moreover, that what he now saw as the twin figure had appeared regularly in the patient's material for some time. There had been a man who was similar to the patient in many ways but who did not have his symptoms; a homosexual brother-in-law who nevertheless was attracted to the patient's wife; a man with whom he played tennis; and students of his who were 'psychological cases'. In this last example, the patient seems to suggest that he and Bion were 'identical' twins on the basis of both working with 'psychological cases', although we had heard that the patient was a teacher.

The 'imaginary' status of the twin figure was accentuated when Bion discovered that some of the exchanges the patient spoke of turned out not to be real: when Bion questioned whether one had actually taken place the patient replied, 'Oh, no … I am just imagining it!' (ibid. 6). Each development of the twin theme emerged after Bion had pointed out changes in the patient's behaviour or way of being. A long-standing feature of the patient's internal world was being brought to the fore.

The patient's freed-up reactions suggest that the improvements seen outside the analysis were now appearing within it, provided that Bion stayed attuned to its form of delivery. Bion was offered a part to play in the 'jocular' sequence 'association – interpretation – association', but the 'depressed' twin was also in evidence. When Bion examined their communications in more detail, he realised that

> the associations were all stale associations inviting a stale response. If I broke the rhythm, he showed signs of anxiety or irritability; if I continued to give the interpretations, which … he both invited and expected, there emerged a sense of having reached a dead end.
>
> (Ibid. 5)

There seemed to be no immediate way of using Bion's new insight to work co-operatively. The next interaction illustrates how Bion used the patient's material to understand his unconscious messages: he commented that the patient's associations expressed concisely what the patient felt was happening between the two of them. Additionally, the patient seemed to be suggesting that he was hearing Bion's interpretations as 'vague complaints', with his own associations being 'designed to keep me [Bion] employed without bothering him [the patient]' (ibid.). For the patient, Bion's interpretations were the psychological equivalent of amytal.[5]

Nevertheless, Bion pointed out, the current unsatisfactory state of affairs must be serving some purpose. He pointed to the main clue to the 'twin' theme, the 'jocular' rhythmic structure 'association – interpretation – association'. This 'indicated that I [Bion] was a twin of himself [the patient] who supported him in the jocular evasion of my complaints and thus softened his resentment' (ibid. 7–8). Abruptly, the patient appeared to revert from being intermittently cheerful and co-operative to the demoralised state in which he had originally presented himself – depressed, tired and 'unclean'.

> The change was so sudden as to be disconcerting. What on earth, I wondered, had happened to the twin [the jocularly alternating rhythm] and the complaining parent [whom Bion had felt the patient to be treating him as]? It was as though he had swallowed them and was suffering the consequences.
> (Ibid. 8)

The term 'swallowed' expresses the concrete bodily way in which unconscious relationships with internal objects are experienced. The jocular exchange seems to be a defence which protected the patient against the toxic effects of introjecting the family, but this was the first occasion when Bion had seen such a 'dramatic' exhibition of it. Bion's interpretation of this sudden change was followed by the continued relinquishing of the patient's defences. We shall not examine the whole of this complex process here, but in the subsequent session the patient reported a 'terrifying' dream – presumably in reaction to Bion's interpretation. The patient dreamed that he was driving behind a car he intended to overtake, but found himself following it and copying its movements instead. He parked as it parked, but right up alongside it so that he was trapped inside his own car. A 'menacing' figure loomed over him, the driver of the adjacent car. The patient 'woke in terror, to remain filled with anxiety throughout the waking day' (ibid. 8).

Here, the twin figure is showing destructive rather than protective traits, as with the family introjection, and again, a lengthy interpretation was to have a significant impact. Bion explained that in serving to make the analytic situation tolerable, the twin was preventing the patient from entering into the outside world, or external reality (i.e. getting out of the car). Moreover, 'The twin was imaginary because my patient had prevented the birth of the twin – there was in fact no twin' (ibid.). The figure appeared threatening for the same reason – because he, the twin, had not been allowed to be born but remained a split-off phantasy figure.

> His use of the twin to alleviate anxiety was therefore illegitimate [a phantastic rather than a realistic action] and the twin was determined that he, the patient, should not now be born, or to put it in other words, achieve freedom or independence. He was thus shut in, both by the twin and by his own act in parking his car so near the twin's car.
> (Ibid. 8–9)

Like all phantasy figures, the 'imaginary' twin had 'real' effects. Bion was suggesting that in the dream, the patient was both himself and the twin, with the twin also representing the analyst, and the car, the analysis. The dream indicated that the patient was preventing Bion from emerging into the analysis as a 'real being': 'the dream showed his fear that in the previous session I had become alive only to block his escape from analysis by using me as a personification of the bad part of himself from which he wished to be dissociated' (ibid. 9). Bion had become the bad, frightening twin in order to stop him leaving analysis. The twin figure, the result of splitting and projection, held the function of reducing the patient's anxiety by providing a receptacle for aspects of himself he could not accept. When Bion exposed this defensive manoeuvre, the figure was revealed as the patient's 'bad self' with its 'menacing' guise. The patient could no longer pretend that the twin was anything other than his own aggressive self.

As with most interpretations, Bion's both aroused and reduced the patient's anxiety. Even when they were not accurate, the fact that they highlighted the patient's internal world provoked anxiety in him, while Bion's continuing presence alleviated it. Once Bion was interpreting more in line with the patient's immediate anxieties, his self-awareness began to increase. Each new insight brought relief because the anxiety was defined rather than left formless and nameless; yet it also disturbed the patient because it demonstrated to him that he needed to face up to aspects of himself he felt afraid or ashamed of. Eventually, this heightening and diminishing of anxiety induced the patient to venture more willingly into his internal world. He appeared more integrated and more connected with reality, as his split-off and projected ego-parts were gradually drawn into the main body of the ego (ibid. 12).

For Kleinians, the major part of any analysis or psychotherapy consists in 'working through' the anxiety released as the therapist's interpretations help the patient become more self-aware. The dream of the 'menacing' twin was followed by such a period, in which the 'prominent features ... were exhibitions of introjection and projection, splitting, and ... personification of the split-off portions of his personality' (ibid.). Working through each defensive structure enabled the patient to repair the split-off parts of the ego and take back the projections; by gaining familiarity with his emotions and his internal world he built the confidence to explore further. As the denied aspects of the patient's personality became better integrated, he became psychologically healthier and communication became easier: Bion, and others in his life, became separate people for him.

Second interpretation

We now come to the second interpretation, focusing on the theoretical nucleus of the paper – the connection between physiological and psychical development, the 'eyes' and the 'I'. Bion's proposition is that as binocular vision develops, so also does the ability to 'see' persons as whole objects. It is only a small step further to see their context – that other people are also players in the oedipal situation, with all its tumultuous conflicts. Bion is now writing of the later period of analysis, when the patient was speaking more freely and could readily explain or expand on points when asked. His view of Bion was also changing:

> Throughout this period it was clear that I was felt to be present and indeed my presence was even regarded as necessary. But I was not to interfere ...

> incursion into the realms of diagnosis and treatment was resented; but I could be myself, not just a twin to be fashioned into a shape he desired.
>
> (Ibid. 14)

The main theme of this phase of the analysis concerned students whom the patient had to send to different specialists. One student had an eye problem, which necessitated referral to two eye specialists. The first 'eye man' thought it was an infection for which nothing could be done; the student's father accordingly requested Bion's patient to arrange a second opinion, which meant he was 'landed with a whole lot of work I don't want to do; she's a nuisance' (ibid. 12). Bion interpreted that the student represented a damaged internal object, requiring 'a whole lot' of psychological work the patient wished he didn't have to be bothered with.

The patient's story continued:

> The second eye man doesn't think it's much different clinically from what the first eye man says, but he thinks it's worth doing something. The first eye man didn't think it worth bothering and that is why her father thought him a bit slack I suppose. Anyway I have to do this now. She must get a blood test done to see if she has syphilis. She should have done it before.
>
> (Ibid. 12)

The mention of syphilis recalls the patient's central anxieties of sexuality and contamination: sexual feelings had made him feel poisoned and unclean as well as aroused. This theme was part of the oedipal material discussed superficially in the first years of the analysis. It was now to be dealt with at a more mature and sophisticated level.

We only learn of the patient's material through Bion's interpretation, or rather, his series of linked interpretations. In these, Bion clarified what he took to be the unconscious meaning of the patient's communications, assessed by his reaction to the interpretation as well as the surrounding material. Bion stated that: 'I [Bion] was the first eye man who said, in effect, that the injured girl was an internal object, infected by the bad objects inside him, for which nothing could be done' (ibid. 12–13).

In other words, Bion interpreted that the patient felt he (the patient) had contaminated his female internal object through his 'bad' inner objects or features, and that this state of affairs could not be remedied. The 'first eye man' was presented as having superior knowledge, in the initial linking of the eyes and the mind, or knowledge.

Bion continued:

> I was also the second eye man who said that the injured girl was injured by his faeces [cf. the infectious diarrhoea], spirochaetes and bacilli [bacteria causing syphilis, amongst other conditions, and feeding off dead or toxic matter], all varieties of bad penes, for whom nothing could be done but for

> whom he would have to do it just the same. He would have to cure her with his penis, since I would not repair damage done by him and it was his object in any case; and he would have to cure her without any pleasurable gain.
>
> (Ibid. 13)

The second 'eye man' had gone into more detail, and the patient now started referring to him as an 'eye surgeon' (ibid. 14). This 'expert' had specified that the female internal object had been damaged by different kinds of bad penis, all versions of an 'unclean' penis consisting of faeces. These contaminating objects could not be rendered harmless, but he would nevertheless have to do whatever it took to make them so (there being no logic in unconscious life). All the patient's internal objects were pronounced to be inescapably his responsibility, however hopeless the outlook; his analyst, in particular, would not do any work connected with them. It was up to the patient to repair his female internal object and neutralise his contaminating faecal penes. The instrument of repair was also the penis – the good or genital penis – suggesting the beginnings of a move from anal to genital functioning.

Bion continued:

> I was also the eye surgeon who threatened him with castration. He had spent some anxious hours on correspondence to see that no question of jealousy or friction marred the relationship between the two eye men and between them and himself. So the twins were to be brought into harmonious co-operation.
>
> (Ibid. 13)

The more expert 'eye man' had become an 'eye surgeon', in a continuation of the levels of status and expertise opening up between the two 'eye men'. The mention of castration and jealousy confirmed an oedipal situation; it was the patient's responsibility to ensure that the relationships between all concerned remained smooth, although he was not part of the eye men's relationship. The eye men now represented parents, imaginary twins and also the patient's two forms of treatment:

> The first, passive eye man represented his previous psycho-therapeutic experiences which had left him and his objects more or less in peace. The second eye man was psycho-analysis that was giving him increased insight, and seducing him into genital sexuality and the threatening situation that went with it.
>
> (Ibid. 13)

The unsuccessful psychotherapy (and psychotherapist) did not force the patient to face his undeveloped 'insight' and the terrors of adult sexuality, whereas psychoanalysis (and Bion) confronted him continually with these difficult challenges. This was a result of psychoanalysis requiring examination of his problems 'with all his senses, including sight and intellect' (ibid. 15). 'Seeing' more clearly also meant understanding the oedipal implications of what he saw: 'The first, passive eye man was the mother and the second, active eye man the father whom he tried to harmonize by his correspondence with both' (ibid. 13). Working with the 'eye men' represented a step along the path of oedipal resolution, as an aspect of the repair of the damage sustained by the ego from its internal bad objects. The patient had to come to terms with the competition, jealousy and threats he faced before 'insight' could be achieved: being 'brought into harmonious co-operation' suggests some resolution or acceptance of oedipal conflict.

Having outlined the content of the material, Bion now turns to 'the manner in which the patient brought this material into consciousness' (ibid.). He states that the themes of contamination and twinship had already been explored 'orally', by and through the mouth – that is, through talking – while remaining at a comparatively superficial level, in the first part of the analysis. Now the same themes are to be investigated through an 'ocular method'. The two eyes are to be brought into co-ordination to achieve a more mature, focused view. Proximity to an object facilitates exploration through touch, taste, smell and sound, but binocular vision requires perspective, or standing back. Bion looks into the connection between the eyes and the mind.

Splitting, projection and denial are the primitive defences of the paranoid-schizoid position. Separateness is denied, as is the knowledge that subject and object are equivalent, individuated beings; instead, figures are felt to be extensions or reflections of the self. It is only with the achievement of the 'three-person' genital or oedipal position that the possibility arises of being excluded from any relationship or connection. Where previously there was only subject and object, there can now be subject and two objects, mother and father. This brings the new emotion of jealousy, amongst others, and the capacity for awareness of the self – the realisation that there is a self to be conscious of, just as one is conscious of other objects, now seen as other 'selves'. Bion is suggesting that the ability to bring the visual image into focus develops in parallel with the sense of seeing people as separate beings, which in turn reveals the oedipal situation. As the depressive position comes to dominate, emotional life becomes more sophisticated and complex, and intellectual life moves to a different level.

In the final part of the paper, Bion brings in other examples (Patients 'B' and 'C') who each showed some of the same features as the first patient (now Patient 'A') and thus tended to confirm these points theoretically. In each case, the 'imaginary twin' figure had been present from a very early stage of ego development but only became important at a certain stage in the analysis. This figure suggests primary splitting, with the merest intimation of 'otherness': 'twin' can easily imply 'identical twin', and does so literally for patient B. This had also been the case in patient A's material, where a number of figures differed in only one respect from the patient himself. The central feature of the twin figure lay in him not being under the subject's control. This is the crux of otherness, the most difficult aspect to accept. Bion concludes that the 'imaginary twin goes back to his very earliest relationship and is an expression of his inability to tolerate an object that was not entirely under his control. The function of the imaginary twin was thus to deny a reality different from himself' (ibid. 19). The twin figure represents a reality which is 'other' but not 'different'.

These points are not immediately obvious on a first reading of the paper. They illustrate Bion's attention to the fine detail of the work – perhaps at the cost of a dramatic presentation. They make sense of the years of psychotherapy undergone by Patient A to little effect, and the two years of work with Bion before progress began to be made. Their subtle, off-beat character illustrates Bion's comments about the therapist's state of mind. Progress only began to be made when he listened to the overall impression, rather than simply listening to the content of the material. The less the therapist's focus is on specific features, whether the patient's history or the earlier part of the session, the more open are the unconscious channels between analyst and patient, and the more receptive each is likely to be:

> The experience of the patient's communication and psycho-analyst's interpretation is ineffable and essential ... The patient's reaction to the interpretation often depends more on this quality of the interpretation than on its verbal meaning.
>
> (Ibid. 12)

To sum up: this paper describes in careful detail the changes the patient made in progressing from being a 'failed patient', out of touch and in a state of perpetual low-grade depression, to a 'successful patient', thoughtful and insightful, able to communicate effectively with himself, his analyst and others. He responded first to Bion's constant and engaged presence before making gradual steps through anxiety and confusion to a position where he could accept Bion's interpretation of the 'imaginary twin' as a primitive way of mitigating his anxiety. This enabled him to re-incorporate both the rage and the otherness lodged in the imaginary twin and proceed to the point at which the 'eye men' introduced him to seeing his objects in perspective, just as monocular vision of the paranoid-schizoid position evolves into the binocular vision of the depressive position. With this change, reality became more important than wish-fulfilment, and the oedipal position, now self-evident, led him to wrestle with the complexities of social relationships.

Bion's proposal that psychological and physiological development progress concurrently is original and thought-provoking. The example given describes how the intellectual capacity for whole-object perception and the recognition of the oedipal process may evolve in parallel with the physiological capacity for focused vision, a proposition supported by the cases of B and C. Bion points out that this supports Klein's redating of the Oedipus Complex from early childhood, where Freud had placed it, to about the third month of life.

Whilst maintaining that the vehicle of therapeutic effect is the developing self-awareness, the emotional significance of the therapeutic atmosphere is also kept in view. The fundamental importance of theory as a guide to practice in Kleinian work is evident, but the emotional flexibility and lateral thinking more often associated with the Independent approach are also in evidence. Bion's account is not always easy to follow, but it includes all the main characteristics of a Kleinian approach.

Masud Khan: 'None Can Speak of His/Her Folly'

This paper, with its intriguing title, was written in 1981 and published in 1983 (1989b: 59–87). It is very different from Bion's paper, as is the work it describes. Where Bion emphasises the fine grain of object relations as they appear in the transference, Khan highlights events in the therapeutic narrative, bringing to life the atmosphere in the sessions, in the therapeutic relationship and in the patient's life. The study describes an example of the 'therapeutic care' Khan offered to those patients he deemed to need something other than standard psychoanalysis. In this type of work, most of the working-through of the patient's problems takes place in the context of carefully thought-out living situations rather than solely in sessions. These living situations were designed in light of the understanding Khan and the patient reached together. As far as possible the situation followed the patient's own sense of her[6] needs, on the basis that each patient held with herself her own 'self-cure'.

Like Bion, Khan includes theoretical discussion: but in Bion's paper the theory is to a great degree intertwined with the material or arising from it, whereas in Khan's, the theoretical aspects are distinct from the clinical material and at a more general level. He begins the paper with a vivacious account of his work with his patient, leaving theoretical factors to the second section: he does not want to 'pre-empt the reader's freedom to experience and evaluate the clinical narrative' (ibid. 59). Here, however, we shall proceed the other way around, beginning with the clinical and theoretical background and following with an account of the treatment. This is to avoid the considerable repetition which would otherwise be necessary, and to connect the clinical and theoretical aspects more smoothly than Khan does.

Background

We shall start by describing the way in which Khan approached therapeutic work, in particular the 'therapeutic care' used in the example described. The main theoretical point the paper goes on to highlight is then set out – the different modes of speech introduced by Freud in the psychoanalytic method.

In his initial assessment of a patient, Khan would consider whether psychoanalysis or 'therapeutic care' was indicated. If the latter, it meant making a major and open-ended commitment to the patient, who was likely to be more disturbed than most. The patient may be living through a 'False Self',[7] with her ways of being based on fitting in with the needs of others. Another possibility, existing separately or together with the 'False Self', is 'cumulative trauma'. Here, the original pathological scenario, constituted by the mother's inappropriate care and the infant's response to it, develops into a destructive pattern which accumulates through childhood and adolescence and into adulthood. The resulting trauma is not triggered by a single event but builds up over time.

These pathologies may exist with or without 'madness'. Rather than seeing madness as psychosis, or psychosis alone, Khan describes it as direct access to the state of mind during which the original pathological scenario or fixation point took place. This may involve states of mind which are bizarre and extreme but not necessarily delusional. It is in this sense that 'madness' is used in this section. Madness arises when the emotions at this point were too difficult or too painful to be processed and integrated. When this occurs before the ego has achieved sufficiently firm boundaries to become an integrated whole, orientation within time and space is left shaky, other people are seen through the lens of the self, and experience is felt as a collection of jagged pieces. Madness is therefore not defensive in nature but the result of development getting 'stuck', although it may continue around the point of madness so that the individual may appear normal, or nearly normal. There is always a weak spot which she is liable to return to emotionally, however, especially under stress. We can see that in Khan's thinking, those patients who need therapeutic care must overlap considerably with those living with his definition of madness, for whom he thought fifty-minute sessions alone were generally not adequate. Whereas most patients are able to regress within sessions and re-integrate when returning out into the world, these patients are fragile in this regard, requiring sustained individualised support. This generally correlates with those who have not progressed securely beyond the 'part object' relationship of the first few months of life into the 'whole object' relationship of the oedipal situation, the depressive position or Winnicott's 'stage of concern' (Winnicott 1963a, in 1982: 73–82).

Thus the care arrangements made by Khan are analogous to those given by the responsive mother to her very young infant. This does not mean Khan devoted all or even most of his time to this single patient; his presence would be symbolised by the supportive context he had organised, making use of people already in the patient's life or who could readily be brought into it. Khan would make himself available to the patient and her significant others for hours at a time if necessary, visiting the patient's home and even, at critical times, receiving phone calls at any time of day or night. As far as possible the length of meetings, the interventions made and the make-up of the holding environment would be patient-led, though interpreted and enriched by Khan and his contributions. The purpose was to enable the patient to relax sufficiently to regress to her original weak spot, live through it anew within a nurturing environment and set of relationships, and take up her psychical development on the basis of the 'True Self'.

Khan's work with 'Judy', his young patient, is a poignant and thought-provoking example of this.

In discussing the work described in this paper, Khan also considers the psychological significance of speech, and particularly the modes of speaking introduced into the psychoanalytic relationship by Freud. The individual's way of speaking, he points out, is overwhelmingly derived from environmental factors – speech is 'very intimately connected with growth, nurture and object-relating from infancy onwards' (Khan 1989: 82). Thus, much can be achieved through communication, and much can be inferred from the patient's manner of speaking – in particular, how and when she uses the three modes of 'talking, telling and speaking' (ibid. 59). 'Anna O', the patient who is said to have 'invented' psychoanalysis in the course of her treatment by Freud's colleague Josef Breuer, called it the 'talking cure', or 'chimney-sweeping' (Breuer and Freud 1895). The therapeutic effect was attributed to catharsis, the release of blocked emotions through free self-expression. Logically, 'talking' requires only one person, but as we now know an external figure is needed for a therapeutic outcome. The next stage, 'telling', is taken from another early case study of Freud's, in which he develops a different basis for psychoanalytic treatment. His patient complained that he 'was not to keep on asking her where this and that came from, but to let her *tell* [Khan's italics] … me what she had to say' (Khan 1989: 83). With 'telling', two people are absolutely necessary, and the main aim is not catharsis but communication and understanding. Khan sets Freud's psychoanalytic method at this level[8] (ibid. 85).

Khan adds 'speaking' as a further development, extending Freud's insights into work with the more disturbed patients who Freud did not think could benefit from psychoanalysis. This, as Khan uses the term, means speaking sincerely and directly: 'speaking from the heart'. Then, communication is imbued with personal authority, and direct connection with the 'True Self' makes 'speaking' a developmental achievement. It is also a striking experience for both speaker and listener, especially if the listener is listening with and from the heart as well. Since the self is intrinsically relational, this mode of speaking, with the analyst listening, constitutes the 'True Self' in action. It allows the authentic centre of the personality to consolidate, grow and develop. 'Speaking' is both the path to resolving past pathological development and a sign that resolution has been achieved.

Khan maintains that the level of 'speaking' is especially relevant to the treatment of narcissistic, borderline and psychotic patients, all of whom are likely to live with madness, in Khan's sense of the term. This is not simply psychosis, although it may include it. The title of Khan's paper indicates that madness ('la folie') involves the loss of the ability to speak authentically – from the True Self. By attending to, listening to and engaging with the patient, it is possible to facilitate the return to the original starting-point of the development of madness; with appropriate support and understanding, the patient's own path to growth and resolution can then configure and emerge. Khan explicitly denies that he is providing a 'corrective emotional experience' (see page 4 of Alexander, French et al. 1980) – he is not trying to be a 'better mother' who is then internalised as a superior maternal figure, or separate good object. His intention is to stay rooted within himself, responding to the patient genuinely and reflectively. He assumes that his responsiveness will include the element lacking in the patient's early care, which she now needs and implicitly asks for. The patient's 'talking' can then develop into 'telling', and later on into 'speaking'. She becomes able to connect with herself and others, receive from them and communicate with them from that most vulnerable point, the true or authentic self. The task of the therapist is to provide an environment and therapeutic relationship which the patient can draw from in order to relax and reach her original fixation point, and then progress from there – without losing more autonomy than is necessary along the way.

'Judy, age fifteen'

'Judy' was the only child in a well-known and wealthy family. She was, Khan tells us, 'compelled' upon him by the girl's physician, whom he had worked with over some years. Judy had attempted suicide a few days previously, having been the subject of a media scandal. The 'compulsion' appears to have come from within Khan, but perhaps also from Judy herself, via her physician. We shall explore Khan's work with Judy by charting her progress from the preliminary level of 'showing', through 'talking' and 'telling' to 'speaking'.

Showing

At first Judy could only meet Khan by 'exhibiting herself' to him. The schoolgirl who arrived at his door, plump, scruffy and rude, was not what he was expecting, given her upper-class background: 'She was wearing the tightest jeans she could possibly have squeezed herself into. Her blouse was unbuttoned to an indecent point' (ibid. 59). We learn that she had been made to put a fur coat over this ensemble to make her look half-way respectable; her normal wear was 'track boots, tight jeans, a shirt or floppy sweater and her favourite football club's long socks' (ibid. 63) – clothes, Khan remarks, which could just as well be worn by a boy her age. Judy had not yet grown into a mature sexual identity, showing an immature and unsuccessful attempt at seductiveness from a position between latency and adolescence.

Khan's impressionistic account of the initial session contrasts markedly with Bion's detailed presentation of his own first meeting with his patient. The experiences of Judy and Khan are both evoked, and it reads more like a diary than a clinical report. Judy's fearful and clumsy defiance makes for painful reading; it is worth looking at Khan's description of this session in some detail. He set no time limit on the first meeting, having little idea of what the therapeutic task might turn out to be or even whether it would be possible for them to work together.

Tacitly pushing the girl to lead the way, they started with 'twenty minutes of mutually provocative silence', with Judy 'showing' Khan her bandaged wrists by continually moving them about. At length she awkwardly forced herself to throw some words his way, with transparently defensive aggression. She was surprised that Khan did not already know about the recent 'scandal':

> 'Don't you read the papers?' 'No.' 'Then what do you read?' 'Books.' 'Well … it will be on the … TV news tonight.' 'I don't see TV either.'
>
> (Ibid. 59)

The first sign of authenticity came when she asked for his help: 'with a strange authority in her voice, she demanded: "If you really want to help me then get me out of school. I cannot go back. I am too ashamed, and I shall really kill myself next time"' (ibid.). This sounds like a sincere communication from someone who feels at the very end of her ability to cope, but who is ready to risk believing that Khan might just possibly want to help her without taking her over. This was a moment of 'speaking' coming out of 'showing', with just a tiny amount of 'talking' to connect them. It suggests that a therapeutic alliance is potentially possible.

Khan acquiesced to her request, but told her to instruct him as to how he should 'get her out of school', to which she replied – with a statement rather than a question – '"Are you a fool. Ring the headmistress and tell her you are advising me not to return to school. And ring my father and tell him you have done it"' (ibid. 60). He asserted his authority, then and there in the session, by speaking first to her father on the telephone and only then to the headmistress, telling them, quite accurately, that he had now 'seen' Judy and agreed with her decision. Khan checked for the signs of triumph which would indicate that he had been manipulated; he detected no such signs, and she now pulled her sleeves down over her wrists, suggesting that she realised that Khan has 'seen' how desperate she was.

Judy thus 'showed' Khan her problems in this first meeting. Her pseudo-seductive style of dress suggests a warily provocative attitude towards the adult world, and she made sure he saw that she had recently been desperate enough to cut her wrists. Khan met Judy by supporting her autonomy and accepting her rudeness as a symptom rather than at face value. However, he maintained his own authority as well as protecting her father's proper position. He comes over as a benign and authoritative father-figure, enabling Judy to contact her neediness and build a modicum of trust.

That first session lasted two hours, leaving Khan 'exhausted', which gives an idea of the power of Judy's emotions. She seemed to have little sense of her own identity but knew that she did not find school a supportive environment. Khan recognised her need for a space in which to find herself. He returned the trust she had tentatively placed in him by allowing an extended weekend before the next session rather than rushing to offer her an immediate follow-up.

Khan saw Judy as someone in close contact with 'madness', the as-yet unknown scenario from early childhood at which her disturbance commenced. He clearly did not see the current situation, distressing as it sounds, as sufficient to explain Judy's state of mind; a psychologically healthy teenager would not have attempted suicide, or related to him so provocatively. Khan took the view that therapeutic sessions alone would not be enough, telling her father that she required 'management' more than psychotherapy as such (ibid.). Without school to structure her days and living in the family context in which she had become disturbed, he believed a supportive overall environment to be a basic necessity for Judy, with sessions with him as an adjunct. He was relying on the normal developmental processes becoming reinstated as the distortions were understood and resolved through sessions with him. Preparing to organise her new therapeutic environment, he invited the two people most concerned with Judy's welfare to come to their next meeting – the physician who had referred her to him, and Judy's father. We might have expected him to tell Judy that he was doing this first, but in fact she found out from her father and may have felt reassured that the adults were prepared to work together on her behalf without asking her permission. Khan was able to inform her of this arrangement before the meeting when she phoned to ask if she could bring a 'girl-friend' with her. This would be unusual for an adult, but more customary for an adolescent; Khan readily agreed.

The most important element of the first meeting was the intense countertransference Khan described. After the session he felt acutely self-critical, with terrible self-doubt, agonising over whether he ought to find out the nature of the scandal or wait until Judy herself could tell him. In the end, he seems to have given in to temptation and asked the physician what the scandal was about, telling the reader that it was indeed very degrading and humiliating for Judy, and would remain in the public eye for a considerable period.

Khan's preliminary assessment was that Judy was 'mad', in the sense that her behaviour, manner and presentation suggested she was in touch with the original, primitive psychic level at which her relationship with herself and her mother had started to go wrong; above this, she had learned hysterical ways of manipulating others. He thought that the madness itself was not the beginning of her pathology: it hid 'an ungraspable psychic pain … which she could neither experience as such nor speak about' (ibid. 61). In addition to her madness, Khan deemed Judy's 'bossiness' to stem from feeling 'utterly resourceless … and desperately needy of help' (ibid.). We might question whether Judy was in fact in touch with her mad point at the beginning of treatment, though she certainly became so later.

Khan's feelings of doubt and inadequacy prompted him to question whether she should be working with someone medically qualified. To his relief, the second meeting turned out to be constructive, however, and a containing structure was arranged: Judy would study with a tutor for two hours a day, help out in her friend Linda's shop for half a day a week and attend a session with

Khan five evenings a week. Her father agreed to arrange for a car to drive her everywhere, as she felt too afraid and self-conscious to use any other form of transport.

From talking to telling

Over the next few months Judy moved from 'showing' to 'talking', and eventually to 'telling'. She 'showed' Khan that one of her main defences was self-harm: apart from cutting her wrists, she also injured her elbow. Khan suggested that this was her way of 'coping with her ungraspable psychic pain and physically localizing it' (ibid. 63); apparently such injuries had been a feature of Judy's life since she was five. Judy also 'told' Khan that she was unable to leave home or see friends, and that she could only eat if 'Daddy is there. He makes me eat' (ibid. 64). Khan dealt with this situation at a practical as well as an immediate emotional level by arranging for Linda to take her out to lunch each day, with Judy's father paying for them both.

Khan guessed, correctly, that she also stole, apparently small items from a shop that received considerable income, it is implied, from the family business; making sure that Khan knew this presumably allayed her guilt. Judy's eating inhibition must have been intermittent, or else alternated with compulsive eating, as she was a plump girl. Feeding problems demonstrate early disturbance, including a sense of being deprived, with which stealing is consistent (Winnicott 1984). Judy stole whenever there was an item in the media about the scandal, and Khan inferred that stealing allowed her 'a private unknowable secret that she can live with' (Khan 1989b: 65), rather, perhaps, than secrets from her past which she could not 'live' with – echoed by the 'scandal'. Khan continued to be receptive to Judy's overt and covert communications, providing the empathic presence in which his own authority was combined with support for her autonomy.

So far, there had been no word of Judy's mother. Khan mentioned that there is a 'vociferously intrusive [female] relative, who kept ringing … to tell "all"' (ibid. 66) – reminding us of the 'secret'; but this relative turns out not to be the mother. The implication is that this 'telling all' would have been more in the nature of a controlling action than a useful communication, and Khan had no hesitation in declining the offer: 'I didn't want to know anything that Judy couldn't tell or speak' (ibid.).

Although there was some 'telling' over this period, the main level of communication was 'chitter-chatter', at the level of 'talking': 'she talked about and around herself, and not from and of herself' (63). Khan was happy to allow this to continue so that the therapeutic alliance could strengthen and grow. Unlike Bion, he was relying a great deal on the overall holding structure to provide Judy with stability and safety, to enable her to integrate the insights developed with his help; and whereas Bion's interpretations were central, Khan's were minimal. In his opinion, the 'most palpable and yet unspeakable psychic pain in her was masked by a myriad of little demands and stealing. This derived, I had surmised, from the traumatic and tantalizing deprivation of maternal love and care' (ibid.), for which her father had attempted to compensate by over-indulgence. All the same, Khan saw Judy as a 'very alert, sensitive, healthy person, with a madness inside her, which circumstances over the past years had dislocated into hysterical antics and manipulativeness' (ibid. 64). This seems to be the more accurate diagnosis: Judy had madness 'inside' her, but did not have continual 'direct access' to it.

Telling and speaking

Around the second month Judy told Khan that she had not realised she was seeing him because she was ill. She worried about how much the treatment was costing her father – the first indication of concern for anyone else. Whereas 'talking' involves a subject alone, 'telling' also needs an object to 'hear' what is told, and Judy had now become aware of Khan, her father and by extension herself, as persons. Evidently she wanted to make use of the sessions, and asked Khan to tell her what she should say. Instead of turning the question back to her – which she would have scorned as a 'psychoanalyst's trick' – Khan enquired about her sleeping problems, which her physician had told him of. Judy reacted furiously at the breach of confidentiality, and this break into genuine emotion ushered in overwhelming grief: 'Now I have lost everything except Dad. Tim is dead, and the country house has been sold' (ibid. 66). 'Tim' turned out to be her pony, who had died some years previously, while the loss of the family's country house had deprived Judy of respite from her London life. Khan recognised that the level of work had changed: 'now I would be encountering the ill Judy, and not the one who had come with the alibi of the "scandal"' (ibid. 65). Judy was beginning to communicate authentically.

The most important material concerns Judy's pony. Her father had given Tim to her when she was five, aware that she was already significantly disturbed since she related to no-one in the large household apart from himself and the butler. Tim died when she was twelve. Throughout his life, Khan suggested, she had cared for him as she would like to have been cared for, writing him stories and drawing him pictures. Tim was not an entirely separate creature in her eyes – 'one could say that Tim was Judy's transitional object' (ibid. 67) – and this was reflected in her need to be physically close to him. When her father discovered that she was sleeping in Tim's stable he went to the length of building a stable onto the house, so that Judy could sleep near Tim but in her own bed. Khan gathered that even as a small, unhappy child she had been capable of unusual care and compassion – suggesting that she had received responsive as well as inadequate maternal care – and he noticed that her symptoms abated as she talked about Tim. Perhaps the level of 'telling' also involved some 'speaking', direct communication from the undefended self, which is therapeutic in itself, especially with a sensitive listener to 'hear' what was told.

There was also a dream, which terrified Judy so much that she phoned Khan at 2 a.m. to tell him of it; she was on the 'critical list' of patients who could phone him at any time.

> She is walking in the street. Suddenly she hears a voice shouting, 'Look out or you will fall into the pit.' She looks up and sees her mother with her typical sardonic smile, standing in front of her.
>
> (Ibid. 67)

The dream conveys a sense of an unresponsive and even cruel mother-figure, with catastrophe hinted at in 'the pit' and the accompanying terror. The therapeutic relationship was clearly developing, but Khan restrained himself from offering interpretations. In his view, this would have brought the attention back to himself, interrupting the gradual growth of Judy's trust in him and in her own thoughts and feelings. Judy herself slowed things down by returning to 'chitter-chatter'.

Shortly after this session an angry row erupted between Judy and the 'nosey relative', who had tried and failed to make her dress up for an evening out. Judy went off defiantly in jeans with her indulgent father. Directly after recounting this to Khan she announced that she wanted to talk about her mother. Khan was anxious that it was too soon to explore such highly charged material, but there was little he could do to prevent it. The main dynamic between Judy and her mother appeared to be unspecified highly tantalizing behaviour. This reflects Khan feeling tantalized by not knowing what the scandal was, and passing the same sense on to readers by withholding significant details such as the nature of the scandal, the identity of the 'nosey relative' and almost anything about Judy's mother.

We do now learn, however, that as a child Judy had been violently mistreated by her mother: when Judy was eight her mother had hit her so hard with a stick that her arm had been broken. The mother would follow up such assaults by buying Judy expensive presents, but with no connection with what Judy might actually want. This extreme behaviour suggests that the mother must herself have been very disturbed. The father clearly failed to protect Judy, instead pandering to her whims and setting few clear boundaries.

At this point in the work a childhood friend, now a glamorous, 'jet-setting' young woman, came on the scene. Where Judy would probably have avoided her a few months earlier, she now 'took to her with a manic passion' (ibid. 69) – presumably to divert herself from depression. The two young women went out on the town with a vengeance, sometimes staying out all night. With the father away and despite Khan's remonstrations, the 'nosey relative' then forced Judy to have an intra-uterine device fitted to prevent pregnancy. Judy acquiesced in this, returning to the childlike passivity with which she had endured her mother's mistreatment, but becoming ill and white with shock. Her physical pain was so severe that the IUD had to be taken out, another intrusive procedure, during which Judy's uterus was damaged and became infected. The resulting extreme pain could only be partially treated because of the addictive nature of the medication used to control it. Her mental state continued to deteriorate. Khan realised at this point that the setting organised for Judy was no longer adequate. He arranged for her to enter into a hospital of his choosing, in effect handing over her care to medical professionals. She became fearful and paranoid, however, especially towards the matron (whom she presumably connected with her mother), and ran away from the hospital one night. She was returned home, where Khan visited her daily. Her delusions continued, culminating in her setting her nightdress on fire – recalling the fire which destroyed the country house, her refuge. The regression was now clearly out of hand, and together with the physician, her father and the hospital psychiatrist, Khan called in another psychiatrist who specialised in treating psychiatric problems with physical methods – presumably drugs, narcosis and/or ECT. This ended Judy's symptoms, but not her madness. Although she was no longer hallucinating, 'The girl I saw now was quietly herself and mad' (ibid. 71) – something which we can certainly agree with. Without hallucinations Judy had, it seems, direct access to the confused, fragmented and distraught state of mind of the original trauma. If she could progress from there, she would have a chance of building a new, authentic life for herself through speaking, and then living, from a genuine rather than a defensive self-organisation.

It is interesting to note that Khan had little hesitation in using physical methods in such an extreme situation. Although physical methods alone cannot 'cure' madness, they may enable the symptoms of psychosis to be managed. If Judy's treatment had ended there, her personality would not have matured and she would quite possibly have broken down again and again, like many psychiatric patients. The holding structure was therefore now more important than ever. Judy asked Khan if he would arrange with her father for her to go to live in the country, away from London. 'She was strangely, passively alert and awake' (ibid.), Khan recalled, and remembered little of her time in hospital. However, her request showed that she knew what she needed in order to recover and had shed her previous refractory defences. Additionally, her transference to Khan was not such that she was unwilling to be parted from him – he had succeeded in making the framework as a whole the main therapeutic vehicle, rather than himself alone.

By an extraordinary coincidence, an aunt of Judy's was visiting the family from her ranch in Argentina. Hearing about the horses, people and life at the ranch, Judy was keen to go there. Although this meant discontinuing her sessions, Khan agreed, continuing to give priority to the holding environment and to Judy's choices. Judy stayed at the ranch for three years, writing to Khan briefly but regularly. We do not hear anything specific of this correspondence until Khan tells us of a letter in which she asked him to find her a book on 'horse language'. She could not understand what a foal was telling her, she said, and Khan wondered if her delusions might be returning.

A few months after this letter, Judy returned to London. She had grown up a good deal and presented as a well-balanced, 'almost pretty' young woman: 'her eyes were quietly vigilant and alert … she was discreetly trusting and relating' (ibid. 74). There were no signs of her eating difficulties, nor of the delusions Khan had feared – and she had discovered meditation. Judy had decided, after a good deal of research, that she would like to follow a spiritual path and go to an ashram (retreat) in India which taught the style of meditation she had learned from a friend at the ranch. Khan realised that this would provide further structured space away from her family to continue recovering and growing up.

By another gross coincidence, Khan himself knew of this ashram and felt quite happy about Judy going there. The session during which all this was discussed lasted five hours, and Judy left with Khan's confidence that she would make good use of her time at the ashram. She was to inherit a large sum of money at the end of the seven-year course, and she planned to use this to develop a centre for children and adolescents who would benefit more from working with horses and learning crafts than following a conventional education. She had come across something similar in Argentina which enabled her to plan this in some detail; it sounded like the kind of setting she herself had needed at the time of her breakdown. As a young adult, therefore, her aim was to offer other young people the means to re-orient their lives that had only become available to her through the modified psychoanalytic treatment she had received.

Summary

Judy's treatment was not psychoanalysis or psychotherapy as normally practised, but the overseeing of a series of care regimes for an adolescent whose childhood development had been badly disrupted. The kernel of this provision was a stable and trusting therapeutic relationship, which extended into specially arranged environments where she was appreciated for who she was. These settings embodied what had been missing from her relationships with her parents: basic responsiveness and appropriate boundaries and demands. We have come to understand that, as Khan stated, her family environment 'could not *provide* her with the idiom with which she could *speak* herself' (ibid. 87) – there was no relaxed and habitual space, and no close relationships, within which her voice could be heard and her communications understood. Instead of following her own developmental path, she grew up defending against the trauma and neglect she had been subjected to, drawn into the 'secondary gains' of the over-indulgence which both parents had offered in attempts at compensation. By adolescence she had developed a persona which was not so much 'false' as confused to the point of desperation. A core of integrity had developed through some responsive care she must also have experienced in infancy, which probably contributed to the 'tantalizing' quality of the 'unspeakable psychic pain'. Judy's rediscovery of her 'good' mother was represented in the care she had lavished on her pony, Tim. The overall therapeutic task was to help her establish a relationship of confidence and respect, and then to assist her in arranging situations in which she could live authentically, constructively, settings which included an 'idiom', or ways of being, that she could use to further her own development.

From the start, it was clear to Khan that she needed 'therapeutic care' rather than standard therapeutic sessions. His first task was therefore to engage with her in a relaxed and open-ended way until a relationship of trust had been established. Once the essential distortions in her psyche had been understood and her development set on a healthier path, Judy's own sense of what she needed was sufficient to guide the treatment. Her breakdown appeared to be a return to the inchoate trauma of her original infantile 'privation'[9] – the unspeakable loss that held a tantalizing quality: it was the turning-point in her development. Once her psychotic symptoms had been brought under control, she could enter into a new environment more in tune with her needs and inclinations. She found what was offered at her aunt's ranch inspiring, and drew on it to make a life-plan for herself. The next stage was apprenticeship at the ashram.

Khan's sensitivity is evident in his remark that 'ailments of Judy's type ... are really growing pains of the self and the soul' (ibid. 78); this reflects his belief that what such patients need most is time and space in which to develop in their own way, and without external impingements. He almost always took the cue in the treatment from Judy's own wishes, in the belief that patients hold their own 'self-cure' within. The study also demonstrates Khan's pragmatic use of conventional psychiatry as a way of treating symptoms but without such interventions being confused with the treatment of the condition as a whole.

The most curious aspect of the study is the absence of Judy's mother, although she clearly played a crucial part in Judy's infantile disturbance, and seems at least to have been alive during the time of Judy's treatment with Khan. There is also the 'interfering/intrusive female relative' whom Khan was always trying to keep at bay. Her father seemed to play the part of seductive but ineffectual protector, giving Judy whatever she wanted in a loving if unbounded way. Judy herself had the basic health to choose wisely for herself: she brought an appropriate friend to the meeting at which her first framework was organised, asked to leave London for her aunt's ranch, and knew when to move on and where to. Khan's guiding principles were first to reach Judy at progressively deeper emotional levels, and then to arrange whatever was required to help her hidden self emerge and evolve.

This is a fascinating account of one way of working with adolescent breakdown, where the holding environment is as important as the psychotherapeutic sessions: although the environment appears to take priority, it was predicated on Khan's insight and guidance. This case study demonstrates the acuity and sensitivity of his perception and his willingness to improvise, both clinically and theoretically. For him, the touchstone of therapy is authenticity, his own and the patient's.

We do not hear of any further contact after the seven-year apprenticeship at the ashram and we are left with the impression that Judy's life continued without further crises. Even if it did not, however, this episode illustrates healthy maturation from a severe adolescent crisis. In the case of further outbreaks of madness in later life, Judy would be in the best possible position to make use of psychotherapeutic or even simply personal help, based on a trust of the self rather than an over-dependence on others.

Khan's interventions allowed Judy to experience, as might a baby, a temporary 'experience of omnipotence' (Winnicott 1962a: 57): an appropriate nurturing environment which together with the ordinary developmental processes could release the therapeutic potential of the treatment. At a critical point in the work, for example, when she left the UK for Argentina, he prioritised the setting over sessions with him. By then, the overall environment could carry the sense of the therapeutic relationship within it, whilst also allowing Judy to draw from these what she needed to build a life of her own. By the same token, Khan was anxious for Judy to avoid spending long periods of time in hospital, or at the home in which her difficulties had originated. The hospital would inevitably have elicited from her the identity of 'psychiatric patient', with its own 'career path' and severe distortions of the personality, while considerable change would have been needed to render her home situation sympathetic to her needs as an adolescent struggling to find her own way in life. Without Khan's guidance, Judy's father would have been unlikely to welcome her taking long periods of time out of school, or choosing a meditation centre in India over a university place. As it was, Judy was allowed to continue on the highly personal path her upbringing had inducted her into, rather than the conventional route of the upper-class young woman. A love of horses, personal truth and concern for young people in difficulties became the central points of her young adult life, and she used what she had found in herself and her environment to construct the picture of a truly creative future to move into.

Bion and Klein: similarities and differences

These two papers highlight the features of the Kleinian and Independent clinical approaches very distinctly. Bion's focus on the 'here-and-now transference' is acute and continuous. Bion listens for the relational communications in the patient's material, picking up what he was trying to have understood and interpreting it in a way that the patient could make sense of and accept. He makes a few direct mentions of counter-transference responses, and much of his counter-transference is implied in his interpretations, but otherwise we hear nothing about his state of mind.

The paper presents Patient A's progress as resulting from the integration of his split-off relational structures – he becomes able to experience directly feelings and parts of his personality he had previously projected into other figures, internal and external. This is facilitated through the support of Bion's presence, and the interpretations which help him realise, even at an unconscious level, that the twin figure, for example, is no more than a device to reduce anxiety by distorting his perception of reality. Thus he comes to better accept his aggression in particular, which had always terrified him because of his linking destructiveness with faeces – he had lived through the messy illness which had annihilated his sister, threatened his own life and no doubt devastated his parents, all unspeakable terrors for a confused one-year-old. The patient's emotional development progresses from a paranoid-schizoid level, in which he treated Bion as an extension or double of himself, to a depressive position, from which he can recognise Bion as a whole object. The growth of symbolic thought, the vehicle of psychic integration, leads him to perceive people and relationships more clearly and relate in a more sophisticated and mature way. He recognises the Oedipus Complex in its different guises and in different circumstances, while his ability to view things from different perspectives allows him to envisage situations or relationships in which he is not dominant. All these achievements are included in the burst of creativity that brought the depressive position to prominence. Instead of living in the all-or-nothing, two-dimensional world of the paranoid-schizoid position, he gained entry to the nuances of the three-dimensional world of relationships between equals as well as with those in authority.

Khan, on the other hand, speaks little of split-off or projected ego structures or the transference figures he becomes for Judy: his theoretical contribution concerns Freud's new ways of using speech in psychoanalysis. His reflection on 'talking, telling and speaking' appears to have occurred to him during his work with Judy rather than as a carefully developed proposition. New theoretical ideas may have arisen for him with each therapeutic situation, making his work with every patient a fresh opportunity to revise his psychoanalytic – or psychotherapeutic – understanding. This is very different from the more systematic use of theory by Kleinians. Khan's main aim for Judy was not for her to build a detailed awareness of her inner world but to make an authentic connection with him, and thereby others, which included the relational elements she had missed out on; this would enable her to progress psychologically in her own way.

As with a number of Winnicott's and Khan's 'therapeutic care' patients, the work with Judy involved 'regression to dependence'. This is regression to the point of absolute helplessness, where the psychotherapist takes responsibility for the ordinary matters of external life, leaving the patient to 'live' her regression as deeply as she needs to. Few people manage to allow this level of trust – Khan, for one, did not – but Winnicott and then Khan saw this as the treatment of choice for pathologies in which the 'True Self' is lost sight of. Khan's first aim was to provide Judy with the supportive relationship and environment which she would need to relax her defences and so return to her point of madness.

His interventions allowed her to have, as might a baby, a temporary 'experience of omnipotence' (ibid. 57): an appropriate, nurturing environment which, combined with the ordinary developmental processes, released the therapeutic potential of the treatment. She could then start to build a more authentic self. Regression was not for its own sake: throughout the work, we see Khan helping

Judy maintain whatever ego strengths she could keep hold of – from when he expected her to phrase the request to the headmistress, to when she finally departed for India. When she broke down, the care he was able to arrange was 'good enough' rather than perfect, so that she could add in her own modifications. Her recovery gathered pace when she asked first to live somewhere out of London and then, more specifically, on her aunt's South American ranch. Although this precluded sessions with Khan, their relationship was by then sufficiently established for her to retain him as a figure in her mind.

The work with Judy goes some way to meeting obvious criticisms of Khan's approach – that it was too gratifying to the patient, that he made concrete connection with the therapist too seductive to resist and thus interfered with the patient's autonomy. These might well have been risks with less skilful and sensitive analysts, but Khan was alert to signs of manipulation in the first session, and he would surely have had no hesitation in dealing with it directly. But the study also suggests that when Judy reached a genuine connection with the roots of her madness, this brought with it a sense of her own best interests. She knew where she needed to live in order to continue her recovery, and made good use of what was available to her. It was Judy's first breakdown and she had not yet developed the identity of 'psychiatric patient' that Khan was so concerned for her to avoid. It is difficult to imagine that without Khan's interventions Judy would have managed to mature successfully: Khan was able to follow her wishes, encompassing them within his own more extended understanding. Without Khan's guidance, moreover, Judy's father would have been unlikely to welcome her taking long periods of time out of school, or choosing a meditation centre in India over a university place. However, he was able to go along with Khan's plans for Judy, and thus Judy's for herself.

How would Bion's patient have fared with Khan as an analyst, and how would Judy have managed with Bion? It is not easy to envisage either of these situations, given how closely in each case the work was built around the patient's needs, but it is especially hard to imagine Judy with Bion. Judy could well have been intimidated by Bion's approach, which could have led to an entrenchment of her defences. She does not come over as someone with a close interest in her own inner world – she was too busy fighting with the external world, and then making use of what was available in it. However, this may not be a fair comparison, since Bion did not work with children and adolescents. If he had come across a 'Judy', he might well have used an entirely different approach – as he did, for example, with the traumatised soldiers in his 'Northfields Experiment', where he designed a therapeutic community specifically around their needs (see Chapter 4). It is easier to imagine Bion's patient with Khan, since Khan described working with a number of hopeless, despondent and 'stuck' middle-aged men who went on to 'come alive' under his personal care. Patient A might have improved with Khan, but he would not have developed the acute insight into himself that he did with Bion; though nor, for that matter, would a patient of Bion's have been likely to develop in the idiosyncratic way that some of Khan's patients did.

While both show acute and accurate empathy with their patients, Bion relies on attention to detail in the patient's material, while Khan's style is more broad-brush and intuitive. One can imagine him knowing how to respond to a patient at an emotional level before being able to explain it, whereas Bion is only too aware when his interpretations are even slightly askew. Judy was able to improve without such close attention to detail and drew intelligently on her various environments: changes in Patient A's environment would only have confused him. Just as insight would have formed part of Khan's aims for Judy, so increased authenticity would have formed part of Bion's aims for Patient A; both, however, would have seen them as secondary to their central focus.

Conclusion

One essential distinguishing mark between the Kleinian and Independent forms of practice is what is treated as the vehicle of containment. For Kleinians, it is the analytic setting, with its regular, consistent and relatively frequent sessions, the stability of the meeting time and space and, most of all, the insightful receptivity of the therapist. With these consistently available, the maximum freedom is allowed within the containing structure for the living-out and working-through of issues in the transference; this leads to their gradual understanding and acceptance, and thus to changes in the patient's assumptions and behaviour. The analytic setting is the structural component of the container, and the attuned presence of the therapist the emotional component.

For Independent practitioners, by contrast, the crucial factor is the personality of the analyst, together with the intuitive ability to improvise, so that the setting is fitted to the patient rather than the patient learning to manage the setting. The analyst or therapist bears the responsibility of providing the unique setting or kind of responsiveness needed by the patient to develop psychologically on the basis of his true or authentic self.

Both Kleinian and Independent approaches depend on a combination of self-understanding and emotional maturity in the analyst. The essential change that must take place is in the psyche of the patient, and the central factor facilitating this is in that of the psychotherapist.

Kleinian practitioners and thinkers reach after an ever more detailed and comprehensive understanding of the self, its parts and its objects – seeing every person as a unique manifestation of a universal human psyche, as did Freud. Independent practitioners strive for their own hard-won vision. Rather than focusing on developing further their own model of the psyche, they see this as evolving from the innumerable individual responses drawn out of the sensitive practitioner by each particular patient. For them, there can be no set picture of the human being: alongside, and beneath the common themes, there can only be ambiguity, paradox, question marks.

Apart from their fundamental divergences, the differences between the two approaches are shades rather than rifts, with Kleinians showing imagination in their thinking as much as Independents do rigour. Their respective beliefs provide directions which guide their work. *An Introduction to Object Relations* described the work of pioneers, from Klein and Fairbairn to Winnicott and Balint, placing the work of each analyst in the context of his or her life experience. This book takes up where the *Introduction* left off,[10] exploring the work of a few of the most significant of the next generation of analysts. Traversing the terrains of Kleinian and Independent thought, we can see that these two approaches can continue to develop, separately and to some extent together. Individual Kleinian formulations, such as the concepts of psychical positions and projective identification, have long since been taken up by many different approaches, including the Independents; and Independent ideas such as transitional objects, Green's 'dead mother complex' and Ogden's 'analytic third' are just a few of the many which could also be taken up by other practitioners, including Kleinians. While Independents may have learned to pay closer attention to the transference/counter-transference sphere, Kleinians may now allow more space for other factors.

Yet not all BPAS members define themselves as Kleinian, or Independent, or Contemporary Freudian. Some simply refer to themselves as 'members of the British Psychoanalytical Society'. They hold the assumption that, barring the few points at which they cannot meet, current Object Relations approaches do not have to cancel each other out. The British Society has its own characteristic form of object-relational thinking, shaping the thinking and approach of all British psychoanalysts and psychoanalytic psychotherapists. Perhaps the 'Controversial Discussions' of the 1940s can be followed by ongoing dialogue in the twenty-first century, without avoiding the conflicts and passions which are central to psychoanalysis, but communicating across the divisions.

Notes

1 'Psychoanalytic cure is in direct proportion to the cherishing love given by the psychoanalyst to the patient' (Ferenczi and Rank, 1912).
2 Balint (1968) contrasts the 'benign regression' of the patient who can make good use of flexibility on the part of the therapist with the 'malignant regression' of the patient who cannot. For these individuals, the therapist may continually 'stretch' the frame, but satisfaction never comes to them because they are unable to make use of interventions, symbolically; thus they attach to the therapist with an ever-tightening grip, convinced that to let go means to drown in deprivation.
3 Bion makes a convincing case that these two systems do indeed progress in concert – examples include the increase of oral aggression (the urge to 'bite') in the same period as that in which the teeth come through (the second half of the first year), and the readiness for sexual exploration at puberty.
4 John Keats coined this term in 1817. In a letter to his brothers he wrote that Shakespeare, in particular, possessed it in abundance: 'when Man is capable of being in uncertainties, mysteries, doubts, without any irritable reaching after facts and reason.'
5 Amytal sodium (amobarbital) is a barbiturate, sometimes used in the twentieth century as a 'truth serum' as well as a sedative, since it lessened inhibition. It was sometimes used in criminal cases as well as therapeutically.

6 In this section there is a female patient and male analyst. The general use of 'he' for infants and patients and 'she' for parents and therapists is reversed, to avoid the misunderstandings which would inevitably arise.
7 See Chapter 6 for details on these points.
8 Freud added free association to 'telling', with the patient saying, from whatever level, anything that comes into his mind and the analyst listening with 'free-floating attention' for the underlying themes and conflicts.
9 Winnicott highlights the difference between 'privation', which denotes an original absence of expected provision, and 'deprivation', meaning the withdrawal of a provision that had previously been given.
10 The questions left at the end of the *Introduction to Object Relations*, such as what the basic human unit might be, are not discussed here since they are taken up in some detail in *The Freud Wars* (2005). A summary of this book is given in the Appendix.

References

Alexander, F. (1957) *Psychoanalysis and Psychotherapy*, London: George Allen and Unwin.

Alexander, F., French, T., et al. (1980/1946) *Psychoanalytic Therapy: Principles and Application*, Nebraska: University of Nebraska Press, first published in New York: Ronald Press.

Balint, M. (1968) *The Basic Fault: Therapeutic Aspects of Regression*, London: Tavistock.

Bion, W. (1950) 'The Imaginary Twin', in *Second Thoughts* (1984).

——— (1984a) *Second Thoughts*, London: Karnac.

——— (1984b) 'Commentary', in *Second Thoughts* (London: Karnac).

Breuer, J. and Freud, S. (1895) *Studies on Hysteria*, S.E.2.

Ferenczi, S. and Rank, O. (2012) *The Development of Psycho-Analysis*, Eastford, CT: Martino Fine Books. First published 1924, New York: The Nervous and Mental Disease Publishing Co.

Freud, S. (1917) 'Fixation to Traumas – the Unconscious', in *Introductory Lectures on Psycho-Analysis* S.E.16: 273–285.

Hopkins, L. (2006) *False Self: The Life of Masud Khan*, New York: Other Press.

Joseph, B. (1985) 'Transference: The Total Situation', in M. Feldman and E. Bott Spillius eds, (2005) *Psychic Equilibrium and Psychic Change: Selected Papers of Betty Joseph*, London: Routledge, 156–157.

Khan, M. (1986) *The Privacy of the Self*, London: Hogarth.

——— (1989) *Hidden Selves*, London: Karnac.

Klein, M. (1952) 'The Origins of Transference', in *Envy and Gratitude and Other Works* (1988), London: Virago.

Little, M. (1985) *Psychotic Anxieties and Containment: A Personal Record of an Analysis with Winnicott*, Northvale, NJ and London: Jason Aronson.

Segal, H. (1986) *The Work of Hanna Segal*, London: Free Association Books.

——— (2006) in *American Imago* 63, No. 3, Fall: 283–292.

——— (2007a) *American Imago* 64, No. 1, Spring: 121–124.

——— (2007b) *Yesterday, Today and Tomorrow*, London and New York: Routledge.

Winnicott, D. (1959) 'Review of *Envy and Gratitude*', in *Psychoanalytic Explorations* (1989: 443–446), London: Karnac.

——— (1962a) 'Ego Integration in Child Development', in 1982: 56–63.
——— (1962b) 'The Aims of Psycho-Analytical Treatment', in 1982: 166–170.
——— (1962c) 'A Personal View of the Kleinian Contribution', in 1982: 171–178.
——— (1963a) 'The Development of the Capacity for Concern', in 1982: 73–82.
——— (1963b) 'Psychiatric Disorder in Terms of Infantile Maturational Processes', in 1982: 230–241.
——— (1971) 'Dreaming, Fantasying and Living: A Case-History Describing a Primary Dissociation', in *Playing and Reality*, London: Tavistock Books.
——— (1982) *The Maturational Processes and the Facilitating Environment: Studies in the Theory of Emotional Development*, London: Hogarth Press, first published 1965.
——— (1984) *Deprivation and Delinquency*, London and New York: Tavistock.

Appendix

Foundations for psychoanalysis

This appendix is a summary of my second book, *The Freud Wars: An Introduction to the Philosophy of Psychoanalysis* (2005). This has been mentioned several times in this book, and an outline of its arguments may be of interest to some readers. *The Freud Wars* looks back to the questions left at the end of *An Introduction to Object Relations*. Both Object Relations and psychoanalysis depend on Freud's concept of the unconscious, and neither can do without it. The essential question is therefore how we account for Freud's 'unconscious': is it a physical or a mental concept? In everyday language, does this concept, and psychoanalysis itself, belong to the empirical world of science or the interpretative world of the humanities?

Categories of knowledge

In Western traditions of thought, subject matter has long been divided into two categories: the physical and the mental, or that which can be looked at and understood from the outside, and that which can only be approached from the inside. Until the nineteenth century, 'science' was held to mean 'knowledge' as a whole; it is only since then that, in everyday thinking, the term 'science' has been confined to the 'empirical' sciences, separating it from the 'humanities'.

This division reflects the mind/body, subjective/objective distinction: matter cannot be experienced personally, and subjective reality cannot be fully described or understood from an external perspective. Additionally, the idea of cause and effect is different for each category. In 'common-sense' or 'everyday' psychology – the assumptions we live by in ordinary life – our notion of 'science' sees reality as composed of identical particles, organised on the principle of determinism. According to this, each and every event is the inevitable result of a specific cause, which then becomes the cause of the next event; thus all events and objects have their place in a perpetual and immutable causal chain.

In 'common-sense' psychology again, human beings are differentiated from the rest of the world (barring perhaps some of the 'higher' animals) by being attributed free will, or autonomy – as being the independent cause of their own actions. We assume that, rather than being trapped within the inevitable chain of cause and effect, human beings can choose to go against temptation or inclination, even under severe pressures such as fear or hunger. This implies that the subjective aspect of ourselves, the mind, is based on personal rather than mechanical principles. We see ourselves as beings holding values which inform our choices, rather than being enslaved to any causal force.

The empirical approach to knowledge can be termed 'physicalistic', and involves identifying and analysing the (sometimes extremely complex) chains of cause and effect. The 'mentalistic' approach rests on subjective understanding: we cannot understand why someone performs a certain action, or experiences a particular emotion, unless his reason for doing so makes sense to us if we put ourselves in his position. This kind of explanation applies to cultural, literary and artistic subjects – the subjects which explore the world of the mind.

The only apparent anomalies are the social sciences, which study group behaviour from an empirical point of view. Whereas the actions and responses of individuals have to be understood at a personal level, group events or tendencies can be understood objectively, in a way which is closer to natural events: for example, the correlation between household income and voting intention can be measured in much the same way as the link between certain months and the likelihood of rain. This is because human beings, like all animals, have a core of biological determinism around which personal autonomy develops. Predictive tests of group behaviour can be made which centre on this biological communality, where they cannot be made of individuals; and with predictive tests come 'conjectures and refutations', Karl Popper's widely accepted definition of the approach of empirical science (Popper 1962). Thus group tendencies, unlike individual impulses, can be viewed from the outside; combined into a single average or range, they are treated in the same way as material events, rather than as a collection of individual thoughts.

In our everyday, 'common-sense' ways of thinking, therefore, all knowledge is based essentially on ways of understanding either the body or the mind.

Psychoanalysis as a special subject

The fundamental question about psychoanalysis has not yet been definitively answered: is it a scientific or a humanities subject, a physicalistic or a mentalistic discipline? That is, is it reducible to matter, or solely to mind? Intriguingly, Freud does not come down fully on either side of this division, but offers a unique resolution. Perhaps his most important and original idea lies in the statement that the task of psychoanalysis is to act 'as an intermediary between biology and psychology' (Freud 1940, S.E.23: 144–145), suggesting a reconciliatory role in an overlapping area. This would make psychoanalysis, the study of psychical reality, unique in being situated in the zone where the physical and the mental coincide. This must be at the centre of any authentic foundation for psychoanalysis.

It could be argued that by definition, such an area cannot exist: perhaps mind and matter can only be defined against each other as alternative hemispheres of knowledge, reality looked at from the inside and from the outside. Freud's assertion rests on there being a way in which they can be seen as continuous with each other – a zone in which each becomes the other. We shall have to provisionally accept the validity of this intermediate zone in order to give Freud a fair hearing.

From its earliest days, psychoanalysis was integrating new epistemological concepts into an overall theory which viewed the mind and the mental as embodied rather than solely abstract. Its central idea, the unconscious, is made up of processes emitting from the psyche, or 'psychic apparatus', and continually proceeding beneath the level of consciousness. These processes have features in common with both the scientific and the subjective views of reality. As with the physical world, we have no immediate access to them so can only learn about them through their effects; yet like subjective experience, they hold personal meaning. Psychical reality differs from both ordinary mental reality, which is conscious, and material reality, which can never become conscious.

Nevertheless, the only way we can understand unconscious psychical processes is by treating them mentalistically, as we do conscious processes:

> if, for instance, we say: 'At this point an unconscious memory intervened', what that means is: 'At this point something occurred of which we are wholly unable to form a conception, but which, if it had entered our consciousness, could only have been described in such and such a way' [i.e. as an 'unconscious' memory].
>
> (Ibid. 197)

By definition, we have no immediate access to unconscious processes, so they have to be explained in terms of another kind of reality – and Freud argues that the closest we can get to them is to ally them with conscious mental processes, for which we have a ready vocabulary.

This might seem to suggest that Freud sees psychoanalysis as a hermeneutic or interpretative discipline, based on the principles and concepts of language, communication and culture. He also argues, however, that the concept of unconscious processes

> explains the supposedly somatic [bodily] concomitant phenomena [of mental processes] as being what is truly psychical, and thus in the first instance disregards the quality of consciousness.
>
> (Ibid. 158)

Freud is saying that psychical processes are not necessarily conscious – we are to 'disregard the quality of consciousness'. We have to presume that conscious mental processes are also physiological processes which we are as yet unable to describe. A moment's thought reveals that this too is an everyday assumption: emotions, impulses and thoughts must have physical aspects – when something is going on in the mind we assume it is also going on in the brain. Otherwise, 'unconscious mental processes' would be a contradiction in terms, located in neither mind nor body. Freud saw psychical processes as the 'supposedly somatic' processes which we presume to be a more complete version of our patchy conscious life.

Psychoanalysis, Freud argues, is concerned with an aspect of the natural world to which we have no direct access. We infer the unconscious nature of the psyche and its functioning through 'observation alone' (Freud 1914, S.E.14: 77) from which, he maintains, all sciences develop: this is his reason for claiming that psychoanalysis is a science, albeit of a very unusual kind. But unlike normal empirical sciences, psychoanalytic knowledge develops through subjective understanding as well as objective reasoning. We need our thinking and reasoning capacities to take an objective view of clinical material and build a theoretical structure of the psyche and its functioning; but personal sensitivity and empathic imagination are also necessary to understand the complex world of the psychoanalytic patient. This takes forward psychoanalytic treatment, which in turn feeds back into the theoretical knowledge informing treatment. Thus psychoanalysis, unlike other subjects, appears to be both mentalistic and physicalistic, hermeneutic and scientific. How can this be possible?

The levels of psychoanalytic theory

Freud's concept of the psychical introduces a third area of reality, between the physical and the mental. Its enigmatic midway position means that it has no language of its own. Psychical reality is neither physical nor conscious, but since we have no way of conceptualising this sphere directly, we have to use either physicalistic or mentalistic terms. The overall theoretical framework of psychoanalysis makes use of both.

Freud presents an 'upper' and a 'lower' theoretical layer of psychoanalysis: the clinical theories and the metapsychology. The clinical theories are the most immediate, and can be deduced directly from material arising in the clinical setting. They include the best known ideas of psychoanalysis, such as transference, repression and resistance. These are unconscious actions or operations, expressed in the 'mentalistic' or first-person terms of subjective reality. However, we know nothing of the disturbing thoughts, emotions and impulses we keep out of consciousness, and it is only when the material they hold breaks through into awareness that we 'recognise' it first-hand.

Underlying the clinical theories are the metapsychological theories and processes, again with an upper and a lower layer. The uppermost layer of the metapsychology states what is necessary for a complete description to be made of the psychical processes formulated in the clinical theories, while the lower layer explains the clinical theories themselves: what has to be the case for the clinical theories to make sense?

Taking the upper level first, Freud sees the psychical processes described in the clinical theories as having three aspects: 'when we have succeeded in describing a psychical process in its dynamic, topographical and economic aspects, we should speak of it as a metapsychological presentation' (1915, S.E.14: 181).

The 'dynamic' aspect of psychical processes is expressed through the principle of defence, which Freud explains as the automatic self-regulation of the psyche: it protects itself from being flooded with psychical energy by operations such as repression, which push particularly disturbing ideas out of reach so that the psyche is not overwhelmed. The 'topographical' aspect of psychical processes describes where they are located in the psyche, or psychic apparatus – in the ego, id or super-ego, and in the conscious, pre-conscious or unconscious systems. The 'economic' aspect, finally, involves viewing them in quantitative terms, expressed through the theory of the drives or instincts. Initially, Freud postulates the ego drives, which serve to protect the individual – hunger and self-protective aggression, for instance – and the sexual drives, which preserve the species itself. Later, however, he develops the Life and Death drives, expressing the pressure towards constructive or destructive ends that all psychical impulses are thought to embody. Psychical processes are made up of different combinations of these contrasting forces. A basic 'metapsychological presentation' of an individual's oedipal conflict, for example, might be the following:

> *The dynamic aspect* is expressed through the defences – here, that would include the repression of feelings which are too morally unacceptable, too conflicting or too intense for the ego to encompass in its current state; for example, erotic yearnings for one parent and extremes of hatred and fear for the other. Further defences, such as splitting and projection, may also be involved. Together, they maintain psychic balance; if they fail to do so, they escape into neurotic or psychotic symptoms which form the starting-point for psychoanalytic treatment.
>
> *The topographical aspect* describes their location. Hatred and fear of the first parent are likely to be partly conscious, so located in the conscious part of the ego. The repressed emotions – excessive hatred and fear of one parent and forbidden yearnings for the other – would be located in the unconscious layer of the ego, fed from the 'seething cauldron' of the id. Guilt, the fear of one's own destructive feelings towards the powerful parent who is also loved, emanates from the superego, the internalisation of the hated and feared figure of one parent, stereotypically the father. The accompanying wish to live out our own values comes from the ego-ideal, the figure we would like to be – stereotypically the mother. The superego and ego-ideal are semi-detached from the ego, helping to maintain a balance between seeking to gratify the drives and meeting the demands of reality.
>
> *The economic aspect* involves the Life and Death drives; the specific energy for the complex and changing oedipal states of mind comes from the ratio of one drive to the other in their ever-changing fusion.

Metapsychological descriptions enable clinical concepts to be fully expressed, but in spatial terms rather than the first-person perspective of the clinical concepts themselves: we speak of an impulse being located in the ego, for example, as if it were a place in the material world. The physicalistic perspective of the metapsychological theories counters the mentalistic perspective of the clinical theories, bringing into doubt the view that psychoanalysis must ultimately be a theory of either mind or matter.

In the absence of scientific or philosophical development, Freud resolves the question of the status of psychoanalysis in a purely conceptual way. At the deepest ('lower') level of the metapsychology are the two 'fundamental hypotheses' and the 'basic assumption' of psychoanalysis. These are what have to be true, in an abstract sense, for the metapsychological models to claim validity. Freud expresses the first fundamental hypothesis as: 'We assume that mental life is the function of an apparatus to which we ascribe the characteristics of being extended in space and of being made up of several portions' (1940, S.E.23: 145). He is saying that psychological processes do not come from an actual physical body, but from an entity, the psyche (or 'psychic apparatus') that we have no alternative but to think of in spatial terms and as divisible into parts. The second fundamental hypothesis brings out the opposite principle: 'The majority of philosophers … declare that the idea of something psychical being unconscious is self-contradictory. But this is precisely what psycho-analysis is obliged to assert, and this is its second fundamental hypothesis' (ibid. 158).

In Freud's time, the term 'psychical' was equated with 'mental' or 'conscious'. Although it was believed that conscious thoughts emerged from something underlying, this was held to be a straightforwardly physical or somatic 'disposition' to produce conscious data. Freud is saying, rather, that underlying the broken patches of conscious mental life there must be continuous processes which are unconscious, subjective and in some way 'somatic', though not in the same way as are normal physiological processes. It is their psychical nature that leads them to be expressed mentalistically and conceptualised physicalistically.

Thus each fundamental hypothesis upholds one side of the physical-mental nature of psyche and its functioning. The final 'basic assumption' of psychoanalysis affirms that logic alone dictates the necessity of the dualistic nature of the psyche and its processes:

> We know two kinds of things about what we call our psyche (or mental life): firstly, its bodily organ and scene of action, the brain (or nervous system) and, on the other hand, our acts of consciousness, which are immediate data and cannot be further explained by any sort of description … Our two hypotheses start from these ends or beginnings of our knowledge.
>
> (Freud 1940, S.E.23: 144–145)

There is no doubt, Freud is maintaining, that mental life is closely connected to both the brain and consciousness: psychoanalysis studies the intermediate area between them. Even today, we have no option but to see the concept of psychical processes as both physicalistic and mentalistic – unconscious, as are ordinary bodily processes, yet holding meaning, like all conscious experience. Freud has pointed out that our everyday mode of thought presupposes the existence of this enigmatic area. Nevertheless, the metapsychology has always been the least accepted aspect of psychoanalytic theory. Even in Freud's own time the death drive, for example, was treated with doubt and disquiet; later, the whole of the metapsychology began to be seen as an optional extra, with a leaning towards seeing psychoanalysis as a hermeneutic or interpretative subject with only mentalistic grounding.

Why abandon the established perspectives?

Our questions turn on whether psychoanalysis ultimately sees psychical reality as mental or physical in nature, scientific or hermeneutic. Since Freud places his central concept not in but between these two categories, we might expect problems whether a scientific or hermeneutic perspective is chosen – and this is indeed the case. These difficulties are illuminated in a heated exchange in *The New York Review of Books* in the mid-1990s (NYRB 1993–1995). The topic under discussion is the validity of psychoanalysis, but since psychoanalysis in the US has traditionally been more scientifically orientated than in the UK, the question actually discussed is whether psychoanalysis is a legitimate science; that it might be a valid subject without being scientific does not seem to occur to any of the contributors. Nevertheless, the two main parties either denounce psychoanalysis altogether or hold it in high esteem.

The initiator of the debate, Frederick Crews (1993), uses the work of the philosopher of science Adolf Grünbaum to construct his case. Grünbaum argues (1984) that psychoanalysis is properly scientific, but only in its method. He does not try to make a case for psychoanalysis being based on biology and he rejects the metapsychology outright. Instead, he bases his claim that psychoanalysis can count as a science purely on its methodology, pointing to a number of its propositions which he asserts are scientifically testable. He declares, for example, that one of the central propositions of psychoanalysis is that trauma results in repression; therefore, if psychoanalysis lifts repression, a cure should always and inevitably come about – and of course it does not. Another instance is Freud's linking of repressed homosexuality and paranoia in the Schreber case (1911, S.E.12). Since homosexuality has become far more socially acceptable than it was in Freud's time, it is reasonable to infer that there is less need for it to be repressed. If this is the case, then again this should lead to an equal diminution in paranoia – which again has not happened. In his view, these hypotheses validate psychoanalysis as a science, but since they have never been met, he concludes it to be a failed or failing science.

The problem with Grünbaum's claim lies in how he views psychoanalytic material. He understands that the strict determinism of the natural sciences could never apply to human actions, so he treats psychoanalysis as a social science. Within this category, human events can be treated in the looser terms of 'probability': a similar validation procedure is used, but can only be applied to groups – and the larger the group, the more reliable the statistical probability. In the examples above, comparison with a control group should demonstrate clearly enough whether or not the links put forward by Grünbaum hold in a significant proportion of cases.

First, however, Grünbaum's examples lie at the margins of psychoanalysis rather than at the centre. Even if they are shown not to hold, the validity of psychoanalysis as a whole and its central tenet, the unconscious, are not affected. Additionally, the philosopher of science Karl Popper argues convincingly that psychoanalysis cannot be treated scientifically because there is no way of setting up predictive tests: psychoanalytic material concerns the interpretation of individual subjectivity rather than the observable tendencies of group behaviour. Another way of putting this is to say that Grünbaum treats human responses objectively, as part of our universal constitutional makeup, while psychoanalysis also treats them subjectively, as part of our individuality. We can see that this comes down, again, to seeing human actions and responses as arising from the body or the mind, and viewing them from the outside or the inside.

If we accept Freud's dictum that psychoanalysis lies between body and mind, biology and psychology, psychoanalytic subject matter cannot be viewed entirely from the outside; nor can the constant causation of empirical science apply. Thus Grünbaum's purely physicalistic foundation is not adequate for psychoanalysis, even if all that is aimed at is to cast it as a failed science.

Taking an entirely mentalistic perspective improves matters, but still leaves problems. *The Freud Wars* examines an influential presentation of psychoanalysis as a 'hermeneutic science', a system of knowledge based on culture and symbol rather than the material world. This is set out in two chapters of *Knowledge and Human Interest* (1971) by the German social philosopher, Jürgen Habermas. He surveys and critiques the forms in which knowledge is organised, all of which he terms 'science'. There is knowledge which derives from a technical perspective, 'empirical science'; personal, subjective knowledge, which he terms 'hermeneutic science'; and a special category of knowledge which offers a continually renewing critique of itself, through examining its own foundations. These are the 'critical sciences', in which Habermas includes philosophy, Marxism and psychoanalysis.

Habermas' presentation of his new conception of psychoanalysis is a bravura performance and convincing in its own terms. However, it entails a cost to psychoanalysis which is unacceptably high. If psychoanalysis is to qualify as a purely interpretative subject, all connections with physicality have to be jettisoned, leaving its concepts hanging in abstraction. Moreover, it cannot count as a study of the human psyche as such, but only of how a particular historical and cultural group conceive of themselves: in common parlance, it reverts from proposed 'fact' to 'opinion'. Without its intermediate psychical status and despite the critical edge that Habermas brings to it as a self-reflective 'science', psychoanalysis appears a less interesting and original mode of thought. Within these limitations the hermeneutic view of psychoanalysis nevertheless holds validity.

An entirely new model for knowledge seems to be required to do justice to our subject. The American philosopher Thomas Nagel appears to introduce just this in his riposte to Grünbaum's work in the NYRB, together with a separate paper on psychoanalysis. Nagel argues convincingly for the importance of psychoanalysis as a 'revolution' in our way of thinking: 'what Freud achieved was a vast expansion of psychological insight, rooted in common-sense psychology and employing some of its concepts, but going far beyond it' (Nagel 1994 in Gomez 2005: 139). For example, the formative nature of early life and the experience and concept of the ego, or 'I', have entered into everyday Western thinking, while the force of the sexual and aggressive drives described by Freud is exploited to the utmost by the advertising industry. Yet Nagel goes on to claim that psychoanalysis can also be seen as a kind of empirical science, using the evidence of 'common-sense psychology' in its explanations. But how can common-sense psychology count as scientific?

In ordinary life, Nagel points out, we depend on being able to understand other people as persons like ourselves, who feel and act for 'reasons', as discussed above. This can be seen as a form of scientific explanation, he asserts, since it is based on causality. However, the form of causality used is not determinism, nor is its mode of validation the experimental method of physical phenomena and normal empirical science. Nor is Nagel an 'eliminative materialist', like Patricia and Paul Churchland, who believe that all mental phenomena can in theory be fully expressed in physical terms, rendering the mental framework and all its terminology obsolete (see Patricia Churchland 1986 and Paul Churchland 1988). Nagel discounts this extreme move: there would always be an experiential factor which goes beyond the physical, such as the taste of chocolate, the feeling of sadness, the thought of tomorrow, which cannot simply either be treated as matter or set aside. Instead, he believes that it is enough to say that physical explanations and mental explanations can coincide, like patterns on a double-sided fabric, without one being reducible to the other:

> A psychological theory need not ... be a rough sketch of the underlying physiological or physical structure. So long as there is no inconsistency at the level of particular causal connections, it may be that both levels of description and explanation can be true, without anything like a reductive relation between them.
>
> (Nagel 1974: 13, in Gomez 2005: 47–48)

Freud's psychical processes are conceived as having two such levels of description and explanation, the material and the mentalistic; or rather, aspects which can only be imagined in material or in mentalistic terms. Thus, Nagel argues, although we have to use the same terms for unconscious and conscious mental processes, we assume that because mental processes as such can be thought of organically as well as mentalistically, they must exist in the same 'objective' way as other organic processes.

It is here that Nagel introduces his most interesting idea. What unites all empirical sciences is the hypothetico-deductive formula, *Law + Conditions = Event to be explained*.[1] Grünbaum has shown that psychoanalysis cannot conform to this principle: the formula only fits physicalistic subject matter, where reality is assumed to be made up of identical particles which can be manipulated arithmetically. This means that only concrete actions can be scientifically tested – and psychoanalysis is overwhelmingly concerned with what can be experienced. Even phenomena such as the ego, projection and regression are conceived mentalistically. If science cannot deal with mentalistic material, how can Nagel's contention help?

Rather than holding the hypothetico-deductive model as his conceptual template, he hopes to work towards a representation of reality in which what is subjective and what is objective can be shown within the same conceptual framework. He disagrees with privileging the physical over the subjective:

> The subjectivity of consciousness is an irreducible feature of reality – without which we would be unable to do physics or anything else – and it must occupy as fundamental a place in any credible world view as matter, energy, space, time and numbers.
>
> (Nagel 1986: 7–8, in Gomez 2005: 34)

A sign of this distant goal appears in our dual use of the adjective 'objective'.

> Objectivity in any area of thought requires some method of confirming or disconfirming the observations or judgements of one individual by reference to those of another. But the particular way we do this for physical data is determined by the nature of those data and should not be identified with objectivity in general.
>
> (Nagel 1995: 88 in Gomez 2005: 36)

We can see, therefore, that Nagel's ultimate aim is not unthinkable. He is imagining a representation of reality based on objectivity in its broadest sense. Although mental and physical phenomena can only be described through their respective conceptual schemes, we assume nevertheless that the reality in which they exist is single and intact. As yet, we can give no unitary account of it; and if we could, it would be in different terms from those we currently use. Nagel is suggesting that, eventually, subjective realities such as time and emotion, might be included in the same conceptual scheme as their physical counterparts. He conjectures that psychoanalysis may be a step in that direction, as may his own work. Until then, however, it is neither a contradiction nor a tautology to say that every mental state is also a corresponding bodily state: they are saying the same thing using different conceptual frameworks.

Nagel proposes taking a third perspective on reality as the basis of theorisation. He terms this 'dual aspect theory', a single category covering both the current viewpoints. This can only develop, he suggests, by taking physical science to a point where it can incorporate mental concepts. His hope is that psychoanalysis, and his own work as well, might eventually lead not just to new theories but to new *kinds* of theory, built around the inclusion of the mental into the material.

However, we should not forget Freud's intriguing 'dual-aspect' concept of the unconscious, composed as it is of unitary processes with psychological and organic 'sides'. Is this the same as Nagel's idea? Might it hold the key to the founding principle that psychoanalysis needs to give it authority as a subject in its own right, without cutting off either its mental or physical roots?

Filling out Freud's foundations

Explicit justification of psychoanalysis

We have seen that Freud positions psychoanalysis and its central concept, the psychical, 'between psychology [the mental] and biology [the physical]' (1913, S.E.13: 182). He does not discuss its conceptual status in detail but there are intermittent thoughts scattered throughout his writings which can be brought together to begin to form some possible foundations for psychoanalysis. These would rest neither on the physicalistic basis of empirical science nor on the mentalistic basis of hermeneutics, but on the psychical basis of the enigmatic yet compelling zone between the two. This area is unconscious yet subjective; holds meaning and is yet embodied. What would such foundations look like?

We can now build up a picture of these foundations. Looking into the context for Nagel's thinking, we find an approach which differs from his dual-aspect theory. Instead of developing either the physical or the mental conceptual sphere, Freud's third perspective goes back to *before* the division is made into mind and body, mental and physical, hermeneutic and empirical. His thinking is original but incomplete, and holds out the promise of a single, coherent psychophysical category: psychical reality. Our foundations are constructed in three stages. First, we investigate and explicate this category; next, we draw out a conceptual framework offering a practical foundation and principle for a unitary concept of psychoanalysis; finally, the practical foundation provides the basis for a theoretical or substantive foundation which can be linked with other conceptual frameworks in a consistent overall system of knowledge. We know that other areas of knowledge do not, at present, need these novel foundations; but without the possibility of extension into other areas, Freud's psychoanalysis would be left conceptually stranded as a one-off oddity.

Apart from Freud's own thoughts, we shall draw on the work of the British philosophers Sebastian Gardner, who specialises in psychoanalysis and the mind, and Peter Strawson, a Professor of Metaphysical Philosophy in the 1950s. Freud, Gardner and Strawson lead us towards a perspective on reality in which psychoanalysis appears as a unique form of enquiry which is philosophically as well as personally innovative. It takes our everyday knowledge of ourselves far deeper in a systematic and authoritative way while illuminating the ground of unity between the empirical sphere of matter and the interpretational world of mind.

Freud's philosophical outlook

Freud's writings contain explicit and implicit foundational (bedrock) elements. He offers a practical vindication of his concept of the dynamic unconscious in common-sense psychological terms, together with indications of his philosophical perspective, or overall view of reality. But everything between the practical vindication and overall perspective is left unsaid. Although he suggests a way of accounting for psychoanalysis in practical terms, he gives no specific foundation for it – no unifying practical or theoretical principles in which to ground it. In this section we shall work towards deducing a practical foundation for psychoanalysis in general, and for his concept of the psychical in particular, which fits with Freud's fragmentary philosophical writing.

Freud's implicit vindication of psychoanalysis consists in the psychophysical unity he places at its heart. Without unconscious mental processes there can be no psychoanalysis, and without a bodily setting there is nowhere for these processes to exist: 'unconscious mental processes' would be a contradiction in terms, like saying 'unconscious conscious processes'. Freud's view of the psychical must be psychophysical through and through.

The reason why Freud did not give an explicit rationale for psychoanalysis is that he saw himself as a scientist rather than a philosopher. In 1938, he declared that 'Psychoanalysis makes a basic assumption [that there are unconscious mental processes], the discussion of which is reserved to philosophical thought but the justification for which lies in its results' (1940, S.E.23: 144–145). He is saying that the practical usefulness of his concept of the psychical is sufficient justification; but we cannot agree with this. He is proposing a new conceptual category of psychophysical unity in place of the traditional physical/mental duality, and this needs a new foundational principle. It is therefore essential to at least try to fill in some of the discussion Freud leaves to 'philosophy' to give psychoanalysis its own intellectual legitimacy.

Freud's justification for the psychical unconscious is threefold: he states that 'our assumption of the unconscious is *necessary* and *legitimate*, and that we possess numerous proofs of its existence' (1915, S.E.14: 166). Taking his last point first, the 'proofs' he mentions lie predominantly in post-hypnotic suggestion, in which people carry out actions they have been ordered to do while they were under hypnosis. They do not remember the hypnotist's commands, but unless they contravene the individual's own values, they obey them while coming up with thin rationalisations for their actions. This shows that the unconscious is dynamic rather than static – actively decision-making rather than simply a series of states. Second, the 'legitimacy' Freud accords the unconscious is only equivalent to that of everyday practical thinking: in according unconscious mental processes to ourselves, he points out, we are doing no more than when we accord consciousness to others (ibid. 169). This makes his concept practically valid, but not scientifically so.

Freud's statement that his idea of the unconscious is conceptually 'necessary' provides the strongest argument: conscious states cannot be explained without it, since consciousness holds only a single fleeting element at any one time. The rest of our thoughts and assumptions are not conscious, but since some are more or less readily available, they must exist somewhere. We know that the philosophical mode of thinking current in Freud's time was to see these 'out of consciousness' states as 'physical dispositions' to produce conscious thoughts, rather than anything psychological. But Freud argues that this approach cannot do anything more than provide a location for where and perhaps how in the brain these processes happen. But comparing them to conscious mental processes enables us to understand them by making sense of them to us as human beings. This makes the psychological approach more directly explanatory and useful than the physical approach.

The validity of this point enables us to go straight to the 'bedrock' level of Freud's 'basic assumption' of psychophysical unity. The 'necessity' of his concept of the unconscious means that it has already been allotted an implicit space in our overall view of reality. We assume that unconscious mental processes occur within the reality we share, and that they do so in the brain as well as in the mind or psyche. In doing so, we take them to exist objectively; and since they are as much psychological as physical in nature, just saying *where* they happen – in the brain or in the mind or psyche – is not enough.

Freud's philosophical outlook is not set out methodically, but when he touches on it he expresses himself as a materialist and a realist – a believer that the reality outside us is genuinely there, rather than a figment of our imagination, and that it is physical in nature. This is clear in his 1895 *Project for a Scientific Psychology*, where he sees psychical processes as reducible to the material, and continues to his late *Outline of Psychoanalysis*, where he describes them as unitary processes with both psychological and 'organic and biological' sides (1940, S.E.23: 195). But on closer inspection, his version of reality does not go back to physical matter: it goes back to the unconscious registration of reality in the psyche. What we call 'reality' exists primarily as something within the psyche, and only secondarily as something we infer to be outside it (although he believes external reality to exist, as well).

An ordinary material realist would hold that the most basic form that exists is matter. Mental phenomena and the mind would be epiphenomena, or by-products, of the material brain, rather than realities in themselves. But Freud, as a 'psychical realist', holds that the most basic form of existence is what we register unconsciously: the psychical unconscious is our bedrock, from which we infer the reality of both matter and mind. For Freud, consciousness is one mode in which the psyche functions, and not even the primary way; nevertheless, it is only through consciousness that we can know anything at all.

This sets Freud's psychoanalysis within an approach which is neither purely empirical nor solely hermeneutic. Like hermeneutics, it begins with the perceiver rather than the perceived; but like empirical science, it acknowledges the priority of 'matter' over 'consciousness'. Instead of the brute alternatives of physical or mental theorisation, he offers us the third possibility of psychical theorisation. The psychical is set *before* the dichotomy is made into empirical and hermeneutic, or body and mind, and therefore holds elements of each.

Towards a psychical foundational approach

Thus 'psychical realism' is at the root of Freud's thinking, and supplies the psychophysical unity his theories call for. We can now begin to develop what is missing from his account, beginning with the practical foundation of psychoanalysis. This is the active framework and principle which could give psychoanalysis its own authority. If these are to succeed, they must reflect the psychical nature of his thinking and should also be prior to the division into the mental and the physical aspects of reality. The main source book used is Sebastian Gardner's *Irrationality and the Philosophy of Psychoanalysis* (1993).

In Gardner's view, psychoanalysis and common-sense psychology both rest within a 'neutral' theoretical mode – one that is neither fully hermeneutic nor wholly empirical. Psychoanalysis begins and ends in the practical domain, he says, with its interpersonal setting and its use of the ordinary ways in which we interpret subjective states and processes. However, common-sense psychology would not be sufficient to make up a valid foundation for Grünbaum or Nagel, for example, and the difference between Freud and Nagel opens up here. Nagel endorses subjective reality as 'objective' because he sees it as a window onto the reality which exists outside the mind: it is this external reality that he sees as basic. From Nagel's perspective, only empirical science, with physics as the dominant perspective, could offer psychoanalysis – or any subject – a solid ground. Gardner, by contrast, suggests that empirical or hermeneutic principles are irrelevant to psychoanalysis: everyday practical psychology is its only conceptual ground, and psychoanalytic thinking begins where common-sense psychology gives out.

Like Grünbaum and Habermas, Gardner is setting psychoanalysis at the level of the clinical theories – resistance, repression and transference – which restricts his scope as it does for them. But taking common-sense psychology as its basis and starting-point gives him more room for manoeuvre than the other two. Gardner defines psychoanalysis as a distinctive adjunct to common-sense psychology, taking it from a pre-theoretical to a theoretical level. This means that he does not see psychoanalysis as either an empirical or a hermeneutic subject but a theoretical venture on its own. 'Psychoanalytic explanation is shown to be a coherent extension of everyday forms of psychological explanation, and scepticism about psychoanalysis is met by exhibiting this continuity', he states (1993: frontispiece); adding elsewhere, 'There can be no pretending that psychoanalytic theory is defensible except on the assumption that ordinary psychology is cogent' (ibid. 202).

Like Freud's psychical realism, common-sense psychology assumes an initial oneness between body and mind: the ordinary idea of a person assumes both body and mind together. This cannot be challenged by either empirical or hermeneutic principles, because it assumes less rather than more than either: common-sense ways of thinking about reality – beginning with the person – are set prior to the division into body and mind, physical and mental, empirical and hermeneutic. They are derived from our ordinary idea of the person, rather than coming after it.

But can Gardner's 'common-sense' perspective develop into a practical foundation and principle? Can it lead to a better understanding of the psychical, particularly its causal mode, than either the empirical or the hermeneutic systems? If not, it is of no use to us.

The 'neutral' account of the psychical: psychoanalysis as pre-propositional psychology

Gardner comments that although psychoanalysis builds on ordinary psychology, it is not just a way of saying the same thing in a more complicated way: 'it explains things that ordinary psychology cannot explain, and does so by employing a distinctive form of explanation which is foreign to ordinary psychology' (ibid. 87).

The philosophy of the mind and the mental is normally known as 'propositional psychology'. In ordinary, non-neurotic life, mental phenomena (thoughts, decisions and to some extent emotions) are viewed philosophically in 'rational' terms, with the 'reason' as the mental equivalent of the physical 'cause'. What makes mental phenomena distinct from physical phenomena is that they are governed by subjective understanding – the possibility of empathy – rather than by endlessly replicable or publicly observable experiments. A mental state is understandable, or rational, if we can see the 'reason' for it. Reasons, unlike physical causes, are in principle unlimited, depending on the individual and his social/cultural context. Propositional psychology sees mental life as made up of elements that involve meaning: values, intentions and to some extent, emotions. A mental explanation is successful if what we are trying to explain fits into a rationally coherent personal scheme – if we can see that the emotion or action 'makes sense' in that person's terms, even if we do not share them.

But psychoanalysis does not fit well into propositional psychology. Often it is concerned with emotions and actions which do not have readily understandable reasons – neurotic acts or phantasies which may be overtly self-destructive or seemingly without relation to the matter in hand. This is where Gardner takes things up: he proposes that psychoanalysis should be viewed as 'pre-propositional psychology' – as concerned with the apparently irrational bedrock that underlies ordinary rationality.

In fact, Gardner says, psychoanalysis rests on the supposition that dynamic and purposive states of mind exist that are linked, but not rationally linked, as they are in propositional psychology. 'And it does so, remarkably, by positing a causal link between mental phenomena which reflects neither the determinism of the physical world nor acting, feeling, or thinking "for a reason"' (ibid. 88). Strange as this may sound, this kind of causal/reason link is already familiar in the everyday, pre-theoretical, common-sense psychology that we all live by. We know it as 'wishful thinking': we are prone to believe what we want to believe, even when it means going against the available evidence and especially if we find aspects of ourselves or others disturbing. Ignoring the need for a visit to the dentist in the hope that the pain will 'go away in the night' is one example. Another is seeing ourselves in a better light than others would, or even as we ourselves might on a braver day. Phobias and delusional states are a step on from these ordinary occurrences, taking common-sense psychology into psychoanalytic territory.

This kind of mental happening can only be explained by traditional propositional psychology as normal mental functioning gone wrong. But psychoanalysis sees rationality as merely a veneer, allowing Gardner to posit these events not as aberrations of the mind but as the breaking through into consciousness of the pre-propositional, pre-rational realm. This is Freud's domain of the psychical, lying between the physical realm of the normal physiological processes which we have no consciousness of, and the propositional level of ordinary conscious rationality.

The 'psychical' causal mode

Gardner defines the basic component of this level of mental functioning as the 'motivational state'. It is not a conscious state of wanting or desire, but the unconscious ground from which desires arise. In physical terms, for example, the cause of thirst would be seen as a shortage of fluid in the system; in mental terms, it is expressed as the need or desire to take in liquid. The 'motivational state' is the connecting link between the two: there must be some point at which the physiological becomes not conscious, but subjective. It is really only significant to us when what we want is not easily understandable or controllable, even to the person concerned – the stuff of psychoanalysis. But since the motivational state underlies rational as well as irrational states, we can talk about it in more readily accessible terms.

The simplest motivational state is what psychoanalysis terms 'the wish' (as in dreams and symptoms being unconsciously 'wish-fulfilling'). But a wish is not simply an isolated urge: its immediate product, or partner, is a picture of its own fulfilment. Wishes are always for something specific, and the fulfilment of the wish is almost a part of the wish itself – with both existing at an unconscious level. The wish and its implied fulfilment include both mental (psychological) and physical (or biological) sides. A lack of food normally brings with it the urge to eat, the experience of hunger; but what we wish to eat, or imagine ourselves ideally eating, varies enormously. The picture of fulfilment of one person's hunger would be imagining eating something that someone with a different mental or cultural 'set' would find disgusting – dogs or pork, cattle or insects.

The relation between the bare 'wish' and its implied 'fulfilment' is beginning to sound like the 'hybrid' causal link we have been looking for: one in which what is mental and what is physical coexist, the link between biology and (common-sense) psychology. But isolated wishes like hunger are not all there is to psychical life. We have wishes for fame and fortune as well as for our basic physical needs to be met, and even the experience of hunger can become disordered or be overridden. Thus the wish and its fulfilment are rooted in a context that is both physical and mental, biological and cultural.

Simple motivational states join with others to become the complex stream of psychical life that psychoanalysis terms 'phantasy'. Unlike the simple wish, however, the workings of phantasy are open to feedback. The kind of breast the baby first encounters will modify his inbuilt sense of what he next wants when hungry, and phantasy itself, moreover, is dimly accessible to consciousness. As psychoanalytically savvy adults, we know that it is involved when we feel impelled to act, react or perceive in a certain way, especially if it is against our conscious wishes or our obvious self-interest. Psychoanalysis is based on the knowledge that we can report on, reflect and, crucially, alter the workings of our minds at this level, although it is very difficult and usually requires the special setting and interpretative help of the psychotherapist. Both insight and 'working through' demonstrate the possibility of intentional psychical change through self-knowledge alone.[2] This means that the 'psychical' is not a purely abstract conjecture but has, in principle, as tangible an existence as anything else that we can perceive first-hand.

The practical foundation of psychoanalysis now falls into our hands. In Freudian terminology, it is the 'pleasure principle', contrasting with the 'reality principle' of propositional or rational psychology. Philosophically, the pleasure principle is based in the fulfillability of wishes, at least in imagination. The ground of psychoanalysis is thus the same as that of the ordinary psychological framework we live by in everyday life. Psychoanalysis extends the range of ordinary psychology and lifts it to the level of theory, while psychoanalysis 'repays ordinary psychology for its extension, by assisting in its vindication' (ibid. 23); it shares the authority it holds with its pre-theoretical counterpart. Psychoanalysis has its own causal mode, lying between the physical 'cause' (e.g. the need for food) and the rational 'reason' (the wish to eat something imagined as 'nice'). The psychical cause/reason is what links the wish with the picture of its fulfilment.

This way of looking at 'the psychical' brings clarity to a process which cannot be satisfactorily explained by either empirical or hermeneutic means. Phantasy and wish fulfilment carry both the inevitability of physiological processes which are not open to consciousness, and the volitional control, however limited, that applies to ordinary rational mental processes. Wish and wish fulfilment are never found apart; and psychical processes remain, as Freud declared, an original unity which can only be divided into mental and physical 'sides' in the abstract.

The theoretical foundation of psychoanalysis

Since Gardner's purpose is different from ours, he does not offer us much beyond this point. But like all practical foundations, his own carries theoretical inferences – the substantive implications which can be drawn out from the practical foundation of psychoanalysis. What kind of being is psychical, or wishful, by nature, in the way that we have described?

The substantive foundation of psychoanalysis must be the same as that of common-sense psychology, since they share the same conceptual framework. This cannot be the 'mind' of the hermeneutic framework, nor the 'body' of the biological framework. It can only be the 'person', defined briefly by Gardner as a 'psycho-physical being' with 'substantial unity': a subject of experience with a tangible existence, which can only secondarily be divided into its mental and physical aspects.

The concept of the person

Peter Strawson's *Individuals* (1959) helps us take our exploration further. This is a highly influential work which is not concerned with psychoanalysis but which gives close philosophical attention to the concept of the person, as one of the most basic of all concepts. Strawson's book is subtitled 'An Essay in Descriptive Metaphysics', meaning that it describes or brings clarity to our basic assumptions about reality, without offering any new concepts; this would be 'revisionary metaphysics', since it would revise our assumptions. 'Descriptive metaphysics' is thus foundational in itself: before offering any new concepts, it is necessary to clean up the most basic.

Strawson takes as his starting-point that the pictures of reality that human beings can come up with are variable, but not infinitely so:

> there is a massive core of human thinking which has no history … categories and concepts which, in their most fundamental character, change not at all. Obviously these are not the specialities of the most refined thinking. They are the commonplaces of the least refined thinking; and yet they are the indispensable core of the most sophisticated human beings.
>
> (Strawson 1959: 10)

Particulars, bodies and persons

Strawson proposes that our overall conceptual scheme – the framework for human experience – depends on 'particulars'. Unless we could distinguish different phenomena within the general flow of perception, nothing specific could be identified or re-identified, and nothing could be perceived, experienced or thought about with any distinctness. This applies to all mental as well as physical phenomena; but the 'basic particulars', Strawson declares, are 'material bodies', or things (ibid. 39).

These physical lumps of matter are further subdivided into inanimate objects on the one hand and 'persons' on the other. Strawson is proposing that the 'person' is one of the few universal categories in human experience, although the *kinds* of person that can be drawn out from this are many and variable. The very notion of the person is psychophysical – or rather, the concepts of psychological and physical have not yet been formulated: the person is by necessity mind and body as one. 'Hermeneutic' and 'empirical' simply apply to the concepts of mind and body taken up to a theoretical level. They too depend ultimately on the concept of material bodies, inanimate (things) and animate (persons).[3]

The theoretical properties (defining characteristics) of the person

Strawson goes on to ask in what respects these two basic particulars differ: what can be said of persons but not of material bodies? First, Strawson suggests, it seems to be a 'natural fact' – a fact of human nature – that 'persons' can sometimes recognise each other's subjective intentions through bodily movements alone: they may be 'writing a letter', or 'coiling a rope', for example (ibid. 111).[4] This 'person-predicate' is made up of a physical component (bodily movement), united with a mental adjunct (subjective intention), making a unity that is readily understandable by others. In societies without writing or ropes, these intentions would not be recognisable – but there would be other examples which would be.

Second, the very idea of the 'person' implies the existence of other 'persons'. We could not recognise our own emotions, for example, unless they were also attributable to others – we would simply have them without knowing what they were, or what they meant. And as Winnicott points out when he takes up the concept of the 'nursing couple', without a caring adult ensuring our physical survival, no human infant is viable. The most basic human category, therefore, is not simply the person, but the 'person-amongst-persons'. In both Strawson's person-predicates – the recognising of intention from bodily movement alone, and the necessity for relationship with other persons – the physical and the cultural are united, just as with wishes and their fulfillability.

A psychophysical context for psychoanalysis

Thus the most fundamental theoretical unit in everyday common-sense psychology, and in its extension into psychoanalysis, is the necessarily psychophysical 'person-amongst-persons'. However, where Strawson sees the concept of the 'person' as secondary to that of 'material bodies' (ibid. 38–58) – the junior partner in his duo of 'basic particulars' – it is also possible to see the situation the other way around. Conceptually and empirically, the person-amongst-persons can be seen as the primary particular, with material bodies coming second.

Conceptually, the idea of a material body (or matter) can be derived from the psychophysical idea of the person-amongst-persons, but the full psychophysical idea of the person-amongst-persons cannot be derived from the concept of material bodies, or matter, alone: the mental or subjective aspect is missing. Empirically, every parent knows that children have to learn that some 'bodies' are not animate, where others are: the table does not hurt when we kick it, but we hope that the other person does. In phantasy, things do not even have to get to the stage of action. Just imagining harm to another body is sufficient to convince us that we have damaged it. We can check this through our own, just accessible phantasy life, especially in the more neurotic of our symptoms or habits.

Thus a unitary foundation which can be drawn from Freud's own writings is not unthinkable: one version comes from developing the hints he gives us of his own undeveloped philosophical framework, in this particular way. The practical foundation of this unitary conception of psychoanalysis is the fulfillability of wishes. The basic practical unit is the wish, and the intimate relation of the wish to its (imagined) fulfilment demonstrates the psychophysical, or psychical, causal mode: you cannot have a wish without it giving rise to, or causing, a picture of its fulfilment. It comes from the physical and cultural worlds as one.

The theoretical or substantive foundation of psychoanalysis is personhood. The basic unit is the 'person-amongst-persons', which simply cannot be divided into mental and physical 'parts' without distorting it. With these foundations, the pre-theoretical subject of common-sense psychology, the assumptions we all make whatever our philosophical preferences, could develop into the fully theoretical subject of psychoanalysis. It could, in theory, be extended into a complete view of reality, taking in both the sciences and the humanities, all built on Freud's 'psychical' centre and implicit assumptions.

In practice, this is not going to happen; but Freud's originality of thought is both thorough-going and deep. His concept of the psychical can be seen to begin with the most basic of all our experiences of reality: the unconscious registration of ourselves as a 'person-amongst-persons', defined and recognised by the unity of the physical and the psychological in that most human of all of our features, the capacity to wish. Even more than we are physical or mental beings, we are wishing beings.

Conclusion

To go back to our original subject: the legitimation of Freud's psychoanalysis is based in a controversial ground, the metapsychology. Through investigating hints and comments dotted through his writings, however, Freud directs us to his most original idea in the psychoanalytic concept of the psychical. It cannot be reached from either the physical starting-point of matter or the hermeneutic platform of mind, but arises out of the 'common-sense' notion of the person. This concept is the ground and origin of the ideas of both body and mind; it is utterly foundational and irreducibly psychophysical, yet psychoanalysis has shown that it is capable of theoretical development without diverging into either the hermeneutic or the empirical path.

We cannot explore further here, but although psychoanalysis is their most natural home, the practical–theoretical foundations of psychoanalysis do not have to end at this point. The theoretical properties of personhood could extend into further theoretical development within the psychophysical framework to form the basis of a psychophysical picture of reality. This would be the fullest development of Freud's psychical realism, the conclusions of practical reasoning about the only reality available to us. The concept of the person would mediate between theoretical development into the non-human material world on the one hand, and the non-material human world, on the other. The transmutations between inanimate, animate, psychical and rational states would appear more self-evident and less mysterious, and the categories we now call 'matter' and 'mind' less antithetical. The 'person-amongst-persons' holds them together; the mental/physical distinction wrenches them apart.

This psychically based view of reality is simpler than Nagel's dual-aspect theory. In giving ultimate priority to reality conceived as independent of the mind, Nagel privileges physical theory over practical conceptualisation, whereas Freud appears to do the reverse. It is of course possible that Nagel's aspiration may one day be realised; in the meantime, there may be other ways of approaching the same objective. Both Nagel and Freud were captivated by the realisation that there are parts of our reality which we can barely begin to explain – the psychical unconscious being primary amongst them. In the practicalities of everyday living, the link between our mental and physical worlds cannot be doubted, yet when we try to explain it we find ourselves at a loss, even – or especially – when considering ourselves. 'We conceive the body from outside and the mind from inside, and see no internal connection, only an external one of correlation or perhaps causation' (Nagel 1998: 346). In aspiring to a theory which reflects practicality, we should not be satisfied until the continuity between physical and mental reality is as transparent to us as that between the idea of a substance and its chemical composition, or the mind and its propositional network of thoughts, intentions and emotions. Only then will we make sense to ourselves; the sole acceptable alternative is to understand why, being the creatures we are, this possibility is permanently, structurally, closed to us.

We have gone from Freudian thinking to the roots of psychoanalysis itself. This suggests one way in which Freud's notion of the psychical holds within it the seeds of its own approach to reality. Personhood itself is built on the unity of the mental and the physical, hermeneutics and science, a unity which can only occur in relationships within and between people.

Notes

1 Applying this to Newton's example: Law (gravity) + Conditions (apple detaching from tree, no counterforce such as upward wind etc.) leads to/equals Event (apple falls to ground).
2 Freud's self-analysis shows this, and it has been repeated by others (e.g. John Sutherland).
3 We shall come to animals very soon.
4 When animals are trained to do such things they have been conditioned (by people) to act *as though* they had these intentions.

References

Churchland, Patricia (1986) *Neurophilosophy: Towards a Unified Science of the Mind-Brain*, New York: Walter de Gruyter.

Churchland, Paul (1988) *Matter and Consciousness*, Cambridge, MA and London: MIT Press.

Crews, F. (1993) 'The Unknown Freud', in *The New York Review of Books*, 18 November.

Freud, S. (1895) *Project for a Scientific Psychology*, S.E.1: 281–387.

——— (1911) *Psycho-Analytic Notes upon an Autobiographical Account of a Case of Paranoia (Dementia Paranoides)*, S.E.12: 3–82.

——— (1913) *The Claims of Psycho-Analysis to Scientific Interest*, S.E.13: 163–190.

——— (1914) *On Narcissism*, S.E.14: 67–104.

——— (1915) *The Unconscious*, S.E.14: 166–215.

——— (1940) *An Outline of Psycho-Analysis*, S.E.23: 139–208.

Gardner, S. (1993) *Irrationality and the Philosophy of Psychoanalysis*, Cambridge, UK: Cambridge University Press.

Gomez, L. (2005) *The Freud Wars: An Introduction to the Philosophy of Psychoanalysis*, London and New York: Routledge.

Grünbaum, A. (1984) *The Foundations of Psychoanalysis: A Philosophical Critique*, Berkeley: University of California Press.

Habermas, J. (1971) *Knowledge and Human Interests*, trans. J.J. Shapiro, London: Heinemann. First published (1968) as *Erkenntnis und Interesse*, Frankfurt am Main: Suhrkamp Verlag.

Nagel, T. (1974) 'Freud's Anthropomorphism', in *Other Minds* (1995): 13–25.

——— (1986) *The View from Nowhere*, New York: Oxford University Press.

——— (1994) 'Freud's Permanent Revolution', in *New York Review of Books* 41, no. 9: 34–38, and in *Other Minds*: 26–40.

——— (1995) *Other Minds: Critical Essays 1969–1994*, New York: Oxford University Press.

——— (1998) 'Conceiving the Impossible and the Mind–Body Problem', *Philosophy* 73, no. 285: 337–352.

Popper, K. (1962) *Conjectures and Refutations*, London: Routledge and Kegan Paul.

Strawson, P. (1959) *Individuals*, London: Methuen.

The New York Review of Books, 1993–1995.

Index